MW00829944

'Few subjects are as crucial as those covered in *Disru* understands them better than Roger Spitz. As value through change, this book is essential reading for le ensure sustainable value creation in a fast-changing world.'
Sebastian Bihari, venture capitalist and General Partner, Vektor Partners

'A must-read for anyone navigating uncertainty. Roger Spitz masterfully equips decision-makers for the steep slopes, crevasses and hazards of the world's fast-changing environments. There are no better frameworks to help build resilience for the shocks while seizing the windows of opportunities as you creatively shape your future.'
Benedikt Böhm, Executive Board, Oberalp, CEO, Dynafit, and extreme ski mountaineer

'Organizations more than ever need to be vigilant about navigating uncertainty and disruption – their relevancy is at stake if they don't! Roger Spitz's Disruptive Thinking Canvas is an essential practice all organizations need to employ if they want to shape the future with impact and be around to see it. This is the "go to" guidebook for businesses who want to successfully navigate the modern world.'
Kara Cunzeman, Director of Strategic Foresight, The Aerospace Corporation, Co-Founder and Chair, Federal Foresight Advocacy Alliance, and Director, USA Hub for Teach the Future

'Uncertainty, disruptions, cascading change... Roger Spitz is uniquely qualified to address these challenges. Backed by fascinating research, practical frameworks, and his original Disruptive Thinking Canvas, *Disrupt With Impact* is your operating manual for unpredictability.'
Cathy Hackl, tech futurist, author, and CEO of Spatial Dynamics

'Makes the case for organizational leaders to adopt new ways to anticipate and act in an era of exponential change. Old methods no longer suffice in our hyperconnected world. Roger Spitz gives readers the tools to flourish through systemic disruption.'
David Jonker, Vice President, SAP Insights Research Center

'A roadmap to visionary leadership, and Roger Spitz is the guide we need. He encourages leaders to think not only about surviving the next wave of disruption but about shaping it to their advantage – and for the greater good.'
Michael J Keegan, Leadership Fellow, IBM Center for The Business of Government and host of *The Business of Government Hour* podcast

'A compelling book that illuminates the complexities of our uncertain world. Through engaging examples, Roger Spitz skilfully provides practical insights that resonate deeply with today's fast-paced environment. Whether you're a seasoned professional or just starting your journey in strategic foresight, *Disrupt With Impact* provides tools to not only survive, but excel.
Quentin Ladetto, Head of Technology Foresight, Swiss DoD, and Co-founder, atelierdesfuturs.org

'Today, boards are operating in uncharted territory and navigating through unprecedented challenges and uncertainties. It is crucial for them to learn how to turn disruptions into opportunities, leveraging innovation and strategic foresight to drive sustainable growth and resilience. *Disrupt with Impact* is a perfect guide for our boardroom community. It provides comprehensive, sector-specific insights that are crucial for today's leaders. The book introduces new concepts for governance through engaging case studies and well-explained nuances.'

Manoj K Raut, CEO and Secretary-General, Institute of Directors, India

'Roger Spitz has done it again! *Disrupt With Impact* is an indispensable guide for navigating today's unpredictable business landscape. Roger provides actionable strategies and profound insights that empower leaders to make tough decisions with confidence. Truly a must-read for anyone looking to thrive in the face of constant change.'

Jake Sotiriadis, Director, Center for Futures Intelligence, National Intelligence University

'Roger Spitz is a visionary in strategic foresight and systems innovation, whose insights have consistently pushed the boundaries of what's possible in business and technology. Having known him from Singularity University, I have seen firsthand his ability to inspire and challenge leaders to think deeply about sustainable futures. This book is a vital resource for anyone aiming to navigate and thrive amid disruption.'

Pinak Kiran Vedalankar, global technology leader

'Roger Spitz, with his unique multi-lens perspective, offers insights on embracing disruption as a frequent phenomenon that can both destroy and create value. *Disrupt With Impact* provides a practical roadmap for leaders aiming to strengthen their "impossibility muscles" and make the world a better place.'

Doris Viljoen, Director, Institute for Futures Research, Stellenbosch Business School

'Combining strategic foresight and systems dynamics principles, *Disrupt with Impact* offers a framework and tools for confidently moving ahead in an uncertain world. Readers will find value in case studies on business themes from bluetech to open banking, lessons from successes and failures, and new opportunities. This book will help you to harness "gray rhino" challenges ahead in order to become a disruptive force for good – instead of being trampled.'

Michele Wucker, author of *The Gray Rhino*

Disrupt With Impact

Achieve business success
in an unpredictable world

Roger Spitz

KoganPage

First published in Great Britain and the United States in 2024 by Kogan Page Limited

2nd Floor, 45 Gee Street
London
EC1V 3RS
United Kingdom

8 W 38th Street, Suite 902
New York, NY 10018
USA

www.koganpage.com

Kogan Page books are printed on paper from sustainable forests.

ISBNs
Hardback   978 1 3986 1690 5
Paperback   978 1 3986 1688 2
Ebook   978 1 3986 1689 9

British Library Cataloguing-in-Publication Data
A CIP record for this book is available from the British Library.

Library of Congress Cataloging-in-Publication Data
Names: Spitz, Roger, author.
Title: Disrupt with impact : achieve business success in an unpredictable
    world / Roger Spitz.
Description : London ; New York, NY : Kogan Page Inc., 2024. | Includes
    bibliographical references and index.
Identifiers: LCCN 2024023746 (print) | LCCN 2024023747 (ebook) | ISBN
    9781398616882 (paperback) | ISBN 9781398616905 (hardback) | ISBN
    9781398616899 (ebook)
Subjects: LCSH: Success in business. | Creative ability in business
Classification: LCC HF5386 .S7533 2024 (print) | LCC HF5386 (ebook) | DDC
    650.1–dc23/eng/20240614
LC record available at https://lccn.loc.gov/2024023746
LC ebook record available at https://lccn.loc.gov/2024023747

Typeset by Integra Software Services, Pondicherry
Print production managed by Jellyfish
Printed and bound by CPI Group (UK) Ltd, Croydon CR0 4YY

CONTENTS

PART THREE The future of artificial intelligence, strategic decision-making and technology

LIST OF FIGURES AND TABLES

Figures

Tables

ABOUT THE AUTHOR

Roger Spitz (BSc Econ, MSc, FCA, APF) is a bestselling author and world-leading authority on strategic foresight and systems innovations. Spitz has given hundreds of keynotes globally, is frequently published and quoted, and has guest lectured at many of the world's most prestigious institutions. He serves on multiple boards focused on anticipatory governance, sustainability, AI and ethics, venture capital (VC) and academia.

Spitz is President of Techistential, the pre-eminent foresight practice, which advises CEOs, founders, boards and shareholders on evaluating their organizations' strategy under uncertainty, anticipating disruptions ahead and sustainable value creation. Spitz is also Chair of the Disruptive Futures Institute (DFI) in San Francisco, an expert advisor to the World Economic Forum's Global Foresight Network, and sits on the Teach The Future board. Spitz lectures and publishes widely on anticipatory leadership, futures intelligence and strategic foresight. He has authored five books, including the acclaimed collection *The Definitive Guide to Thriving on Disruption*, and his frameworks have featured in *Fast Company*, Gartner, *INC. Magazine*, Institute of Directors, *MIT Technology Review, WIRED* and World Economic Forum.

Renowned for his pioneering work in climate foresight, with bestselling books on green business and sustainable development, Spitz is a Climatebase Fellow and board member of Lux Carbon Standard (Brazil's first carbon credit certifier). Spitz's DFI Sustainability & Climate Academy equips leaders to accelerate the energy transition for sustainable futures through transformative change and capacity building for resiliency.

A recognized expert, speaker and investor in the AI field, Spitz founded the Techistential Center for Human & Artificial Intelligence, and is known for coining the term 'techistentialism'. Spitz writes extensively on the future of AI and strategic decision-making, serves on the AI Council of the Indian Society for Artificial Intelligence and is a CogX Ambassador.

A strong supporter of the startup ecosystems, he is partner at Vektor Partners (impact venture capital, Palo Alto and London), and LP investor and advisor of Berkeley SkyDeck's fund. Spitz was the former Global Head of Technology M&A with BNP Paribas, where he advised on over 50 transactions with deal values of $25 billion. He launched the bank's US M&A practice in San Francisco and built its European Technology & Digital Investment Banking corporate finance advisory franchises in London and Paris.

Bilingual English and French, Spitz has lived in 10 different cities across three continents.

LIST OF ABBREVIATIONS

4G/5G	fourth-gen/fifth-gen mobile communications
6 i's	intuition, inspiration, imagination, improvisation, invention, impossible
AAA	antifragile, anticipatory, agility
AGI	artificial general intelligence
ANI	artificial narrow intelligence
AR	augmented reality
ASI	artificial superintelligence
BMaaS	business-models-as-a-system
CBO	chief bridging officer
CEO^2	chief existential officer
DaaS	disinformation-as-a-service
ESG	environmental, social and governance
EV	electric vehicle
eVTOL	electric vertical take-off and landing
IoE	Internet of Existence
IoT	Internet of Things
LLM	large language model
M&A	mergers and acquisitions
MVF	minimum viable fields
RaaS	ransomware-as-a-service
RLHF	reinforcement learning from human feedback
SDG	sustainable development goals
STEEPE	social, technological, environmental, economic, political, ethical
TRL	technology readiness level
UN-VICE	unknown, volatile, intersecting, complex, exponential
VC	venture capital
VR	virtual reality
VUCA	volatility, uncertainty, complexity and ambiguity
XR	extended reality

Introduction

As we learn to navigate increasingly fast-paced and complex environments, we must extend our gaze beyond the immediate horizon. We need to anticipate the underlying forces that will shape the futures and understand how these transformations can create cascading effects. The true impact of innovation isn't in its disruptiveness; rather, it lies in its ability to ignite hope, unlock new possibilities and catalyse positive transformations across systems.

I've dedicated my career to advising boards, leadership teams and investors on strategy under uncertainty. As the president of Techistential, a leading climate and foresight consultancy, and in my capacity as chair of the Disruptive Futures Institute, I empower organizations to become future-savvy.

With over two decades as the global head of technology mergers and acquisitions at a leading investment bank and partner in a venture capital impact fund, my insights have been shaped by a relentless pursuit of understanding the core drivers of change to create sustainable value. This book will provide you with a deep comprehension of decision-making amid uncertainty, anticipating disruptions and sustaining competitiveness.

In these pages you'll find distilled futures intelligence garnered from advising some of the most prestigious organizations in the world. This book does not rely on established knowledge. It discards tired and outdated formulas, recognizing the diminishing effectiveness of pre-cooked playbooks in our unpredictable world. *This is a guide to embracing the futures with resilience and foresight.*

This book is not about either trends or the latest technology fads. The world does not need another generic techno-optimist book focused on formulaic innovation or business optimization recipes. Instead of chasing fleeting trends, we prioritize signals over noise, investigating the fundamentals that propel change. We view disruption systemically, transcending the passing technological hypes emanating from Silicon Valley.

The more I investigate the essence of our world, the more I realize that our systems are not just fragile, but outright ineffective. Everything in our world is constantly evolving – except our organizations, strategies and governance structures. Too often, we act on flawed assumptions, believing in a world that is predictable, linear, stable and controllable. But the cost and missed opportunities from these misconceptions are on the rise.

This book explores opportunities, risks, strategies and tactics to remedy this lack of resiliency. It offers practitioner frameworks and real-world insights to enhance foresight and decision-making in addressing major disruptions, from sustainability and artificial intelligence to geopolitical shifts and cybersecurity risks. Let it serve as your guide for confidently navigating through the turbulent waters of change in the increasingly interconnected yet fragmented global landscape. Be empowered to overcome challenges and seize new opportunities for success and growth.

We will learn to decipher the true nature of the world, not oversimplified narratives engineered for short-lived influence, control and commercial gains. Instead of viewing the future as predetermined or singular, we embrace multiplicity – there are many possible futures in our dynamic world of constant flux. Our anticipatory thinking focuses on enhancing preparedness for diverse scenarios that may unfold, rather than attempting to predict the inherently unpredictable future. We don't overemphasize the future at the expense of the present, because the present is our only tangible reality. We imagine the future as a tool to inform today's actions and short-term decisions.

Faced with relentless change and escalating uncertainty, we empower you with essential tools – principles, concepts and mindsets – in an era of ambient disruption. *Imagine navigating uncharted waters with a compass calibrated for the unpredictable.* This book provides that compass to actively create meaningful change in a world where every swerve feels like nothing that's ever happened before.

Across all aspects of business and society there is no shortage of events which are presented as 'historic', 'unique' or 'unprecedented'. Maybe there should be new parameters for 'unprecedented', as it becomes the norm. In this environment, we can only make relevant decisions by anticipating what might arise, unshackled from the steady state that has been.

Join me on a journey to traverse the ever-evolving landscape of uncertainty. Along the way, we'll discover perspectives that empower us to shape our futures. Together, let's embark on a quest to anticipate and prepare for the uncharted challenges ahead while driving impactful change.

The book is organized into four parts.

Part One: Disruption has always existed – what's different now? In this initial section, we reframe disruption and delve into its dual nature, uncovering both challenges and possibilities. We learn the language of change, adopting new mindsets essential for thriving amidst ambient disruption. By scanning the horizon, we identify elements of constancy and discontinuity, equipping ourselves with early warning systems to anticipate inflection points.

Part Two: How to drive systems innovation and transformational change. In Part Two we unpack how to achieve systems-level change to create sustainable value. Surface-level innovations fall short in addressing the complexity of our challenges. As the world's fundamental paradigms are increasingly changing, we need to account for constant disruption, which is giving rise to monumental shifts in value and business models. Those who fail to embrace sustainable change risk irrelevance. To use systemic disruption as a springboard for creating impact and value, we need to be antifragile, learn from the software industry to beta test our ideas and think across varying time horizons. In this context, we delve into the Greenaissance – an era marked by renewal, momentous innovation and investment opportunities, all aligned with the common goal of achieving a sustainable energy transition. We also explore how the clearly delineated 'sectors' of yesterday are disappearing, as industries converge and new fields emerge.

Part Three: The future of artificial intelligence, strategic decision-making and technology. This section examines the defining technologies of the upcoming decade and their potential for growth, disruption and unintended consequences. We dive into the profound impact of artificial intelligence on strategic decision-making. We also examine 'info-ruption' – a radical shift in the disruption of information, presenting new phenomena like weaponized disinformation and global cybersecurity threats. At the core of our investigation lies the antifragile, anticipatory and agility framework. These essential skills are key to decision-making in an increasingly unpredictable world where machines continuously learn.

Part Four: Unleash your disruptive thinking. This final chapter introduces our practitioner Disruptive Thinking Canvas™. Disruption creates space for novelty, opening doors for fresh approaches. Uncertainty and fast-changing environments drive new opportunities and gaps. Disruptive thinking allows you to find those gaps and explore them to invent the future today. Our proprietary Disruptive Thinking Canvas™ is your dynamic road map – a process to design, implement and drive disruption for yourself, your projects or your organization. It's not just a canvas; it's your actionable toolkit to uncover and create disruptive futures on your terms, with tools designed to develop new mindsets for driving impact.

Part One
Disruption has always existed – what's different now?

1

Exploring the dual nature of disruption

Challenges and possibilities

OBJECTIVES
Reframing disruption

We reframe disruption, recognizing it is more than a discrete or recurring event; it's now systemic, expanding its reach. We explore disruption's dual nature, unveiling both challenges and possibilities.

An era of ambient disruption

Disruption's definition tends to fluctuate depending on its usage. In Silicon Valley business jargon, disruption means radical, technology-driven change to an industry. For example, Amazon redefined retail while Uber upended the traditional taxi market.

Despite *disruption* being one of the most used and abused terms, it remains subjective and misunderstood. We perceive its impact and valence through our own unique lenses and our understanding of disruption has not kept pace with the ever-evolving nature of change.

Disruption is no longer a single or recurring event, but a steady state expanding its impact. In our non-linear world, patterns become harder to interpret. Not only are business incumbents being disrupted – our institutions and humanity's relevance are as well.

There is daily evidence of systemic disruptions coalescing: the World Uncertainty Index shows a clear upward trajectory in the use of the word 'uncertainty'.[1] The 2022 *Collins Dictionary*'s Word of the Year was 'permacrisis', an extended period of instability.[2] IPCC reports conclude that the world is reaching a tipping point, threatening irreversible impacts to Earth's biosphere.[3] The AlixPartners 2023 Disruption Index[4] surveyed thousands of CEOs: 98 per cent believe they need to overhaul their companies' business model within three years; 85 per cent don't know where to start; and 72 per cent say their executive teams lack the agility to deal with it. Jamie Dimon, JPMorgan's longstanding leader, qualified this era as 'maybe the most dangerous time the world has seen in decades'.[5] All this while the debate on the existential risks of artificial intelligence reaches a crescendo.

The negativity of this evidence is not just a reflection of the challenges; it stems from our failure to adjust our relationship with the world. We created the conditions that led to this permacrisis, yet we lack the foresight and adaptability to resolve it. The status quo isn't an option. We need to disrupt the norms with impact, catalysing our agency to influence alternative outcomes. We can no longer be bystanders in our potential demise. The time has come to be response-*able*, agile architects of the future, unconstrained by perceived limitations and defined by boundless possibilities.

In a world of intricate, interconnected challenges, organizations must navigate diverse stakeholders and complex ecosystems. The effectiveness of disruptive innovations hinges on awareness of their potential impacts. Overlooking their cascading effects can render them ineffective, even counterproductive.

Consider today's paradigm shifts: warp-speed information and artificial intelligence (AI) influencing decision-making; climate change as a mounting priority; cybersecurity driving national security; and biotechnology that puts our very beingness into question. While these shifts may seem gradual and disconnected, their effects will be self-reinforcing and disproportionately felt across regions and industries. Systemic change is not just a buzzword; it becomes the imperative filter to navigate this intricate web.

Our society loves bite-sized information. With limited attention spans, one-size-fits-all answers oversimplify every problem.

Simple solutions are an appealing escape from complex environments, which inherently display tensions, paradoxes and contradictions. Addressing complexity requires that we recognize the ambiguities, oppositions and inconsistencies. These arise as we analyse the issues and develop nuanced solutions. With complexity, context is crucial and no solution is universally applicable. These environments defy simplistic dichotomies which are only reliable in dependable, certain and consistent (read: imaginary) contexts.

The challenge? Complex systems hide beneath the surface. Deeply analysing system interactions reveals that explanations and answers may not be straightforward. Achieving consensus on the nature of these environments is challenging, demanding the art of constructive, critical debate.

To address ambient disruption's issues while capturing opportunities, organizations must appreciate the new dynamics at play. Confronting the realities of our complex world means we must embrace systemic change as a key to unlocking sustainable value.

Disruption has always existed – what's different now?

Our legacy systems and leadership structures lack resilience in the face of disruptions, unable to make effective decisions under uncertainty. Current assumptions are becoming obsolete. To handle this, we must raise new questions and accept with humility the realm of what we know – and what we don't.

Deep uncertainty affects us today more than ever before. But disruption is not new. For instance, a person born in 1914 would have faced major upheaval by the time they reached age 30 in 1945. They would have lived through the 1918 Spanish Flu pandemic, which killed over 50 million people, World War I, the Great Depression and World War II. Few years would have been spared from global pandemics, world wars and massive economic turmoil.

The period ending in the 1950s offered little respite: periods of growth and globalization were followed by crises, destructive nationalism, authoritarianism and more wars. This cycle paved the way to the second half of the 20th century, a return to rebuilding, globalization and advancements for much of the Western world.

Today, we are faced with profound questions on the fundamental features of our world. These go beyond the cyclical ruptures experienced in the 20th century. Exponential technologies are cascading at a runaway pace. Unlike previous eras, the velocity and interconnectivity of today's disruptions are self-reinforcing, exacerbating the initial effects.

For the first time, we face an undercurrent of existential threats in a sea of uncertainty about the future. This is a watershed moment for systemic disruption. Preconceived ideas and our references collapse as the future becomes disjointed. The recipe to create sustainable futures may require ingredients that we can't even imagine.

Unfortunately, many of us act on flawed assumptions, such as believing that the world is:

- predictable, changing linearly
- navigable through standard strategies

- comprehensible, accurately represented by our models
- safe to consider with short timescales
- defined by a series of isolated discrete phenomena

Systemic disruption obliterates rules

Common types of industry disruption

Historically, two implementations of disruption are notable. The first is 'creative destruction', popularized by economist Joseph Schumpeter. Creative destruction describes innovation that pushes countries or institutions through cycles of constant reinvention: through industrial mutations, new economic structures, where the destruction of old paradigms creates new ones.[6] We refer to this as Disruption 1.0, treating economic structures as an organic and evolving macro-process of disruption.

More recently, Clayton Christensen's 'disruptive innovation' describes a reliable process of how an innovative product typically disrupts an old market.[7] We label Christensen's specific case of disruptive innovation as Disruption 2.0.

Clayton Christensen's special case of disruptive innovation

Disruptive innovation outlines how small companies with constrained resources can challenge – and ultimately displace – significantly larger and better-capitalized incumbents.

Here, the new product offers lower prices and fewer features, which satisfies a market that was not well served by existing products. The new entrant achieves scale through this, then reaches an inflection point where customers of the incumbent migrate to this adequate solution for greater affordability, customizability and convenience.

Christensen argued that, as established companies grow, their focus shifts from innovating and obtaining new customers to marginal improvements that retain their more valuable consumers. Incumbents maximize revenues from these key customers, driving only incremental growth. This strategy leads the incumbent to focus less on potentially meaningful, but secondary, market segments. Start-ups then focus on innovations to target these overlooked customers. If new functionality and lower prices prompt the new entrant to achieve scale, it can ultimately disrupt the entire industry.

EXAMPLE
Netflix is 'disruptive innovation', but Uber isn't

One often-cited example of disruptive innovation is Netflix, famous for dislodging Blockbuster. Originating as a mail-order DVD service, Netflix's disruptive innovations led it to reshape the entertainment industry.

When Netflix launched in 1997, its initial offering was not appealing to most of Blockbuster's customers, who typically impulse-rented new releases. Netflix's first customers were movie buffs and early technology adopters (DVD players, then e-commerce, then streaming). In 2008, Blockbuster's CEO Jim Keyes famously said that 'Neither RedBox nor Netflix are even on the radar screen in terms of competition.' At that time, the two companies catered to very different needs for their 'respective' customers. Only a few years later, Blockbuster declared bankruptcy when its customers realized that Netflix's innovative platform could serve their needs better than Blockbuster's legacy model.

Uber, however, does not qualify as a disruptive innovation by Christensen's definition.[8] First, Uber did not originate with 'low-end footholds' overlooked by taxi operators. Second, Uber did not primarily target non-consumers of the taxi industry, but served incremental innovations for conventional taxi customers.

Christensen's process describes many industry disruptions, but it is only one type of disruption. Likewise, Silicon Valley's appropriation of the term has often been explained in this narrow context of fast-moving start-ups displacing incumbents.

Looking forward, disruptive innovations specific to a company, market or discrete technology may not represent how entire ecosystems will transform, disappear and emerge. Disruption's scope is broader, its features more nuanced, its speed faster, its shape exponential and its scale larger. Disruption is now systemic.

The duality and opportunity of disruption

From a Japanese perspective, the notion of something being 'broken apart' contains possibility. In the art of *Kintsugi*, practitioners reconnect broken pieces of pottery using gold. Depending on one's perspective, the storms of disruption can be reflected into the sunshine of opportunity.

Disruption is known by many different names:

- In science, disruptions are 'paradigm shifts'.
- Disruptions in game strategy are 'metagame shifts'.
- In technology, we often refer to disruptions as innovations.
- Colloquially, disruption might be called a rebirth, reset or renaissance.

There have been disruptions forever, positive and negative. The invention of the wheel around 3,500 BCE was a major disruption. However, disruptions are occurring in more areas and more rapidly than ever. Accordingly, we should not be surprised if today's rapid pace of change accelerates.

Along our path – from writing around 3,400 BCE, the printing press in 1440, the telegraph in 1830, the smartphone in 2007, to 25 per cent of the world on the internet in 2009 doubling to 50 per cent in 2018 – we discern a pattern: the rate of change is increasing. On this accelerating, exponentiating curve, each disruption arrives more rapidly than the last. This isn't a mere excavation of history – it's the stark observation that we are in an era of constant compounding change.

As we look back upon millennia of human evolution, it's clear that, while the rhythm of change appears slow, its tempo is fast. From the dawn of civilization to the exploration of the moon – and now, Mars and beyond – each advancement is a testament to self-reinforcing effects of innovation.

As this exponential curve steepens, it becomes even more critical not just to observe, but also to actively participate in shaping the futures. Disruption must be assessed as a systemic driver of change. The nature of today's radical changes is more fundamental, deeper and broader than disruptions caused by specific innovations or products. Disruption is no longer an isolated, one-off or recurring event, but a steady state of existence.

The intersecting elements of disruptions are often overlooked when considering next-order implications, especially in our hyperconnected world. This second-order thinking goes beyond direct consequences to consider subsequent effects holistically over time. Together, these create a new context of systemic disruption.

Predictability's inverse relationship with uncertainty

The cost of running businesses as if the world is stable and linear is increasing. As uncertainty grows, it becomes more costly to assume that the world is predictable. Predictability is only viable when parameters are known. The greater the extent of unknown variables, the less predictable the environment.

EXAMPLE

The collapse of Silicon Valley Bank

As the largest bank by deposits in Silicon Valley collapsed in 2023, it marked the second-largest bank failure in US history. Despite the many uncertainties that affected it, Silicon Valley Bank (SVB) relied heavily on its past decade's experience. SVB's downfall stemmed from its unwavering adherence to a few critical assumptions. Although it had a large exposure concentrated in long-term bond portfolios, SVB assumed the low-interest-rate environment would persist. These holdings were vulnerable to interest rate fluctuations and lost value as rates increased. Additionally, the bank counted on continued enthusiasm for the technology start-ups it depended on. When valuations plummeted, SVB faced a surge in credit losses.

Unlike the 2008 financial crisis, social media platforms compounded these challenges. The moment a venture capitalist on Sand Hill Road hinted at avoiding concentration of cash deposits with SVB, news of the bank's troubles spread like wildfire. Reminiscent of the 1946 film *It's a Wonderful Life*, this news triggered a bank run, with large numbers of depositors attempting to withdraw their cash simultaneously. Due to SVB's long-term holdings, it lacked liquidity to meet customer demands, compelling the bank to sell its bonds at a significant loss.

In 2022, the repercussions of Russia's invasion of Ukraine spilled into global markets. Relying on quantitative forecasts that isolate and extrapolate historic numbers carries implications. While data and forecasts are abundant, they failed to shield the world from suddenly experiencing the highest levels of inflation in half a century. The mighty US Treasury admitted its complete

Figure 1.1   The increasing cost of business as usual

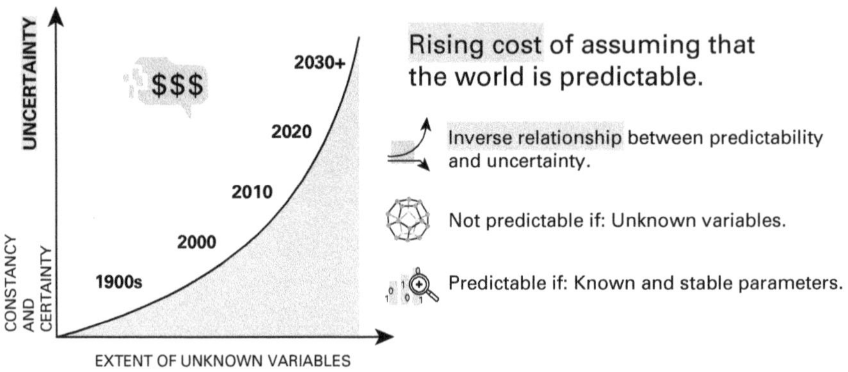

lack of understanding of what it labelled as 'unanticipated' shocks to the economy. Many others were similarly surprised, despite surging inflation being common after extensive 'money printing'.

At any point, the information available for decision-making is historical. Meanwhile the outcomes lie in the inherently unknown future.

Given the inverse relationship between predictability and uncertainty, there is an increasing cost of assuming a stable world (Figure 1.1). As assumptions unravel, the scope of value destruction is growing for those intent on business as usual.

Systemic change is Disruption 3.0

The single most dangerous mistake is looking at disruption as isolated cases or independent episodic events. The complex network of interconnected forces driving disruption reinforces the inherent dislocations, paradoxes and diversity of perspectives, problems and responses.

This environment conjures a new type of disruption, omnipresent and systemic. It establishes entirely new paradigms, which themselves will evolve. We label this Disruption 3.0.

Beyond VUCA: Updating for velocity and connectivity

'VUCA' spread across the US military's leadership from the 1980s. Twenty years later, it made its way to business strategists.

The traits – volatility, uncertainty, complexity and ambiguity – were not new even back in the 1980s. But thanks to their significant increases in magnitude, they have informed decision-making. *In a VUCA world, if you're not consciously confused, you're ignorant. If you're not preparing, you're negligent.*

If you compare VUCA's search popularity in 2023 to a decade earlier, we see interest increased nearly fivefold. In other words, for each time someone searched for VUCA in 2013, there are five people searching a decade later.

Today, VUCA is amplified due to cascading effects from:

- growth in interconnections, networks and ecosystems
- instantaneous communication
- tipping points of artificial intelligence and climate change
- the explosion of emerging and converging technologies

Despite that, the world remains intent on behaving as if structure, control and predictability are still dominant. For a VUCA environment, our tools and systems are becoming ineffectual, from education to governance.

In 2020 a new acronym emerged: BANI (brittle, anxious, non-linear and incomprehensible).[9] While these resonated with many, 'anxious' and 'brittle' suggests an inherent fear of the future, lacking opportunity.

There are many other variations of VUCA. While we do not need additional acronyms, we do need improved methods of understanding our environment to establish suitable responses.

Our world is facing new tensions, contradictions, complexities and uncertainties. This new reality is the basis for our own version of VUCA, updated with two additional features: *intersecting* and *exponential*. In an UN-VICE[10] world (see the following box), these concepts are as important as unknown, volatile and complex. We must go beyond automatically relying on *ad*vice and start forming our own UN-VICE to survive. Proposing yet another acronym is risky – I hope the acronym police will be merciful.

With *intersecting,* cross-impacts determine outcomes. The more connected everything is, the more combinatorial effects will interact. These drivers ricochet into unexpected change.

Exponential refers to the shape of change. Exponential change is initially slow; our cognitive biases expect it to continue linearly. This deceptive nature causes people to miss inflection points after the change swells.

The accelerating connectivity, complex interconnections and rapid evolution of constant changes means that these exponential and intersecting drivers move us to a higher disruptive frequency.

Deconstructing our UN-VICE

What is our UN-VICE in the context of Disruption 3.0?

To sum up, UN-VICE is an updated way of capturing the state of the world. Framing the dynamics of systemic disruption as *un*known, *v*olatile, *inter*secting, *c*omplex and *e*xponential enables an empowering response. We are not helpless victims unable to make decisions – *we have the power to shape our own futures*.

KEY POINTS
Our UN-VICE acronym

- **Unknown: Uncertainty becomes our comfort zone.** Recognize you can't know anything perfectly and many decisions are based on assumptions. Increased uncertainty lowers the value of advice and requires increased self-reliance. Learn how to respond regardless of the lack of precedents.

- **Volatile: Harness change for gain.** Our world, and change itself, are evolving faster than ever before. Volatility is not new; we simply can't ignore its impact. In volatility, we see the shifting speed and texture of the changing environment.

- **Intersecting: Everything connects to everything else.** The broader our lens, the greater the insights gained from realizing how boundaries are disappearing.

- **Complex: Notice emergent properties and adapt.** In complex environments, inputs do not map clearly to outputs. Practitioners must acknowledge emergent properties and reconcile the immediate with the indefinite. Such systems require critical thinking, experimentation and judgement. Evaluate emerging issues, build resiliency and learn to adapt to expanding complexity.

- **Exponential: Pay attention to non-linear types of change that increase in growth rate.** Notice rapid acceleration of seemingly small shifts. Monitoring early on will mean fewer surprises.

Examples of new opportunities deployed for humanity's progress

Disruption 3.0 is impactful. It offers pathways to promising futures, going beyond modern techno-industrial innovation.

- **Vaccine development:** Supported by AI platforms, a new generation of vaccines allows speed and scale from development to deployment, with the promise of eradicating deadly diseases.

- **AI maps out human biology:** AlphaFold is an AI program that predicts biological molecules, including extremely complex protein structures, with unprecedented precision and speed. Google's DeepMind is capable of making predictions for the shape of every single protein in the human body. Millions of scientists already use AlphaFold for insights into curing diseases and solving major problems including antibiotic resistance, microplastic pollution and climate change.

- **Net positive energy fusion:** Dozens of organizations are working to develop nuclear fusion, which would generate more energy than it consumes.

- **First asteroid deflection:** NASA successfully altered the trajectory of an asteroid, a proof of concept for deflecting any dangerous asteroid that threatens to collide with Earth.

New scientific discoveries are driven by the intersection of fields. Technology could redefine humanity's outlook – and what it means to be human.

Each of these discoveries results in value transfers. The volatility, changes and disruptions transform existing industries and create new fields, generating value for some, eroding value for others.

Advice is becoming less replicable

Relying on experts and their advice is less helpful now than ever and their helpfulness continues to decrease. We are not arguing for the systematic dismissal of expertise; rather, we can no longer delegate our decisions and rely on experts alone for all the answers. In the words of the Royal Society, *nullius in verba* ('take nobody's word for it').

In contrast to advice, our UN-VICE is not a suggestion of behaviour or a mandate. Instead, it is a way to decipher changing circumstances imaginatively. All advice should be carefully considered, combined with an emphasis on developing and trusting our own capabilities.

In our increasingly UN-VICE world, the value of recommendations is rapidly decreasing. Systemic disruption has devalued *ad*-vice; instead, we offer our best UN-VICE. We must explore unanswered questions, rather than adhering to unquestionable answers.

Zen Master Suzuki Roshi said, 'In the beginner's mind there are many possibilities, but in the expert's there are few.'[11] Our UN-VICE draws from the three stages of the Japanese martial arts concept *shuhari*. In the first stage, *shu*, the student masters the established fundamentals. In the second stage, *ha*, the learner practises and experiments with novel approaches, guided by their own unique perspectives. In the third stage, *ri*, they break loose from confining rulebooks to adapt freely to any situation. *Shuhari* is a journey, a continuous process of learning, experimenting and letting go.

Nothing can be your substitute

The third stage of *shuhari* is the hardest but most important in our present-day world and imminent futures. No external structures can replace your individual accumulation of knowledge and perspectives. *You'll have to learn and adapt for yourself.*

Science enables the treatment of many debilitating diseases, illustrated by the record-fast development of Covid vaccines. Thanks to science, we have harnessed electricity, built aeroplanes, 3D-bioprinted functional organs, put humans on the Moon and rovers on Mars. Science is nothing short of miraculous.

However, this expertise often exists in narrow fields and specific circumstances. Experts are most helpful in controllable, ordered and predictable environments. Here, cause and effect is understood beforehand, models are reliable, forecasts accurate and solutions replicable. In these knowable environments, expertise is invaluable.

But the world is no longer controllable and understandable. Rather, it is increasingly unpredictable, and there are not always right answers at the onset. Here, reliance on expert analysis alone is limited.

We are faced with novel challenges for which there are no established experts. The deeper the uncertainties, the greater the divergences of existing expert views. This is the case for social inequalities, mitigating climate change and transformational technologies, which demand different thinking. We should embrace the latest science while appreciating the limitations of our knowledge.

We must also be wary of the flood of misinformation and unsupported opinions. Those who face the future by denying reality and science will fare poorly compared to critical thinkers. The emerging features of our new environments are not understood. Even experts may not know or agree on the potential challenges, outcomes or solutions.

Not knowing is uncomfortable. We humans like to verify everything empirically. We crave certainty. Enduring the unresolved can be distressing. Yet, we can harness this unpredictability to drive novel ideas and original responses.

The permission to wander around, imagine, ask questions and challenge assumptions makes the magic happen.

Let's unpack the constituents of UN-VICE: unknown, volatile, intersecting, complex, exponential.

Unknown

No one can perfectly predict the future just as no one can perfectly know the present. *In an unknown situation, humility about one's knowledge is paramount.*

In VUCA, 'U' stood for uncertain and 'A' for ambiguous, describing a lack of confidence in how events might unfold. Together, these two elements articulate that the field of behaviour is confusing and that agents lack 'knowledge'.

'Knowledge' has always been prized in Western philosophy, in contrast to its near neighbours, supposition and opinion. Knowledge is not just confident, accurate belief; it is a state of alignment between the agent and the world that enables successful thought and action. Agents with 'knowledge' thrive.

Environments, agents and their relationships are increasingly liminal. Liminal spaces are blurry in-between boundary zones where old and new coexist. With ambient disruption, it is folly to believe one will 'arrive at the other side' of any transition. We live in a state of liminality, navigating between the certain and uncertain. We can no longer differentiate between known and unknown, digital and physical, natural and artificial, truth and fiction, reality and simulation, competitors and partners, science fiction and science fact. Liminal spaces are growing and evolving.

Entire industries, especially strategic consulting, sell frameworks to define, tier and quantify levels of knowability. However, these calculated bets tend to be modelled on assumptions, rendering them useless or even dangerous. Dynamic changes have impacts that can be disproportionate and incomprehensible. *Relying on assumptions does not quantify the unquantifiable or make the unknowable known.*

Rather than rely on specific outcomes, we need to plan for many eventualities. Relentless curiosity demands a strong tolerance for ambiguity. We must adjust mindsets and accept that our questions may have fewer answers. The value lies not in the answers we formulate, but in our questions.

Perfecting imperfections

We need to become 'perfect imperfectionists'. Western culture is stubbornly attached to perfectionism; Eastern philosophy finds beauty in imperfection. The Buddhist concept of *wabi sabi,* and other similar approaches, accept incompleteness, transience and emptiness to form a transcendental comprehension of the unknown.

Leadership once meant having the right answers. Now, it means asking insightful questions. In these liminal spaces and nebulous relationships, those who have a healthy relationship with the unknown, including within themselves, will thrive. They will have knowledge despite – or because of – the unknown.

Deep uncertainties propel us into the unknown

Today, increasing unpredictability is evident everywhere, from the Covid pandemic, to emerging technologies that disrupt incumbents, to predicting military operations and their outcomes, to cascading effects of geopolitical change.

Deep uncertainty means we lack visibility of the type of events that may happen, let alone their likelihood. How do energy turmoil, food insecurity, high inflation, pandemics, China's rise, Russia's war in Ukraine, spillover from Middle Eastern instability, polarization, rising autocracies, emerging technologies and extreme weather interact? What are the transversal consequences of climate change across society? What happens as the impacts of advancing AI systems, the space race and brash cyberattacks on critical networked infrastructure collide?

The world we live in is deeply uncertain – we are better off building resilience. *Relying on probabilities, certainties or crystal balls will fail us.*

EXAMPLE
96 per cent is far from certain

Despite widespread AI hype, the 2022 Australian Tennis Open reminded us of the pointlessness of relying on predictions.

During the final match, Rafael Nadal was struggling against Daniil Medvedev. After Nadal lost the first two sets, bookmakers looked at the data: only in five previous situations had a player made a comeback from here in a Grand Slam final. It seemed very unlikely, almost impossible, that Nadal would win. Accounting for Nadal's recent injuries, age and other variables, the algorithm assigned Medvedev a 96 per cent chance of winning. In fact, Medvedev did nearly win – he had three different opportunities to win the match with a single point, but Nadal persisted.

The technology did not factor in the unpredictability of life, mental state and composure of humans. Nadal made a comeback and won. Human behaviour is not predictable or replicable. Humans are complex adaptive systems, chaotic by nature.

Statistics, AI and our cognitive thinking develop predictive models based on assumed known parameters, but our current world is deeply uncertain and unpredictable. Any predictions about the future should be carefully evaluated, as no one knows how the future will unfold. *Put simply, there is no data on the future.*

Volatile

Not only is the world changing faster than ever, *change* is evolving faster than ever.

Something that is volatile changes rapidly. In economics, a volatile investment swings widely in value. In chemistry, a volatile substance evaporates quickly. Humans typically fear change rather than desire it, so we generally conceptualize volatility as negative. This is inaccurate. *In truth, neither volatility nor change have an inherent valence.*

Just as chaotic times can be ruinous or spur needed transformation, our volatile world is simply experiencing more rapid evolutions. Change is gaining new footholds and transmuting trends. Across domains, change is shifting in speed, volume and texture. Some harness this volatility for gain; others suffer from it. Alan Watts, a Western proponent of Eastern philosophies, observed: 'the only way to make sense out of change is to plunge into it, move with it and join the dance'.

Intersecting

As boundaries disappear, formerly separate areas connect. Intersecting elements come together, overlap or interact. For example:

- In civil engineering, an intersection is where two roads meet.

- In mathematics, an intersection is the overlap between two sets.
- In sociology, intersectionality analyses how various aspects of identities intersect to create emergent properties that shape personhood.

Intersections can create an emergent whole greater than the sum of its parts, permitting deeper and broader innovation than before. In a systemic world, the notion of discrete events is obsolete; every impact intertwines, weaving a tapestry of interconnectedness.

Creations emerge when diverse perspectives intersect, making connections between ideas and experiences.

Magic happens when intersections create new combinations

Intersections are the crucible from which novelty emerges. Whether inseparable or independent, the power of associative thinking amplifies when diverse individuals, fields or technologies interact.

Consider the intersection between technology, manufacturing and biology that led to a 3D-printed miniature heart at Tel Aviv University. This interdisciplinary emerging field called synbio (synthetic biology), comprising biology, advanced materials, engineering, medicine and technology, allows humans to create new types of life.

Likewise, the fusion of AI, genetic engineering and robotics is revolutionizing drug discovery. The emergence of biotechnology AI platforms is radically transforming the pharmaceutical industry. Similar convergences of cross-fertilizing innovations are redefining entire sectors.

In a digitized world, semiconductor chips manage electricity consumption, track locations and operate systems. A chip manufacturer today might become the automotive industry's engine tomorrow, with a car's operating system representing most of its value. An automotive manufacturer developing electrification, energy storage and flying vehicles is not alone, as an aerospace supplier will be doing the same. *Distinct sectors may no longer be discernible as industries intersect.*

To respond, organizations need more awareness than ever, respecting that everything connects. A competitor may emerge from anywhere and they might become a partner or customer. This transdisciplinary approach underlies our UN-VICE world, emulating nature itself as diversity breeds creativity.

Complex

People tend to believe that the world is governed by either obvious simplicity or impenetrable complexity. Reality is not so cut and dry.

At its simplest level, complexity limits our understanding:

- In *complex* systems, typical analysis tools don't work: Complex systems are dynamic, unpredictable and have no predefined outcomes. No predictable path can be established in advance and relied upon with certainty.

- *Complicated* environments are predictable: 'Complicated' refers to a high level of difficulty that can be understood and solved. Here, we can rely on expertise because problems can be broken down and reassembled. There is a range of right answers – we know what we don't know.

Something is complex when it has unknown unknowns, multi-source causality, co-dependent variables and moving parts that simultaneously seem interconnected and interdependent. Complex systems like cities, social networks and financial markets are dynamic. They constantly morph and generate emergent properties unexpected at the outset. *The whole is not merely different from the sum of its parts – the whole lacks a clear relationship to the parts' sum.*

The industrial, mechanical world that relies on technical expertise is complicated. But the Amazon rainforest, where species become extinct, weather patterns change abruptly and which will be affected by an infinite number of interactions between its parts, is complex. Any type of project involving nature, such as rerouting rainforest water sources, is subject to unexpected changes from an unknowable number of sources and must account for complexity (Table 1.1).

Table 1.1   Contrasting complicated with complex

Complicated – examples	Complex – examples
- Linear relationships - Voltage and current in an electrical conductor - Programming a computer - Building an aircraft - Repairing an engine - Sending a rocket to the Moon or probe to Mars - Highways, roads, bridges - Oil or mineral exploration - Wikipedia	- Ant colonies, termite mounds, fish schooling - Brain, immune system, human genome - Bacteria, disease and pandemic outbreaks - Raising a child - Social networks, World Wide Web, network effects - Disinformation, misinformation, conspiracy theories - Countries, planets, universe - Traffic management, cities - Amazon rainforest, global biosphere - Markets, geopolitics

Complexity is non-linear

In non-linear systems, small inputs can result in large effects. Here, one rogue actor, insignificant event or small error can trigger a disproportionate amplifying effect. Thus, most people do not anticipate – and are even surprised by – the magnitude of the consequences of change in complex environments (Table 1.2).

Systemic change can be unsettling due to its inherent complexity. Non-linear phenomena, coupled with the velocity and multiplicity of interconnections, ramp up complexity's effects.

Since complex systems contain unclear connections, causality can only be established retrospectively. You must appreciate the dynamics between elements, even if you can't identify them. Actors can probe complexity via safe experiments. This trial and error should incorporate multiple hypotheses from diverse perspectives, incorporating feedback into an evolving understanding of emerging patterns, all while adjusting behaviour based on results.[12]

Adapted responses to complexity often create autonomous, decentralized and self-organized networks rather than hierarchical structures where the top dictates action. Instead of waiting for consistency, the successful actor must learn to operate in uncertain and ever-changing environments.

With complexity, we move away from a reducible Newtonian view of the world. Shifting from this mechanistic view to one where there may not be straightforward solutions is challenging for everyone – including businesses, institutions and policymakers. We are moving from what 'may', 'might' or 'could' to actually having to prototype these futures.

Table 1.2 Comparing linear to non-linear

Environment	Definition	Terms
Linear	Outputs directly **proportional** to their inputs.	Additively, anticipated, direct, extrapolation, gradual, growth, homogeneity, incremental, predictable, sequential, simple, straight, summation, superposition
Non-linear	Effects (outputs, behaviours) **not proportional** to their causes (inputs). Effects could be larger or smaller.	Change, chaotic, collapse, counterintuitive, disruption, exponential, multiple, network, overshoot, shift, snowball, sudden, surprise, swerve, transformation, turbulent, unpredictable

Certainty is fleeting, but through experimentation, systems innovation and trial-and-error, instructive patterns emerge as guidance.

EXAMPLE

Relying on technology and standard instruction manuals

On 1 June 2009, Air France Flight 447 crashed into the Atlantic Ocean between Rio and Paris, killing everyone on board. In the chain of events leading to the crash, many factors eventually led to human errors.

Ice had accumulated outside the aircraft, affecting the pitot tube sensors, which measured speed. Erratic airspeed readings caused the flight computer to disconnect the autopilot when there was significant turbulence. These failures led the plane to stall. Specific manual intervention was required to remedy the stall, but the pilots relied on information systems that indicated the plane was not stalling.

The pilots excessively relied on technology in two ways. First, in terms of pattern recognition, they were unaccustomed to manual intervention in these challenging conditions. Second, the pilots failed to recognize the stall because the computer systems indicated no such issue; they couldn't fathom that the technology was unreliable.

Unfortunately, overreliance on machines and adherence to standard play-books means that humans often operate in 'autopilot' mode. When we are not accustomed to unexpected environments or needing to experiment to find the answers ourselves, we risk overreacting or underreacting as new situations spiral out of control.

Complexity allows for emergence as an alternative to operating on auto-pilot.

While the tragic example above is atypical, the business world is plagued by experts who misapply their knowledge of complicated situations to complex ones. MBA-style playbooks are bound to be limiting, if not obsolete, when transposed to UN-VICE environments.

The case of CNN+: With a little help from McKinsey?

McKinsey, the consulting firm, is believed to have advised CNN on the launch strategy for streaming service CNN+ in 2022. After the launch failed,

Axios reported that the shuttering of CNN+, just 'weeks after the subscription service launched, will be remembered as one of the most chaotic moments of CNN's 40-year history'. Shortly after the launch, concerns emerged about the app's costs and business plan. The strategy had projected two million US subscribers in its initial year, growing to 15–18 million after four years. After underwhelming sign-ups, they were forced to scale this back dramatically.

In these situations, a consultancy's typical scope includes an analysis of the competitive landscape, a deep dive into the historical data of competitors, forecasts based on the assumption of replicating a comparable brand's business model, extrapolating peers' track records into the future and a comparison of these trends and business plans to the client's model. These data-driven findings are presented in a polished report containing detailed market analyses, which provides reassurance to executives and board members. The consultancy typically has no skin in the game and is compensated for a formulaic report that confirms the client's preconceived notions, regardless of any flaws, potential challenges or conflicts of interest.

Beyond consulting, IDEO, a founding innovation firm behind design thinking, went through a major turnaround in 2023 as it experienced less demand for its services. Maybe pre-cooked recipes, from strategic consultancies to designers' toolkits, are no longer relevant for handling complex environments. Complexity's biggest dangers arise when we are mired in old ways and assumptions instead of adapting to new patterns.

Exponential

In mathematics, something is 'exponential' when it grows based on its size. The term is used colloquially to mean any growth that accelerates.

Humans operate on millennia-old hardware. We can comprehend linear relationships, but have trouble processing accelerating rates of change. While linear change may feel comfortable, exponential growth feels like a surprise. In *The Sun Also Rises*, Ernest Hemingway echoes this: 'How did you go bankrupt?' 'Two ways. Gradually, then suddenly.'

Exponential growth made its mark on the 20th century and will be even more impactful in the 21st. Technology grows at an exponential rate: Moore's Law states that the number of transistors on an integrated circuit doubles every two years. Social connections do too: Metcalfe's Law states that a network's effect is proportional to the square of the number of users.

From compound interest to compound learning, paying attention to rates of change is critically important (Figure 1.2). If you miss an exponential curve, there's no catching up. For example, while 30 linear steps take you around 30 meters, 30 exponential steps (doubling in length every time) take you around the Earth more than 25 times.

EXAMPLE
Exponential water lilies

Figure 1.2   A month at the pond

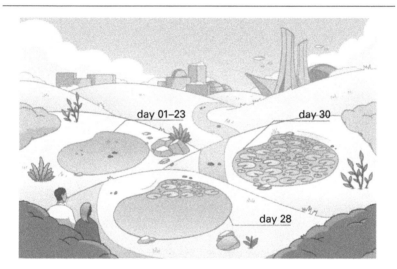

Observe the power of exponential growth through the story of water lilies:

- **Despite doubling every day, the initial effect is barely perceptible:** If lilies in a pond double daily for 30 days, they will cover less than 1 per cent of the pond for 23 days.

- **A gradual process:** On day 28, lilies cover only 25 per cent of the pond.

- **A sudden finish:** 75 per cent of the growth occurs on days 29 and 30, when the lilies rapidly cover the rest of the pond.

In the early stages of a pandemic, a social upheaval, or as a new technology emerges, let Monet's famous 'Nymphéas' paintings from Giverny remind you of the subtle onset of exponential changes.

As science fiction writer William Gibson puts it: 'The future is already here – it's just unevenly distributed.' Though the future cannot actually be here, exponential growth makes it feel like it is. Fragments of the future exist in the present, growing gradually… until one day they've suddenly already taken over.

Due to the velocity of change, the lifespan of ideas, products and policies can contract sharply and unexpectedly. In our exponential world, we must pay attention to the cumulative effects of change, which can have both positive and negative impacts.

The best UN-VICE you can get

Table 1.3   Insights and responses to our UN-VICE acronym

	Acronym	Insights	Response
UN	**UNknown**	• Need to learn from oneself • Uncertainty + ambiguity = lack of knowledge	**Achieve knowledge despite the unknown**
V	**Volatile**	• Abrupt change • Shifts speed, texture and magnitude • Neither volatility nor change have an inherent valence	**Be aware of and harness volatility for gain**
I	**Intersecting**	• As boundaries disappear, separate areas connect • Intersections create new combinations, as elements converge, overlap and intersect	**Respect that everything connects to everything else**
C	**Complex**	• Limits our understanding • Constant flux, unpredictable • Disproportionate impacts	**Acute sense-making, constant adaptation, notice emerging issues**
E	**Exponential**	• Gradually, then suddenly • Early developments – even if doubling – barely perceptible	**Pay attention early to rates of change**

Our UN-VICE? Emulate the octopus

When approaching the unknown futures, it helps to assemble a strong team. We have therefore selected the octopus as our mascot.

Uniquely suited to the role by remaining relevant for 296 million years, our squishy friend helps you navigate our UN-VICE world (Table 1.3).

As is necessary for relevance, the octopus is an encapsulation of opposites:

- **Vulnerable, yet strong:** Acting in varying circumstances as predator or prey, octopuses pull from their vast capabilities to camouflage, distract, dodge, solve and strike.

- **Intelligent, yet short-lived:** Octopuses are incredibly intelligent, but live only up to three years, a stark contrast to other intelligent animals. As a species, the octopus has flourished, in part through adaptation trade-offs. For instance, the loss of a shell around 275 million years ago enabled them to become better problem-solvers but opened them to predation.

- **Leisurely, yet swift:** Octopuses prefer to move slowly along the ocean floor, sometimes literally crawling, spending little energy. However, an octopus can draw water into its body and shoot it out to propel itself at speeds up to 25 miles per hour.

- **Powerful, yet agile:** An octopus's body is around 90 per cent muscle, with no bones, giving them great strength and agility. An octopus's tentacles can grab and hold nearly anything; some species have lifted 40 times their body weight.

Physically agile, this squishy strategist and tentacled tactician uses its intelligence and agency to intuit situations, anticipate outcomes, invent solutions and improvise, remaining relevant for nearly 300 million years.

Notes

1 World Uncertainty Index. www.worlduncertaintyindex.com (archived at https://perma.cc/3YQ7-K4NJ)

2 D Shariatmadari. A year of 'permacrisis', Collins Language Lovers Blog, 1 November 2022. blog.collinsdictionary.com/language-lovers/a-year-of-permacrisis (archived at https://perma.cc/RC5N-FHPD)

3 IPCC. AR6 synthesis report: Climate change 2023, IPCC, 2023. www.ipcc.ch/report/sixth-assessment-report-cycle (archived at https://perma.cc/KR2P-8CJS)

4   AlixPartners. 2023 AlixPartners Disruption Index, AlixPartners, 2023. docs. alixpartners.com/view/397725974 (archived at https://perma.cc/LJF3-7KHW)

5   T Espiner and N Sherman. JP Morgan's Jamie Dimon warns world facing 'most dangerous time in decades', BBC, 13 October 2023. www.bbc.com/ news/business-67104734 (archived at https://perma.cc/SL2Y-UEWU)

6   J A Schumpeter (1942) *Capitalism, Socialism and Democracy*, Harper & Brothers Publishers, New York, NY

7   C M Christensen (1997) *The Innovator's Dilemma: When new technologies cause great firms to fail*, Harvard Business School Press, Boston, MA

8   C M Christensen, M E Raynor and R McDonald. What is disruptive innovation? *Harvard Business Review*, 1 December 2015. hbsp.harvard.edu/product/ R1512B-PDF-ENG (archived at https://perma.cc/Q996-6V8W)

9   J Cascio. Facing the age of chaos, Medium, 29 April 2020. www.medium. com/@cascio/facing-the-age-of-chaos-b00687b1f51d (archived at https:// perma.cc/U8LK-DUMQ)

10   R Spitz and L Zuin (2022) *The Definitive Guide to Thriving on Disruption: Essential frameworks for disruption and uncertainty*, Disruptive Futures Institute, San Francisco, CA

11   S Suzuki (1970) *Zen Mind, Beginner's Mind*, Weatherhill, Trumbull, CT

12   S E Page (2009) *Understanding Complexity*, The Great Courses, Chantilly, VA

2

Embracing new mindsets for thriving on uncertainty and disruption

OBJECTIVES
Learning the language of disruption

The dynamics of change are evolving. By mastering its language, we cultivate new mindsets and capabilities crucial for thriving in uncertainty amidst ambient disruption.

Widen the aperture, multiply lenses

Understanding the world depends on our windows to it. This chapter widens the aperture, allowing us to shift mindsets and change the narrative around uncertainty.

When exploring complex issues we must dismantle silos, because everything is connected. Global supply chains, artificial intelligence, automation, social media, climate change, existential risks, geopolitical reshuffling, societal paradigm shifts, work, education and more – none exist in a vacuum and we can't treat them as such.

Disruption is not sporadic; it's now our constant reality, permeating domains with unprecedented speed. The degree of surprise we face depends on our mindset toward change. An anticipatory mindset with critical thinking and diverse perspectives diminishes astonishment. Exploring multiple future scenarios enhances our preparedness for any potentiality.

Mindsets for surviving surprises

By its very nature, disruption is surprising. According to the wisdom of Seneca: 'The man who has anticipated the coming of troubles takes away their power when they arrive.' Disruption shatters what we consider normal. In times of radical change, our understanding of the world must evolve; otherwise, we risk perpetual surprise. *The impacts of disruption depend on your perspective, preparation and response* (Figure 2.1).

CHECKLIST
Reducing surprise

How can we prepare for something that could always surprise us?

- **Anticipate more.** By gaining perspective, we are more inclined to challenge the status quo and test assumptions.

- **Explore with curiosity.** Investigation uncovers changes sooner rather than later.

- **Initiate the change yourself.** Agency is the ability to take action. By exercising agency, we become response-able, escaping the victim mindset to deal with constant change. When you initiate change, you are unsurprised by the swerves.

- **Timely response.** Given exponential change, failure to respond when disruption rears its head can be disastrous. Adaptation is a fundamental determinant of evolutionary success.

The surprise you experience from disruption is inversely tied to your preparedness and willingness to question. An anticipatory mindset diminishes astonishment when change occurs. By recognizing the duality of disruption, thinking critically and questioning assumptions, we reduce shocks and uncover opportunities.

Disruption's impact hinges on three factors: your perspective, your preparedness and the effectiveness of your timely response.

Figure 2.1   Factors that impact the degree of disruption

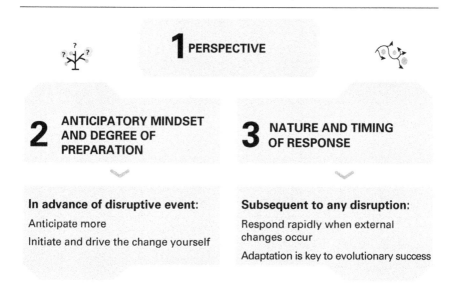

The 6 i's

How do we rise above resilience to actually thrive on disruption? In the quest to make an impact, how can we have a passionate, effective and flourishing experience?

The language of disruption is rooted in action. Unlock the mindsets necessary to embrace uncertainty with the 6 i's – keys to not just surviving, but thriving (Figure 2.2):

- **Intuition:** Explore ambiguous environments without straightforward answers by tapping into curiosity, avoiding preconceptions.

- **Inspiration and imagination:** Encompassing broader futures, be inspired by asking profound questions and breaking from the present.

- **Improvisation:** Experiment through improvisation, mistakes and ambiguity, seeking authenticity.

- **Invention:** Nothing is predetermined. We have an open canvas to create our futures.

- **Impossible:** With the courage to wander and fail, you can stumble upon – and achieve – the impossible.

These are our 6 i's to thriving on disruption: intuition, inspiration, imagination, improvisation, invention, impossible.[1]

Figure 2.2   The 6 i's to driving and thriving on disruption

1 **INTUITION** Avoid preconceptions, trust yourself and your judgement

2 **INSPIRATION** Explore – be curious, inspired and imaginative

3 **IMAGINATION** Ask broad questions, break from the present

4 **IMPROVISATION** Experiment with authenticity, mistakes and ambiguity

5 **INVENTION** Nothing is predetermined: we invent our futures

6 **IMPOSSIBLE** Confidence to wander, fail and stumble upon the impossible

Intuition, through the beginner's mind

In Steve Jobs' Stanford commencement address, he told the tale of following his intuition. Stumbling upon a love for calligraphy early in his career, he realized its importance a decade later – when the Macintosh became the first computer with beautiful typography. Computers today – particularly Apple – might not have the same design focus had Jobs not followed his intuition.

Intuition is the ability to recognize patterns through tacit knowledge and apply them without clear reasoning. Daniel Kahneman divides cognition into two systems:[2]

- **System 1:** Rapid, unconscious and intuitive-emotional.
- **System 2:** Slower, conscious and rational.

The effectiveness of relying on analysis is inversely proportional to the degree of uncertainty.

Intuition is neither a luxury nor a shortcut; *in deeply uncertain environments, intuition is a necessity.* We should not reject rational analysis or expert advice, but we must recognize these don't have all the answers in UN-VICE environments.

Different types of intuition

- **Expert intuition:** Based on recognition and experience, expert intuition allows individuals to make quick decisions in familiar situations. When a doctor, engineer or pilot must react swiftly in a known environment, they can do so unconsciously. However, expert intuition's effectiveness may diminish in unfamiliar domains, in which ingrained habits hinder flexible decision-making.

- **Implicit intuition:** This type involves sudden insights that emerge without conscious effort. It is often derived from tacit knowledge or experiences that we aren't aware of.

- **Non-local intuition:** Also known as inner wisdom or instinct, this intuition taps into a spiritual connection with the universe. This is observed in entrepreneurs who make impactful decisions beyond the bounds of reason or experience.

Shoshin: *The beginner's mind*

The Zen Buddhism concept of *shoshin* (the beginner's mind) is a reminder of intuition's importance. From the Japanese *sho* (初), meaning the first time and *shin* (心), meaning mind and spirit, *shoshin* values approaching each situation with an open, curious mind. In the 14th and 15th centuries, Zeami, Japan's greatest playwright, initiated the famous Japanese Proverb '*shoshin wasuru bekarazu*' (never forget the beginner's mind).

Shoshin prizes childlike naivety. With no outside influence or preconceptions, you can follow your intuition. For these reasons, Henry Ford said, 'I am looking for a lot of men who have an infinite capacity to not know what can't be done.' John Lennon said, 'Every child is an artist until he's told he's not an artist.'

Following your intuition requires a culture of trust. We should be encouraged to explore changing the world through action and experimentation. With the courage to trust our abilities, we can follow our intuition to new heights.

Prior experiences, credentials and conventional solutions no longer suffice in tackling systemic challenges. The courage to learn through trial and error is not just essential; it is imperative for unlocking outsized discoveries.

Imagination, curiosity and resourcefulness are the enduring skills of resilience and innovation.

The indeterminate environments of today require new decision-making, new types of leadership and new operating models. *Ultimately, the beginner's mind offers humility as a place for learning.*

Reversible decisions

As uncertainty takes centre stage, the information needed for informed decisions becomes increasingly elusive. Here, distinguish between reversible and irreversible decisions – a concept articulated by Jeff Bezos in his letter to Amazon shareholders.

Assessing a decision's reversibility provides valuable perspectives into the risk associated with relying on intuition. Two questions emerge in this evaluation:

- What are the consequences of this decision?
- Can this decision be reversed, and if so, for how long?

With limited consequences, we can make reversible decisions rapidly and gain a competitive advantage. The inherent flexibility of reversible decisions allows for agility in the face of uncertainty. Harnessing intuition can expedite the process. Leveraging feedback loops transforms outcomes into learning opportunities, eliminating the concept of failure. Reversible decisions are two-way doors that allow us to continuously improve decision-making.

Conversely, when assessing consequential irreversible decisions, we must defer commitment in order to delve deeper because the stakes are higher. These decisions are one-way doors with no turning back, even if the consequences prove undesirable.

Intuition does not substitute investigation, but complete certainty is often unattainable, irrespective of how many experts we consult, the data we have or the time we take before deciding. Bezos states you can make most reversible decisions with 70 per cent of the information you wish you had. For irreversible decisions, such as launching a major product or signing a long-term lease, you should not require more than 90 per cent optimal knowledge. If you wait to obtain more information than that, you may be too late.

Bezos' own decision to launch Amazon was based on his ability to return to his former Wall Street job if it failed.[3] Years later, his decision to launch Amazon Prime was based on intuition.[4]

KEY POINTS
Ingredients of intuition

When cultivating intuition, follow these six concepts:

- **Confidence:** Trust yourself and your judgement.
- **Avoid preconceptions:** Relax and release your worries. Cultivate a beginner's mind.
- **Be curious:** Make attempts and have confidence in your abilities. Expand your experiences to find unexpected connections.
- **Accept the two components of trial and error:** First, readiness to experiment and second, willingness to fail.
- **Zoom out:** Take a step back and remember what matters most.
- **Reversible decisions:** Stakes aren't equally high for all decisions. Rely on intuition for reversible decisions.

Inspiration unbound: Passion's spark for creativity

With inspiration, we generate timely creative ideas. In our hyperconnected digital world, anyone can access as much information as a CEO, world leader or academic researcher, anywhere, at any time.

Diverging perspectives unleash inspiration

Diversity is a key driver to inspiration. Tapping into different cultures and eclectic fields enables richer experiences, all available at our fingertips.

When we connect with multiple perspectives and diverging views, we unleash inspiration.

Satisfying curiosity is easy if we intentionally open our mind to new activities and possibilities. What does a curious mindset look like?

- **Cross-fertilization:** Intersections create richer textures of innovation as cross-impacts prompt new outcomes.
- **Exploration:** Scan emerging signals and connect the shifting dots to imagine new bridges.
- **Some knowledge, but not too much:** It is easier to be curious about topics we have some awareness of, as opposed to none. Conversely, if we are already experts, we may believe we know it all. The middle path breeds inspiration: basic knowledge leads to curiosity, inquiries lead to exploration, and so on.
- **Serendipity:** Cultivating our ability for fortunate discovery by chance can be the ultimate inspiration.
- **Curiosity is contagious:** Surround yourself with open-minded people.

Visionaries across disciplines, like Thomas Edison, Albert Einstein and Steve Jobs, exemplify how a curious mindset ignites the flames of inspiration. Leonardo da Vinci, the quintessential 'Renaissance man', excelled in various fields despite having no formal education. His findings across diverse disciplines revealed the importance of connecting unrelated concepts. Da Vinci's curiosity spanned anatomy, engineering, botany, astronomy and more. He was not only one of the greatest painters of all time but also the inventor of numerous engineering breakthroughs, including conceptual designs of the first flying machines.

Serendipity is key to inspiration

Serendipity researcher Christian Busch notes that nearly half of all inventions and innovations emerge through serendipity. He defines serendipity as 'enabling dots to emerge, connecting them and acting on them; it turns unexpected discoveries into outcomes with value'.[5] Well-known serendipitous inventions include nylon, Velcro, Viagra, Post-it notes, X-rays, rubber and microwave ovens.
Busch identifies three core characteristics of serendipity:

- **Initial trigger:** When an extraordinary or unusual moment presents itself (through a conversation or encounter).
- **Linkage:** Like a bridge, a link between the patterns observed and the event's potential value.
- **The dots connect:** An individual's curiosity and tenacity generates a new innovation, realizing the event's value.

Not all luck is created equal. We can distinguish between 'blind luck' (pure chance) and 'active luck' (enabled by our actions). Busch concludes that an open mind is core to making discoveries and creating serendipity. This is consistent with a quote often attributed to Roman philosopher Seneca: 'Luck is what happens when preparation meets opportunity.'

In *The Medici Effect*,[6] Frans Johansson examines how and why ground-breaking ideas occur at the intersection of different cultures, industries and disciplines. Johansson derives insights from Renaissance artists, scientists, poets, philosophers and bankers who shaped historic ages of profound innovation. While the Medici family did not intentionally drive the extraordinary creativity of the Renaissance, they significantly contributed to it by enabling others' serendipity.

Passion is everything; inspiration will follow

True passion – intense desire or enthusiasm – inspires and motivates unconditionally. Steve Jobs believed that 'people with passion can change the world'. Passion prompts action, driving inspiration in the process. Howard Schultz, Chairman and CEO of Starbucks for over two decades, never considered his company to be in the coffee business. He was inspired by using Starbucks as a vessel to foster unique and innovative experiences.

Passion drives you to immerse yourself in a field, with curiosity sparking inspiration. As you explore, your passion might overflow to broader applications, just as Steve Jobs blended art and design with technology. Make your passion glow for partners and teams and they may be inspired to find their own.

KEY POINTS
Ingredients of inspiration

Our five laws of inspiration:

- **Passion:** Start with the passion of an explorer, then amplify, develop and share it. Passion is naturally contagious.
- **Diversify:** Seek a variety of perspectives – diverse ideas, ecosystems and individuals.
- **Novelty:** Intentionally open your mind to newness. Mechanically repeating your routine won't inspire.

- **Make connections:** Build bridges and explore intersections. Uncover patterns and connect the shifting dots across unrelated fields.
- **Embrace serendipity:** Create opportunities to be lucky. Breathe happenstance and cultivate chance.

Imagination above everything else

Albert Einstein ranked imagination above most other cognitive acts. While knowledge is more readily defined, it is limited. *Imagination is infinite*. It enables creativity and allows you to explore the undefined present and even the non-existent future.

In *How Google Works*, Eric Schmidt and Jonathan Rosenberg advocate imagining the unimaginable.[7] They suggest we ask ourselves what could be true in five years. What inconceivable thing is actually imaginable after rejecting conventional wisdom?

Certain questions play an important role. Science fiction, for instance, enables you to prototype 'What if?' scenarios. The world's most innovative companies ask 'How might we?' to imagine. These questions are open, have no targets, foster curiosity and can be asked without judgement.

Slack, boredom and play: Imagination's incubators

Slack, buffers and redundancies give you the space for unconstrained imagination. Prioritizing efficiency and optimization entails a high opportunity cost. If you restrict your energy, mindset and time, you miss out on new explorations.

Research supports the value of 'gratuitous play' – recreation with no immediate goals. The biologist Andreas Wagner researches the relationship between imagination, innovation and playfulness.[8] Wagner found that play is an iterative process. It suspends judgement, allowing us to 'descend into the valleys of imperfection to later climb the peaks of perfection'.

Even boredom can spark creativity and imagination. Constant digital stimuli and packed schedules prevent us from roaming freely, exploring new ideas or fostering imagination.

Einstein, Newton, Descartes and Poincaré solved important problems while not actively working. *Before insights arrive, one must undergo an in-*

cubation period. By following labour on a challenging problem with a less-taxing activity, our mind can coagulate a solution. This is why many innovations occur while walking, driving or even in the shower.

Unleashing imagination with a clear mind

Zen philosophy uses *mushin* (無心 – no mind) and *muga* (無我 – no ego) to describe a pure state of mind free from plans, attachments or emotions. When our minds are truly relaxed and empty, they can solve our most intractable problems.[9]

Meditation practice (*zazen*; 坐禅) develops an increased awareness of *mujō* (transience). Acknowledging impermanence during meditation can 'reset' your mind, which has many benefits. You can forget yourself and your ego, experiencing perfect peace. When someone starts meditating, their mind often races. They can't keep attention on their breath even for a few minutes. *Mujō* helps one realize these difficulties will pass. Over time, the mind calms and recognizes deeper impermanence.

Life is inherently indeterminate. Seeking to constantly control our thoughts and environments is futile. Practising awareness of one's breathing, relaxing and avoiding distraction can act as a catalyst for intuition, flow and imagination.

The 20 per cent rule

We all experience time constraints. Like any scarce resource, prioritization is crucial for effective time management. As distractions vie for our attention, the 20 per cent compounded time rule suggests allocating a fifth of our time to exploring new ideas beyond our expertise – even without specific focus.

The magic of a small – but regular – investment in time is its compounding returns. As you plant insignificant seeds today, your ideas grow considerably over time. Isolated fields and ideas naturally connect and become powerful drivers of imagination.

Daily exploration offers numerous advantages. It fosters ideation, encourages contemplating 'What if?' scenarios and reveals intersections between diverse fields. Most importantly, it attracts serendipity, offering unexpected opportunities for those insightful explorers who venture into the unknown.

Google's renowned 20 per cent time policy, which let employees pursue projects disconnected from their primary work, is a testament to the power of unstructured time in fostering innovation. Many imaginative thought leaders, including Bill Gates and Steve Jobs, were also known for cultivating curiosity and spontaneity outside of rigid schedules.

The 20 per cent rule encourages imagination and sparks chance, extending beyond mere optimization.

KEY POINTS

Ingredients of imagination

According to Einstein, imagination ranks above everything else. Here are five laws for harnessing it:

- **Ask broad, open questions:** Imagination starts with 'What if?' and 'How might we?'
- **Use science fiction:** Challenge assumptions, reframe perceptions and suspend disbelief. Unlock speculation and creativity by leveraging the science fiction genre as a catalyst for imagination.
- **Break from the present:** Imagine longer time horizons and discontinuities.
- **Be bored and playful:** Grow comfortable in seemingly unproductive scenarios. Cultivate environments that lack judgement or failure.
- **Explore the edge:** Spend 20 per cent of your time outside your domain. Seek activities beyond your daily routine, where the outcomes may not be predetermined.

Improvisation, and all that jazz

Keith Johnstone, author of improvisational theatre book *Impro!*, captured the value of improvisation: 'There are people in the world who habitually accept offers; they say yes. And there are people who habitually block offers; they say no. The people who say yes are rewarded by the adventures they get to go on, and the people who say no are rewarded by the safety they attain.'[10]

In a remarkable instance of improvisation, jazz musician Keith Jarrett turned a routine piano concert in the Cologne (Köln) Opera House into a legendary performance. Facing exhaustion, hunger and an untuned piano, Jarrett initially contemplated cancelling the show, but decided to proceed. The inadequate piano pushed Jarrett to improvise in new ways, unlocking his creativity. Despite the conditions, this performance became the best-selling solo album in jazz history.

Improvisation is not limited to jazz. At Stanford University, one improvisational theatre ('improv') class is consistently oversubscribed because students seek its renowned magic.

Since the 1950s and 1960s, improv has been increasingly appreciated as a creativity strategy. Founded on the principle of 'Yes, and', improvisers accept incoming information and add new gifts to the scene. *Improvisers are unaware of what is about to happen until it occurs, spontaneously creating as they go along.* They follow intuition, trust their partners and have faith in the performance's success.

Improv combines quick connections with rapid actions in stressful scenarios. While preparation may seem antithetical to improvisation, it is actually key to improving. As the adage goes, 'The more I practise, the luckier I get!'

KEY POINTS
Ingredients of improvisation

The more you practise thinking on your feet, the better you can react to future scenarios:

- **Permission:** Act on ideas you usually filter out. First, you might act on these uncensored ideas for fun. Soon, you may find yourself reframing your approach to everyday life. Constant control is impossible. Become comfortable with ambiguity.

- **See mistakes as gifts:** Unusual additions bring opportunities.

- **Accept issues:** You can't stop the show because you flubbed a line, nor can you undo a bad investment. Accept the truth and continue with the best of your ability.

- **It's better to give than receive:** Improving the experience of others is more satisfying than self-promotion.

- **Be authentic and trust:** We're all performing in life together; we must have faith in our collective ability.

Invention, and open futures

In contrast to *innovation*, which builds on something that already exists, *invention* is the true creation of novelty.

Inventions are made all the time, from technology to medicine, art, communication, transportation and culture. Just as the internet, periodic table and Covid vaccines are inventions, so too are the piano, telegraph, locomotive, democracy and even language.

As invention creates something new, it is by definition an unknown, novel phenomenon which may not have been predicted.

Nothing is written in stone

Necessity is the mother of invention, not least in the invention of our own existence. The most empowering aspect of the open futures ahead is the opportunity to create our selves – our 'beingness'. We can constantly invent ourselves, create our reality and our essence, a freedom only possible by virtue of the indeterminacy of life. Invention can arise from deep uncertainties.

In our UN-VICE world, the futures are wide open. We continually create our essence and define ourselves through curiosity, innovation and experimentation.

Alan Kay stated that 'The best way to predict your future is to create it.' As we rewire to anticipate disruption, we become less fearful of the futures. Rather than seeking to predict them, we invent and build the futures we want.

Inventing our beingness

Understanding the limits of our vision is not the same as accepting them. The world's lack of certainty does not deprive us of choice.

Our human condition has a direct connection to invention. From Jean-Paul Sartre's famous lecture 'Existentialism is a humanism', existentialism is the power (and responsibility) of humans to make free choices; it allows human value to be self-created, not predetermined.[11] That opportunity literally allows us to invent ourselves and change our lives. You are free; you make choices; you invent.

Whether in art, morality, technology or our lives, every area has creation and invention in common. Unpredictability simply means that an area is yet to be determined or invented. That process of invention is freedom. Despite the anguish of unpredictability, uncertainty is empowering and optimistic. It is a philosophy of action wherein we make ourselves what we are, building our way forward.

Of course, this freedom does not turn humans into magicians – certain realities may be fixed. It *does* reinforce the importance of our responses, even to events outside of our control. We can anticipate and respond to events with curiosity, experimentation and exploration. In short, we can choose. Our choices define our future. Our freedom exists in our ability to emerge in each and every uncertain moment, rather than through predetermined responses. *Uncertainty is a prerequisite to our agency and freedom.*

CASE STUDY   Afro-optimism: Agency and a Silicon Savannah

Despite Africa's challenges, the youth defy gloomy clichés, exhibiting strong agency, responsibility and entrepreneurship.

Ghanaian economist George Ayittey coined the term 'Cheetah Generation' for energetic young leaders with a fresh perspective, reframing Africa as a continent rich with opportunity.[12] They reject their corrupt post-colonial governments (which Ayittey labels the 'Hippo Generation') and tackle issues with a beginner's mind.

Africa's Cheetah Generation take ownership of their futures. They radiate positivity, celebrating a dynamic 'Africanness' and prioritizing technological progress for economic growth and political reform.

To invent a new Africa, innovative hubs across the continent enable collaborative problem-solving. Successful start-ups have emerged from Kenya, Rwanda, Nigeria, South Africa and more. Kenya's Silicon Savannah, powered by innovations in mobile money through M-Pesa, leapfrogged outdated infrastructure and reshaped the country's financial landscape for the mobile age.

Malawian inventor William Kamkwamba deserves mention for his invention of a windmill at age 14. Inspired by a picture in a book, he built it to bring his village power. Amidst a devastating food crisis, Kamkwamba defied odds to invent a solution for his community.[13]

The Cheetah Generation imagines a new Africa, framing social problems as business opportunities, leveraging technology for positive change and overcoming issues that have plagued the continent for centuries.

Failure and invention go hand in hand

Failure is a key ingredient to creativity. When inventing, we must embrace failure. Jeff Bezos said, 'Failure and invention are inseparable twins... But the problem is, people also are afraid of failure. If you already know it's going to work, it's not an experiment. Only through experimentation can you get real invention... The most important inventions come from trial and error with lots of failure.'[14]

Failure is a necessary ingredient of invention. In *Life Finds a Way*, Andreas Wagner draws analogies between failure and evolution: 'If we are honest with ourselves, we understand that we are failing more often than we are succeeding, and that is a very Darwinian concept... Even very successful scientists have a lot of failures.'[15] For example, Thomas Edison made thousands of attempts before perfecting the light bulb.

Accepting failure cultivates the resilience and self-belief necessary to generate inventions. Learning from mistakes is invention's fuel. Creating a list of what you learn from your failures can capture positive lessons on the road to success.

Each of us has a greater role in creating the future than ever before. Decentralization and networking empower individuals and small groups. As products are increasingly developed collaboratively, we all have the potential to be inventors.

Still, if we are to invent our futures and ourselves, we must conquer our cognitive biases, overcome our fear of failure, deprioritize short-termism and avoid relying on millennia-old assumptions.

Vertical innovation through breakthroughs

Companies often limit their propensity for invention by relying on flawed assumptions. Clayton Christensen's Innovator's Dilemma theory[16] illustrates that many great companies fail due to their assumptions, not least the assumed importance of listening to customers or the need to continuously improve existing products above anything else. These 'sustaining innovations' upgrade established products for existing customers to gain market share. This allows new players to disrupt established business models through 'disruptive innovations' that are often cheaper, with a more attractive user experience and actual novelty. These upstart companies gradually acquire the incumbent's market share.

We saw this transformation in the telecommunications industry where legacy operators such as AT&T, Verizon and Deutsche Telekom continually improved their historic cash cows (text messaging, international calls) while neglecting to pursue new, disruptive technologies (Skype and, more recently, WhatsApp, WeChat and Zoom).

In his seminal work with Blake Masters, entrepreneur and investor Peter Thiel builds the distinction between 'horizontal' innovation (going from '1 to n') and 'vertical' innovation (going from '0 to 1').[17] Going from '1 to n' iterates on what exists, while a '0 to 1' innovation creates something new. *A vertical innovation will never look like anything that came before – this is invention.*

To create truly novel breakthrough innovations, you must discard your hard-held beliefs. Doing so allows you to see beyond established solutions to build new foundations. True inventions such as the printing press, vaccines, water purification systems, computers, internet and smartphones all required fresh perspectives before they became breakthroughs.

Innovation versus invention

At its core, innovation is incremental. It sustains, improves and exploits what is known. Innovation relies on established beliefs, derived from trends and market research. Innovation's continuous focus comes from thinking by analogy, within the boundaries of convention.

Invention is discontinuous, exploring the unknown, co-creating something new. Invention applies the beginner's mind, asking 'What if?' to reimagine ideas, including crazy ones. Inventions are novel and require a tolerance for many failures. They acknowledge that complex problems may demand fundamentally different solutions (Figure 2.3).

Zen Buddhism as a catalyst for invention

Steve Jobs was close to Zen master Chino Roshi. Jobs implemented a *chisoku* perspective to form Apple's minimalist design and a *shoshin* mindset to reimagine the mobile phone from first principles, innovating the mobile internet.

Salesforce founder Marc Benioff has also incorporated *shoshin* into his company's activities. Salesforce constantly looks for new ideas and has even invited Buddhist monks to help their mindset.

Figure 2.3 The 10 differences between invention and innovation

Innovation

INCREMENTAL	DISCONTINUOUS
SUSTAINING, EXPLOITING	EXPLORING
KNOWN, UNDERSTOOD, IMPROVE	UNKNOWN, NOT UNDERSTOOD, CREATE
ESTABLISHED BELIEFS AND ASSUMPTIONS	WHAT IF? BEGINNER'S MIND
CENTRALIZED, HIERARCHY	CO-DEVELOP, CO-CREATE, DECENTRALIZED
OFTEN INTERNAL	TYPICALLY EXTERNAL (OUTSIDE LARGE ORGANIZATIONS)
EVOLUTION: CONTINUOUS FOCUS	REVOLUTION: REIMAGINE IDEAS, INCLUDING CRAZY ONES
THINKING BY ANALOGY, BOUNDARIES OF CONVENTION	NEW, COUNTER-INTUITIVE, CONSTRUCTION
EXISTS: TRENDS AND MARKET RESEARCH AVAILABLE	DOES NOT EXIST: ENTIRELY NOVEL
SHORT-TERM, RESEARCH, DIRECTION	MANY FAILURES OVER LONG PERIODS

Invention

Jeff Bezos believes that 'Every day is Day One.' On being asked what Day Two looks like, he answered: 'Day Two is stasis. Followed by irrelevance. Followed by excruciating, painful decline. Followed by death. And that is why it is always Day One.'[18] Bezos is applying the beginner's mind:

- **Day One – Fresh eyes:** In your infancy, you see things with fresh eyes, make mistakes, but learn from these as you innovate your way ahead.

- **The agility of the early days:** In the beginning, organizations function with speed, nimbleness and a risk-accepting mentality before slowly morphing into the bureaucracies of large organizations – characterized by slowness, rigidity and risk aversion.

- **Embrace disruption:** Fending off Day Two involves embracing customer obsession, changing trends and high-velocity decision-making. You must constantly try new things – because if you fight disruption, you are probably fighting the future.

The Stanford school for design thinking recommends that its pupils assume a beginner's mind to increase empathy. On assuming a beginner's mind in business, the d.school's Design Thinking Bootleg says: 'don't judge, find patterns, really listen, question everything and be genuinely curious'.[19]

A key aspect of *shoshin* is recapturing the essence of 'the first time'. Recall the first time you truly felt love, or when you first saw snow falling. The feeling of a new sensation is akin to a beginner's mind – free from thought, full of wonder.

After failure or success, we calcify our actions, repeating what succeeded or avoiding what caused harm. *Shoshin* re-opens possibilities, accepting what arose in the process of our journey.

KEY POINTS
Ingredients of invention

By grasping the vast possibilities, we unlock five principles for inventing the future:

- **Indeterminacy births invention:** Be grateful that the futures are unknown, as uncertainty is a prerequisite for inventing.

- **Agency:** Invention is not limited to art, technology or products. Every day we make choices and invent our existence.

- **Our powers are larger than we know:** For the first time, entrepreneurs now have the same power of invention as any large organization. What will you do with these superhuman powers?
- **Failure and invention go hand in hand:** The more we are prepared to fail, the more inventive we can become.
- **Ditch beliefs and assumptions:** See beyond established solutions to the open space in need of invention.

Impossible for breakfast

In Lewis Carroll's *Through the Looking-Glass*, the Queen tells Alice that achieving the impossible requires practice. 'One can't believe impossible things…' Alice claims; the Queen retorts 'I daresay you haven't had much practice… sometimes I've believed as many as six impossible things before breakfast.'[20]

The future imagined by science fiction writers is swiftly becoming reality, propelled by technology, biology and engineering breakthroughs. Envision a world with a cure for cancer, teleportation or true invisibility. Quickly, fictional elements like Harry Potter's cloak, H G Wells' *The Invisible Man* or Richard Wagner's magic invisibility helmet in *Das Rheingold* appear as puzzles awaiting resolution.

The convergence of connective technologies (AI, 5G, IoT), immersive experiences (spatial computing, mixed reality, metaverse) and the human–machine interface promises a multi-sensory digital experience, enabling users to see, hear, feel and even smell virtually.

The physics of the impossible

In *Physics of the Impossible*, Michio Kaku tiers the levels of impossibility to separate actual impossibilities from mere challenges.[21]

Class I impossibilities are impossible today but do not violate the laws of physics (such as teleportation). Class II impossibilities sit at the very edge of our understanding. For example, Einstein's equations showed that time travel is theoretically possible. Kaku writes: 'Once confined to fantasy and science fiction, time travel is now simply an engineering problem.' Class III impossibilities violate the known laws of physics.

It is striking how many existing technologies were once deemed impossible. Some have evolved alongside our understanding of physics; others have emerged thanks to technological advancements:[22]

- **X-rays, radios and disbelief:** Lord Kelvin believed X-rays were a hoax, radio had no future and Earth could be no older than a few million years.

- **Nuclear energy:** Ernst Rutherford discovered the nucleus (1911) but dismissed the idea that an atomic bomb could release its energy. Albert Einstein in 1934 suggested that nuclear energy may be unobtainable. Five years later, nuclear fission was sufficiently understood, leading to the first atomic bomb in 1945.

- **Space flights:** For centuries, leading scientists dismissed the possibility of space flight. Less than a century after Jules Verne imagined using a giant cannon to reach the moon (1865), the first artificial satellite, Sputnik, was launched (1957), followed a few years later by the first manned spaceflight.

- **Black holes:** Even after Einstein's 1915 theory of general relativity, black holes were largely overlooked by physicists, until further discoveries revealed more proof.[23]

First principles: Mental model for the impossible

First-principles thinking has been used for thousands of years by inventors (Gutenberg), philosophers (Aristotle), military strategists (John Boyd), investors and entrepreneurs (Charlie Munger, Elon Musk) to create solutions.

Aristotle defines first-principles thinking as 'the first basis from which a thing is known'.[24] A first principle is a foundational fact that can't be derived from any other. You don't assume; instead, you establish what is absolutely certain to be true. Foundational propositions rely on reasoning that stands on its own. In practice, this requires going deep to break down complex problems into basic components.

Examples of first-principles thinking

First principles are successfully used every day to achieve the impossible:

- **Scaling commercial space:** With SpaceX, Elon Musk challenged the conventions of the space industry by asking himself why a rocket's material costs were less than 5 per cent of the typical price. Thinking from first principles, he proved you can develop and manufacture commercially viable, cost-efficient rockets. The space industry (NASA, Boeing) failed to achieve this despite their decades of experience. Using first principles, SpaceX cut the price of launching a rocket by a factor of 10.

- **Water from thin air:** Watergen applied first principles to produce drinking water from air. By challenging assumptions and focusing on fundamental principles, the Israeli company invented a device that condenses and liquefies humidity to make drinkable water. This 'miracle' device has since been used around the world in the wake of disasters.

- **Mass production of automobiles:** Henry Ford invented the moving assembly line. Prior to Ford, assembling one car took more than 10 hours. By breaking down a car into its basic components, Ford invented moving assembly lines that completed cars in under two hours.

- **The printing press:** Johannes Gutenberg's invention of the printing press in the 1400s combined the engineering of a coin punch with the power of a wine press. Gutenberg looked at the components separately, imagined how they could be combined and invented something new.

KEY POINTS
Applying first principles

Applying first principles takes six steps:

- **Don't think by analogy:** Avoid being a prisoner of established perspectives. Instead, seek conflicting views and new information.

- **Break things into fundamentals:** What are the basics? Can we break them down further?

- **Build differently:** Take things apart, examine how the basic components fit, explore different ways of building and rebuild from the ground up.

- **Practise Socratic questioning:** Explore, assess and challenge. Ascertain the validity of ideas and assumptions. Clarify understanding, probe evidence, consider perspectives, evaluate consequences and, finally, question the questions themselves.

- **There is always a first time:** A lack of existence does not imply impossibility – or even difficulty.

- **Solve real problems:** Those who solve real problems reap real rewards.

Not knowing it's impossible makes it possible

Can ignorance of the impossible make it possible?[25]

The Wright brothers achieved the seemingly impossible task of designing and building the world's first flying machine in the early 1900s. Their lack of formal education in engineering left them unburdened by the project's perceived impossibility, as 'experts' had historically dictated. Their persistent experimentation and willingness to learn from failures played a crucial role, as did their frugal approach, funding their project with their bicycle business. Encouraged from a young age to pursue curiosity for its own sake, their success ultimately stemmed from a commitment to working from first principles.

Clarke's three laws for the impossible

Arthur C Clarke, the famous science fiction writer and futurist who co-wrote *2001: A Space Odyssey*, made observations on the impossible, today known as Clarke's three laws:

- **First law:** 'When a distinguished but elderly scientist states that something is possible, he is almost certainly right. When he states that something is impossible, he is very probably wrong.'

- **Second law:** 'The only way of discovering the limits of the possible is to venture a little way past them into the impossible.'

- **Third law:** 'Any sufficiently advanced technology is indistinguishable from magic.'

Clarke, who popularized space travel and satellite communications, enjoyed comparing those inventions with those he categorized as expected, such as telephones, cars, robots and aircraft. Clarke then compared these expected inventions with those he classified as unexpected, such as X-rays, nuclear energy and quantum mechanics.

Certain ideas will be deemed impossible until they become part of everyday life. Pliny the Elder said it best: 'How many things, too, are looked upon as quite impossible, until they have been actually effected?'

KEY POINTS

Ingredients that make the impossible possible

Our six principles:

- **Be audacious:** Cultivate an unshakeable belief that the impossible is possible – and that you can achieve it. Combine unrealistic goals with experimental short-term actions.

- **Mindset enables the impossible:** A beginner's mind and comfort with ambiguity can reframe the impossible as possible.

- **Exercise your 'impossibility muscles':** Practise thinking of the impossible things that could be achieved. Then apply first-principles thinking, unpolluted by preconceived ideas, to imagine how to achieve them.

- **Grit:** Make the sacrifice to show up, start and persevere. Tenacity makes the difference. Avoid excuses and don't underestimate yourself.

- **Failovation:** Let your passion feed on frequent failures, as they breed innovation. Failure is often the path to success. We call this 'failovation'.

- **Harness the 5 earlier i's:** Follow your *intuition* to experiment and *improvise*; cross disciplinary lines to *inspire* serendipity and *invention*; *imagine* the impossible.

Notes

1 R Spitz and L Zuin (2022) *The Definitive Guide to Thriving on Disruption: Essential frameworks for disruption and uncertainty*, Disruptive Futures Institute, San Francisco, CA

2 D Kahneman (2013) *Thinking, Fast and Slow*, Farrar, Straus and Giroux, New York, NY

3 Amazon Staff. 2016 letter to shareholders, Amazon, 17 April 2017. www.aboutamazon.com/news/company-news/2016-letter-to-shareholders (archived at https://perma.cc/67J3-2GCQ)

4 J Bezos. 2018 letter to shareholders, Amazon, 11 April 2019. www.aboutamazon.com/news/company-news/2018-letter-to-shareholders (archived at https://perma.cc/YS5G-U4VB)

5 C Busch (2020) *The Serendipity Mindset: The art and science of creating good luck*, Riverhead Books, New York, NY

6 F Johansson (2004) *The Medici Effect: Breakthrough insights at the intersection of ideas, concepts, and cultures*, Harvard Business School Press, Boston, MA

7 E Schmidt and J Rosenberg (2015) *How Google Works*, John Murray, London

8 A Wagner (2019) *Life Finds a Way: What evolution teaches us about creativity*, Oneworld Publications, London

9 S Suzuki (1970) *Zen Mind, Beginner's Mind,* Weatherhill, Trumbull, CT

10 K Johnstone (1979) *Impro: Improvisation and the theatre*, Routledge, Abingdon

11 J-P Sartre (1946) *L'existentialisme est un humanisme* [Existentialism Is a Humanism], Les Editions Nagel, Paris

12 G Ayittey. Africa's cheetahs versus hippos, TED, June 2007. www.ted.com/talks/george_ayittey_africa_s_cheetahs_versus_hippos/transcript (archived at https://perma.cc/7D8F-RMCM)

13 W Kamkwamba and B Mealer (2010) *The Boy Who Harnessed the Wind: Creating currents of electricity and hope*, William Morrow, New York, NY

14 T Soper. 'Failure and innovation are inseparable twins': Amazon founder Jeff Bezos offers 7 leadership principles, GeekWire, 28 October 2016. www.geekwire.com/2016/amazon-founder-jeff-bezos-offers-6-leadership-principles-change-mind-lot-embrace-failure-ditch-powerpoints (archived at https://perma.cc/586M-7K6Q)

15 A Wagner (2019) *Life Finds a Way: What evolution teaches us about creativity*, Basic Books, New York, NY

16 C M Christensen (1997) *The Innovator's Dilemma: When new technologies cause great firms to fail*, Harvard Business School Press, Boston, MA

17 P Thiel and B Masters, B (2014) *Zero to One: Notes on startups, or how to build the future*, Crown Business, New York, NY

18 Amazon Staff. 2016 letter to shareholders, Amazon, 17 April 2017. www.aboutamazon.com/news/company-news/2016-letter-to-shareholders (archived at https://perma.cc/T87C-PW89)

19 d.school. Design thinking bootleg, Stanford University, 2018. dschool.stanford.edu/resources/design-thinking-bootleg (archived at https://perma.cc/6YTC-FWV4)

20 L Carroll (1871) *Through the Looking-Glass*, Macmillan, London

21 M Kaku (2008) *Physics of the Impossible: A scientific exploration into the world of phasers, force fields, teleportation, and time travel*, Doubleday, New York, NY; M Kaku, S Rose and F Hepburn. *Sci Fi Science: Physics of the Impossible*, Science Channel, 2009

22 M Marshall. 10 impossibilities conquered by science, *New Scientist*, 3 April 2008. www.newscientist.com/article/dn13556-10-impossibilities-conquered-by-science (archived at https://perma.cc/LH9S-GTL8)

23 A Levy. How black holes morphed from theory to reality, Knowable Magazine, 11 January 2021. www.knowablemagazine.org/content/article/physical-world/2021/how-black-holes-morphed-theory-reality (archived at https://perma.cc/5SG6-9S2V)

24 Aristotle (2002) *Aristotle's Metaphysics*, trans. J Sachs, Green Lion Press, Santa Fe, NM

25 S Brooks. Why did the Wright brothers succeed when others failed? Scientific American, 14 March 2020. blogs.scientificamerican.com/observations/why-did-the-wright-brothers-succeed-when-others-failed (archived at https://perma.cc/8FX4-W658)

3

Scanning the horizon

What's changing and what's staying the same

OBJECTIVES
Constants and drivers of disruption

We investigate the underlying drivers of disruption and explore what remains constant. Scanning enables us to detect emerging signals of changes that could evolve to impact our options and decision-making.

How to detect emerging change

Signals are fragments of the future that can be observed today. Early warning systems can offer a preview of the future to inform short-term decision-making. Strong signals are indicators of imminent change; weak signals are early signs of change that could grow to herald fundamental discontinuity (Figure 3.1).

Because weak signals often arise on the fringe of mainstream knowledge, reactions of disbelief, laughter or even ridicule can act as a filter to identify them. Despite this, weak signals can grow to significantly impact future directions, driving radically different possibilities across strategy, technology, markets or society. Weak signals are often overlooked due to perceived low probabilities or unknown outcomes, even though they may lead to transformational events.

In medicine, individual symptoms are signals, evaluated together to form a diagnosis. Future impacts are better understood from a thorough diagnosis, rather than isolated symptoms.

Figure 3.1 Signals, drivers and scanning

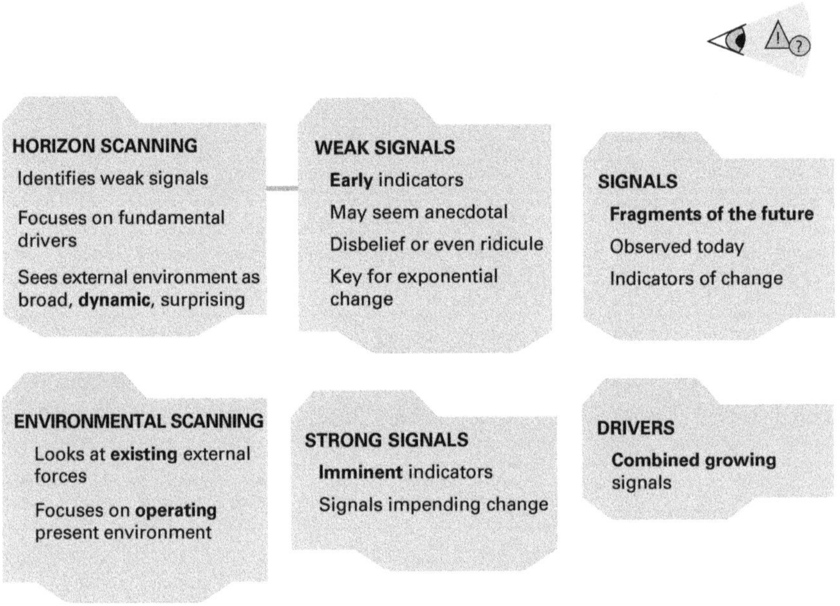

HORIZON SCANNING

Identifies weak signals

Focuses on fundamental drivers

Sees external environment as broad, **dynamic**, surprising

WEAK SIGNALS

Early indicators

May seem anecdotal

Disbelief or even ridicule

Key for exponential change

SIGNALS

Fragments of the future

Observed today

Indicators of change

ENVIRONMENTAL SCANNING

Looks at **existing** external forces

Focuses on **operating** present environment

STRONG SIGNALS

Imminent indicators

Signals impending change

DRIVERS

Combined growing signals

Horizon scanning is the practice of identifying weak signals in advance. Compared with environmental scanning,[1] which looks at existing external forces, horizon scanning is more relevant because it focuses on influences that shape future disruptions. Horizon scanning is diagnosing, acknowledging the broad and surprising dynamics at play.

KEY POINTS
How to scan signals

Golden rules for scanning:

- **Start at the fringe:** Real change begins on the periphery. Seek out the uninhibited, strange and weird. Fringe perspectives do not typically come from experts.

- **Go wide:** Diversify your sources, widen the aperture and multiply the lenses. Follow global opinion leaders across many fields. Check think tanks, research reports, technical publications, experts, generalists and counterculture media. Seek worldviews outside what you know.

- **Go deep and apply the 'So what?' questions:** Focus on deep, transformational currents. What are the origins of the change? What do the changes mean? Is there a pattern? Who might win or lose from potential changes?

- **What's your horizon?** What is the new issue's timeline – and how novel is it really? Consider whether you are observing weak signals or established trends.

- **Connect the shifting dots:** Signals should not be considered in isolation but as clusters. Insights come from connecting the dots between signals, fields and emerging issues. One emerging signal is unlikely to cause fundamental change; combined, they are the drivers of change.

- **Scan continuously** for interesting phenomena without any particular topic in mind. Signals are constantly evolving. Their context is dynamic and relative to their environment. Observe what's happened to past signals over time. What fizzled out and what might we have been wrong about?

Evaluating signals over noise

Signals provide a constantly updated preview of the future: early, small, emerging, qualitative, fringe, anomalous, unstructured. Today's signals are found in research and experiments on genetic engineering, bioprinting, weather controllers, teleportation, advancing intelligent systems, the brain–computer interface and mind uploading.

KEY POINTS
Filters to evaluate signals

One challenge of horizon scanning is the noise from limitless weak, fake and inflated signals. Filters help us qualify signals:

- **Qualify the source:** How credible is the source? Does it seem independent and objective? Who is behind the information and what are their incentives?

- **Likelihood:** What is the signal's momentum? How frequently have you picked it up? Is the signal becoming stronger?

- **Self-confirming bias:** Is it a false signal, selected to confirm your own beliefs?

- **Newness:** Signals have a life cycle. Initial emerging issues grow into significance, then can ultimately fade. Tracking a weak signal's journey can indicate whether it is actually new and evaluate when it might emerge as a strong signal to start making an impact.

- **Compounding:** How do signals interact? Do similar observations confirm and reinforce? Are signals pushing in the same direction? Do the signals conflict or result in polarized messages? Do diverse perspectives validate the signals?

- **Impact:** What could the signals do and to whom? Is any particular sector or demographic most affected?

- **Interconnections:** Do signals seem isolated or interconnected? Are there clusters and patterns emerging? Do the signals intersect across fields?

Signals are invaluable for anticipating new innovations, technologies or ideas that could evolve into significant developments. They provide insights into a future which has not yet emerged. Unlike trends, signals can presage innovations before they mature.

Trends continue... until they don't

A trend is a prevailing tendency for a given category. Trends represent historical change, often measurable, where experts can analyse data to validate the specifics. Examples of trends include 5G mobile subscription numbers, 3D printer sales, virtual reality headset metrics, cybersecurity breach rates and automation software market penetration. Trends can be broad-ranging, covering the way products are sold (e-commerce, digital, physical), points in cycles (recession, boom, stagnation) or evolution of demographics.

Trend analysis can be useful, but *trends only describe our past*, implying some degree of continuity. Many trends die out, replaced by newer, equally ephemeral ones. Because humans are wired to extrapolate linearly, it can be challenging to have a fresh view of the world from trend analysis.

Trend watching and market research are huge industries, but they can conceal the real emerging changes. Projections do not capture underlying drivers or multidimensional impacts, because trends continue until they don't.

Akin to excavation by archaeologists and historians, trend spotting unearths what is expected to happen in the future, although it doesn't necessarily prepare you for any future. Surviving our UN-VICE world requires a perspective shift, prompting questions about alternative possibilities and strategies to realize our preferred futures.

The end of trends?

A primary objective of signal and trend monitoring is to illuminate the longer-term transformations emerging today. As change becomes a constant, trend analysis may unwittingly become limited to past consumption patterns or technology adoptions.

Take the example of fast-fashion company Shein, which produces small batches of products based on real-time social media data, pushing out new designs in a matter of days. These life cycles are increasingly compressed – and this immediacy is beginning to dictate more aspects of business and society. At some point, we may come to experience the collapse of trends in their entirety, replaced by the constant emergence of a multitude of microtrends.

Welcome to the end of trends.

Metatrends or metaruptions?

In his 1982 book *Megatrends*, John Naisbitt defined megatrends as large, transformative processes with global reach and dramatic impact. Today, a megatrend is a slow-to-form, long-lasting, large-scale evolution resulting from a combination of individual trends. Megatrends are high-level driving forces of broad fundamental changes to society, culture and business. They are perceived as relatively certain and fixed.

Similarly, metatrends are beyond individual evolutions; they represent a transformative global impact from a confluence of drivers. The prefix 'meta' represents a higher level of abstraction, transcending silos. Metatrends deeply affect all aspects of nations, economies and individuals. These might be global shifts in macroeconomics, geostrategy, warfare, eroding democracies and the energy transition.

While the definitions of trends, megatrends or metatrends may be subjective, typical trend reports have features in common. First, they are derived from the past, extrapolating history towards the future. Second, even when unrelated, trends are presented as interacting predictably with each other.

Third, trend analysis does not account for second- or third-order consequences, implying continuity and a lack of spillovers.

Extrapolating trends is dangerous, especially when they compound flawed assumptions. With time, assumptions magnify; wrong assumptions cascade and blow up.

Trends are not the finality – they are an initial base on which to build, imagine and explore possible scenarios of the many diverse futures ahead. But the greater the pace of change, the harder it may be to understand the long-term trajectory of a metatrend from looking in the rear-view mirror.

Trends are not disruptions

Systemic disruption forces us to acknowledge unpredictability. Disruption unlocks many futures, as cascading consequences follow the initial shifts. New insights emerge from the knock-on effects of change because cross-impacts determine outcomes.

In contrast to trends, disruptions are discontinuous (Figure 3.2). They acknowledge futures that establish new paradigms, which may evolve in unexpected ways. Systemic disruptions cause ripple effects that ricochet into new, counterintuitive or even revolutionary changes. The inability to understand the implications of the initial impact is why disruption becomes apparent only in hindsight.

Figure 3.2   Contrasting trends and disruptions

METATRENDS	METARUPTIONS
Known, complicated but understood	Unknown, complex so not fully understandable
Assumptions, determinate	Uncertainties, indeterminate
Exist, analysis, research, observed data, past	Novel, synthesis, investigation, exploration, futures
Prediction of specific outcomes given trends	Multiple future possibilities
Continuous, stable, first-order consequences	Discontinuous, surprise, second- and third-order impacts
Observing by analogy, extrapolation, fixed	Counterintuitive, new, emergent
Isolated, combined, grouped as a family	Systemic, intersect, converge, collide, emerge

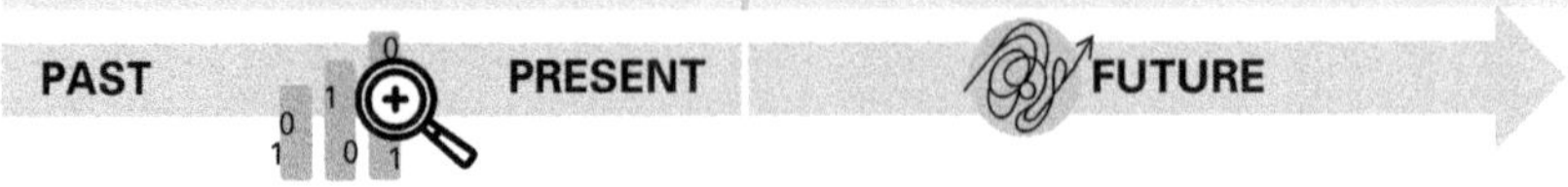

PAST   PRESENT   FUTURE

Systemic disruption means there may be no measurable data to substantiate our understanding. *Here, imagination outshines analysis.*

Disruptions interact at every possible level. The drivers of disruption are interconnected, forming dynamic disruption networks. Disruptions accelerate as their drivers amplify. These systems are too unpredictable for governments or companies to control with hierarchical, short-termist command structures.

The world is not made up of isolated controllable parts. And so the strings, wires and controls used to manage this illusionary world are obsolete.

The reach of systemic disruption

Disruption invites us to look outside our domains as we scan for early signs of change. Systemic disruption can never be evaluated as a single episodic event – its drivers are an interconnected network. Those best positioned to thrive on disruption learn to interpret emerging signals. In these disruptions, however unsettling, there will always be winners and losers.

KEY POINTS
Eight laws of disruption

These eight laws of systemic disruption help decode its reach:

1 **Disruption is omnipresent,** affecting everyone, everything, everywhere. While disruption is not only technology-driven, technology permeates every facet of our world, so disruption and technology are often interlinked.

2 **Disruption is a constant.** It is no longer merely a single event but a steady state.

3 **Systemic disruption establishes new paradigms,** which themselves will evolve, sometimes morphing without warning.

4 **Effects are combinatory and cumulative – not isolated.** Disruptions interact as hyperconnected networks.

5 **Systemic disruptions have non-linear ripple effects.** The initial disruption (input) can ricochet into amplified higher-order effects (output).

6 **Disruption's effects must be explored with extended timeframes.** The consequences of change only become apparent over time.

7 **Left unchecked, disruptions can slip into irreversibility.**

8 **Disruption itself is neither good nor bad;** its impact depends on one's perspective, degree of preparation and nature and timing of response.

Metaruptions drive systemic disruption

Metaruptions[2] is a portmanteau word – an abbreviation of disruption with the prefix 'meta'. A metaruption is a multidimensional family of systemic disruptions, including shifts in the notion of disruption itself. Metaruptions are characterized by the dynamic interactions of subordinate drivers of change.

Metaruptions cause widespread and self-perpetuating effects that extend beyond their initial disruptions. As initial changes spill over, these impacts combine to propagate and modify other elements within the system, ultimately disrupting the disruption itself.

EXAMPLE

Questioning to explore metaruptions

Imagining the interplay of metaruptions is a creative endeavour, not a number-crunching exercise.

Consider future technological developments such as the singularity – the point where AI surpasses human levels. We can use our imagination to explore fundamental questions: What could be the ramifications of AI systems achieving human-level performance? Could AI make decisions against the interest of humans? Beyond the future of work and business, what lies ahead for humanity if computers surpass human intellect? Could technology self-replicate and sustain without human intervention?

It's impossible to fully anticipate the possible outcomes or evolutions of technology in its own right, let alone when we consider the transversal effects of AI on everything and everyone around it. Analysing social media in the age of AI, how do we integrate the profound impact of fake news, deepfakes and other forms of misinformation and disinformation when entangled with a host of other changes?

Metaruptions can have far-reaching consequences, radically altering how information is interpreted and used across all fields. Social media already fuels systemic transformations of society, governments, geostrategy and business. Brexit, the Covid pandemic, US elections and geopolitical events in Eastern Europe and the Middle East reveal how social media can be abused to amplify polarization and populism. As subordinate drivers of disruption interplay with social media, could this lead to the end of democracy, cyberwars and massive social unrest? Or can the world seize this opportunity to drive social change, to create unstoppable movements for good?

Metaruptions acknowledge the absence of answers to these questions, aiding in the distinction between explicit drivers of disruption and the intricate, emergent nature of their unpredictable interactions.

Metaruptions defy rulebooks. We must envision the questions to be asked – and delve into the questions behind the questions. Metaruptions require adaptive problem finding and resilient solutions amidst incomprehensibility.

The current decade will bring unparalleled messiness together with its opportunities. Learning to speak the language of metaruptions means staying engaged as paradigms shift to unravel these possibilities.

Metaruptions and the 10 drivers of disruption

While change can be tortuous, disruptions are powerful instruments to drive transformative outcomes. By understanding and leveraging the metaruptions at play, we can use their power for new beginnings.

Metaruptions are constantly evolving. The signals provide feedback loops that help appreciate how dynamic futures may take shape. However, we need to pay careful attention to compounding forces, which could spill over into irreversible tipping points.

To comprehend disruption, we need to decipher its fundamental drivers, forces and influences. Identifying these drivers and their synthesis as metaruptions can inform decision-making (Figure 3.3).

Figure 3.3 Disruption drivers radar

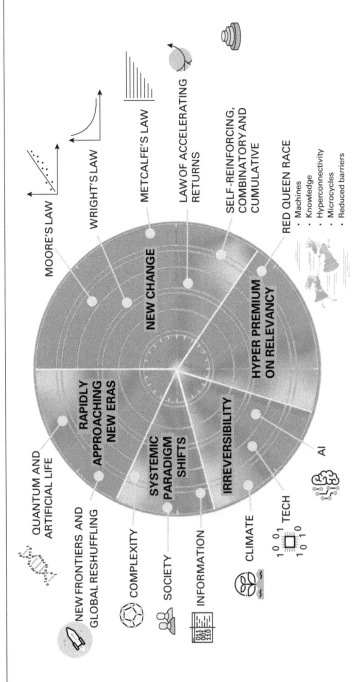

> ### KEY POINTS
> Five metaruptions, 10 drivers of disruption
>
> Here we consider five metaruptions, fuelled by 10 drivers of disruption (numbered with roman numerals):
>
> - **Metaruption #1: New change.** The new nature, velocity, multiplicity and interconnectivity of disruptions generate a runaway pace of change. Despite the inevitable turbulence, (i) *the new nature of change* also unlocks novel pathways to address global challenges.
>
> - **Metaruption #2: Hyper premium on relevancy.** Exemplified by the (ii) *Red Queen Race*, the bar to become and remain relevant is higher than ever. You need to run faster to stay in the same place. Even if you do, you could still end up behind.
>
> - **Metaruption #3: Irreversibility.** However beneficial certain technological developments might be, evolutions in (iii) *climate*, (iv) *technology* and (v) *AI* could advance to such a degree that their impact on society is irreversible.
>
> - **Metaruption #4: Systemic paradigm shifts.** Today, our current paradigms are shifting. (vi) *Complexity* is moving to centre stage, as rigid structures are rejected and non-linearity prevails. Likewise, the evolving expectations of (vii) *society* intersect with shifting values. (viii) *Information* becomes uncontrollable and evolves at warp speed with exploding connectivities.
>
> - **Metaruption #5: Rapidly approaching new eras.** The shadows of new realities are fast approaching. (ix) *Quantum computing and artificial life* could usher in a new epoch of existence. (x) *New frontiers, geopolitical and economic reshuffling* transform space, geopolitics and world economies.

Metaruption #1: New change

Velocity is a key ingredient of new change, the first metaruption. *The accelerating pace of change is now the norm.*

Driver of disruption (i): The new nature of change

In dissecting the first metaruption, we find its driver: the new nature of change. This driver has two main facets. First is the foundation of accelerating change, our four unruly laws. Second is the combinatory and cumulative effects that interact with these four laws. Together, these generate a runaway pace of new change.

Foundations for accelerating change – These four 'unruly' laws fuel accelerating change:

1   **Law of Accelerating Returns:** Ray Kurzweil's Law of Accelerating Returns describes how the rate of progress of evolutionary learning environments increases exponentially.[3] In essence, *advances breed faster advances.* This acceleration is propelled by digitization, wherein entire fields benefit from advancing computing power and converging technologies. For instance, the fusion of 3D printing, materials science and biotechnology gives rise to innovations like 3D bioprinting. As established paradigms reach their limits, novel approaches emerge, building upon prior innovations to sustain acceleration. Fuelled by innovations like AI or, in the future, quantum computing, this perpetual cycle of acceleration illustrates how the exhaustion of current methods triggers novel approaches.

2   **Metcalfe's Law – network effects:** As each additional user joins a network, that network becomes more valuable for the other users. Metcalfe's Law dictates that the effect of a network is proportional to the square of the number of connected users. With over five billion global users, the internet represents an extraordinary network. Here, digital goods, experiences and transformational ideas can be rapidly reproduced or deployed at scale with low marginal cost. While cars, telephones, electricity and television took decades to reach 50 million users, Facebook achieved it in four years, WeChat in one year and Pokemon Go in 19 days. Modern cloud platforms enable instant adoption. For instance, Google introduced Smart Reply to over a billion Gmail users overnight.

3   **Moore's Law – more processing power, cheaper:** Named after Intel co-founder Gordon Moore, Moore's Law illustrates how computers operate with greater speed and capacity at less cost over time. Moore put forward in 1965 that the number of transistors on an integrated circuit would double every two years. Despite this doubling, the cost decreased. Moore's Law supports converging technologies given their cumulative (multiplier) effects.

4   **Wright's Law – learning by doing:** Formulated by Theodore Wright in 1936, Wright's Law provides a framework for predicting cost decreases as a function of cumulative production. In studying aircraft production,

Wright observed that when production doubled, the labour time required to build a new aircraft dropped 20 per cent due to the builder's increasing knowledge.

The importance of the combined impacts of Moore's Law and Wright's Law cannot be overstated. In all technological disruptions, cost stands out as the fundamental driving force. As experience accumulates and technologies advance, the cost of production consistently decreases. To illustrate, the cost of genome sequencing was approximately $1 million in 2008. By 2015, it plummeted to $1,000. More recently, it reached a few hundred dollars.[4] Declining costs democratize access and pave the way for new groundbreaking discoveries.

Self-reinforcing combinatory and cumulative effects – Other accelerators compound with the above laws to further intensify the pace of change:

- **Cognification:** The Internet of Things (IoT), 5G wireless connectivity and AI transform inanimate items into 'smarter' ones. Advancements in robotics, natural language processing and computer vision pave the way for the cognification of everyday objects.

- **Recursive self-improvement:** Breakthroughs in deep learning will automate the creation of software itself. As machines become 'smarter', this recursive loop of innovation will drive further accelerations. Machine learning algorithms are gradually developing the capability to write and eventually maintain their code, enabled by extensive amounts of public training data.

- **Convergence and fusion:** Converging technology platforms are transforming business. Compounding technologies such as machine learning, IoT and 3D printing further leverage cloud platforms by fusing, driving self-reinforcing advancements in all individual technologies.

- **Stacked innovation:** Each generation's defining technology builds upon its predecessors. The internet, AI and mobile platforms democratize innovation, allowing anyone to invent at reasonable prices. Vast datasets covering everything from finance to genetics are available for analysis. Affordable tools empower individuals to solve old problems in new ways, impossible just a few years ago.

Every innovation is linked to, and benefits from, earlier phases. As these technologies converge, cognify and improve, their acceleration compounds – resulting in more powerful, cost-effective solutions with greater reach.

To counterbalance runaway accelerators, certain forces decelerate the pace of change. For instance, cataclysmic existential risks such as nuclear war, asteroid impacts or prolonged breakdowns of infrastructure and networks could conceivably result in a return to the Dark Ages. The future is open to any eventualities, including a decelerating rate of change.

Metaruption #2: Hyper premium on relevancy

The bar to become and remain relevant is higher than ever. You need to run faster to stay in the same place, or even likely end up behind. There is a new premium on staying relevant.

Driver of disruption (ii): Red Queen Race

The second disruption driver is the Red Queen Race, which emphasizes the *hyper premium on relevancy*. This premium is the direct result of intersecting metaruptions. The new change explained above shows the mutating pace of change. The Red Queen Race deals with the increasing difficulty of keeping up.

In 1871, Lewis Carroll published *Through the Looking-Glass.*[5] Simultaneously, the scientific world began to understand the ramifications of Darwin's natural selection. The Red Queen Theory is named for Carroll's royal character who states that 'It takes all the running you can do, to keep in the same place.' This theory of evolution is no different today.

The Red Queen Race underscores the premium of staying relevant. If you simply run faster without understanding the changing nature of the world, you will fall behind. Embracing new imperatives allows you to establish and sustain relevance, seize opportunities and win races:

- **Reduced barriers to entry:** Connectivity fuels perpetual remote work. This decentralizes and virtualizes the workplace, globalizing the talent marketplace. Employees no longer need to relocate for career growth, democratizing access and intensifying competition.

- **Compressed life cycles:** Accelerating change compresses company, product and even career life cycles. Innovation, ideas and speed prevail as constant emergence replaces trends. Attention spans crumble. Everything becomes cheaper and faster. Remaining relevant is at a premium.

- **Competing with machines:** Typically used in automating repetitive tasks, AI is expanding into creative domains. It now plays a significant role in decision-making, even in human-centric fields like healthcare and law.

Current software can analyse, decide and learn; future capabilities may include independent thought.

- **Hyperconnectivity drives events to cascade rapidly:** While rapid scaling benefits sound ideas, it can also cause issues to spiral out of control. Network effects compress time frames, turning years into weeks and reaching millions instantly. This doesn't discriminate between worthy and unworthy information or projects; all can spread like wildfire.

- **Knowledge and learning:** Information is readily available to everyone, often for free. Skills, experience and critical thinking drive democratized opportunities. Rather than relying on formal education alone, the Red Queen Race demands self-knowledge, learning how to learn, and lifelong inquiry for self-actualization.

You need to move not only faster, but smarter. There are abundant opportunities in our rapidly changing world. Decentralization means that opportunities are available to everyone, anywhere.

The Red Queen Race necessitates being fast *and* astute. *Speed alone is insufficient.*

Metaruption #3: Irreversibility

Irreversibility means that outcomes are difficult or impossible to reverse. Furthermore, the consequences of poor decisions and delayed responses are high. If an existential issue reaches irreversibility, it may mean nothing can alter that serious outcome for humanity.

We include climate change, technology and AI in our drivers of disruption, because they pose the greatest risk of irreversibility. Given that these have exponential profiles, their outcomes create larger effects faster than expected. If we are not timely in our anticipatory decisions and mitigation, any transformative developments may quickly – and inadvertently – become irreversible.

Despite their challenges, AI and climate also represent great opportunities for rethinking innovation, work and even life. Many benefits to society can arise from thoughtful advances in technology, healthcare, energy and food systems.

For the existential risks of our own making, humanity is now at a crossroads: we can either seize the opportunity today, or cease to exist altogether.

> **KEY POINTS**
> The three characteristics of irreversibility
>
> - **Possible damage:** Adverse consequences can be highly damaging, regardless of promising benefits.
> - **Timing threshold:** The tipping point when we cross into irreversibility.
> - **Difficulty in reversing:** Profoundly difficult or totally irreversible outcomes.

Driver of disruption (iii): Climate – winning the race against irreversibility

Major global climate risks include extreme weather, failure to adapt, man-made environmental damage, biodiversity loss and natural disasters.

Climate change places all of society and humanity at risk. It affects sea levels, food security and more. *Changes in ecological systems create unpredictable second-order consequences.* Society will collapse unless it has fresh water, clean oceans and secure food chains.

A host of disruptions related to mitigating and adapting to climate change must be considered. These include changing the energy mix to renewable and addressing potential resource shortages.

While the risk of climate irreversibility is real, there is still time to turn the tide. However, this reversal requires effective and timely responses.

There will be entire new sectors, business and employment opportunities from the investment in climate. Innovations and technologies are required, which will offer significant latitude for new models and value creation. These innovations enable every company to become an energy company to reduce emissions, as green becomes the new digital. We call this the 'Greenaissance' era.

Climate change will inevitably be highly disruptive. The relevant anticipatory mindset reinvents extractive production techniques with sustainable and regenerative approaches.

Drivers of disruption (iv) and (v): Technology and AI – sleepwalking into irreversibility

While technology is not intrinsically bad, it invariably brings unintended consequences. Directly or indirectly, our choices surrounding it can lead to irreversibility.

Humanity's lively debate on the limits of AI is a clear indication that we are more sophisticated thinkers than the AI we are building. But we cannot relinquish our agency and must continuously make sense of our complex and indeterminate world.

Despite its current inherent limitations, AI may be one of the most powerful tools ever created. As with any breakthrough technology, we must be thoughtful in its use, recognizing its unpredictability.

AI spans machine learning, natural language processing, neural networks, robotics and facial recognition. AI will ensure that anything that can be automated, cognified or disintermediated will be. These shifts will radically transform every aspect of our lives. Like all powerful technology, AI comes with trade-offs, including job disruption and potential changes to human identity.

No single AI development will be a watershed moment. Rather, we will experience a flow of continuous and ever-larger disruptions as AI evolves.

Exercising choice with AI is more important, difficult and urgent than ever:

- **Evaluating next-order implications:** Technology has become pervasive so rapidly that it is impossible to keep up with its consequences.

- **Decision-making outcomes:** For now, we can calibrate the degree of decision-making autonomy we give to machines. We can choose the contexts in which AI can be used for good and select the contexts in which we wish to avoid AI.

- **Governance and safeguards:** We have choices as to how to regulate the use and building of AI. Today, we can still decide whether – and to what extent – we will continue to add value when partnering with machines.

Leaders must navigate AI's unpredictable evolution with anticipatory governance and agility in mind. To prevent ourselves from sleepwalking into a future written by algorithms, humans need to wake up and make choices for ourselves.

The same features of AI that could help us tackle climate change, feed the world and eliminate genetic diseases pose extraordinary hazards. Stephen Hawking wrote that AI could end humanity. Nick Bostrom[6] and Max Tegmark[7] raise serious concerns about self-improving AI pursuing goals misaligned with human interest.

More immediately, what are the implications of mass automation on work? Will AI really create more employment than it displaces? Social cohesion is at stake. Even with today's artificial narrow intelligence (ANI), AI already has incredible capabilities and can outperform people in specialized areas. AI is taking over areas previously thought too important to entrust to machines, triggering a pathway to widespread job displacement. Massive unemployment could result in the spread of crime and increasing global wealth and power concentration in the hands of individual founders and corporations.

Metaruption #4: Systemic paradigm shifts – complexity, society and information

Our fourth metaruption details *systemic paradigm shifts*. A paradigm in any field represents a particular perspective or ideology. Paradigm shifts impact not only their fields but influence across domains, forcing you to think and act differently. *Paradigm shifts are fundamental changes in our approach.* They can be unstoppable.

Complexity, society and information are defining systemic paradigm shifts. These are dominated by complex systems, with multiple parts interacting to produce unpredictable behaviour and where small inputs can result in disproportionate effects. As complexity is the norm, so is uncertainty; in this environment, humility, curiosity and a questioning mind may be more effective than 'mastering' the preconceived solutions. *In these paradigm shifts, addressing individual parts of a problem will not resolve anything.*

Driver of disruption (vi): Complexity – rigid structures become ineffective

As change accelerates from linear to exponential, our problems and systems move from complicated to complex. Unlike *complicated* problems, *complex* problems do not have established answers. Complex systems like financial markets, technology, society, climate or the human nervous system are not easily understood. In a world of complex and rapidly shifting environments, we need to rethink the implications of ongoing change.

Relying on specific expertise may prove inadequate for the decision-making required to address daily complex situations. Centralized control proves ineffective because complexity is uncontrollable and problematics are holistic. Here, you need to appreciate the system's interdependent moving parts to act effectively.

Adaptive complex systems are resilient. They can withstand shocks and disturbances. At the same time, the non-linear impacts of large systems can result in massive events such as floods, earthquakes, stock market crashes, technology glitches and epidemics.

Governments, institutions and organizations often overlook the nuances between 'complicated' situations and 'complex' systems. Complexity is neglected in education. However, it should not be treated as rare or abstract, but as a fundamental feature of everyday life, taught as a core subject just like mathematics or language arts.

The issue we now face is awakening from the illusion of an orderly world. This imaginary predictable world focuses on preparing for what is known, which leaves us unprepared for turbulence. Today's global leaders fail to decode the complex social and technological networks that drive rapid change.

Complexity is not something to be feared. It empowers agency, fosters novelty and drives the emergence of ideas. Thriving in complexity demands collaborative problem-solving mindsets, creativity and experimentation.

Driver of disruption (vii): Society – immediacy, radical transparency and traceability

Many societal challenges can be defined in terms of equity. Gender equality, wealth equality, racial equality, equality of opportunity and social justice are issues we must address now. We know that the future is not distributed evenly and neither are inequalities. Avoiding alienation in a world of transparency is challenging at a time of shifting societal values, especially when incentive structures drive organizations to short-term decisions.

Extreme inequality, global injustice, corruption and structural discrimination are potent forces that drive systemic paradigm shifts. Our society could thrive or collapse depending on how we respond to these issues. However, *the social justice barometer is impossible to reconcile for everyone.*

Global generational shifts: Millennials, Gen Z and demographics – Generational and demographic changes offer an added perspective on societal paradigm shifts:

- **Labour force:** Millennials, born between 1981 and 1996, are now the largest generation in the US labour force, making up over a third of workers. Together with Gen Z, born after 1996, these generations will represent around two-thirds of the workforce before 2030.

- **Population stagnation** is expected around the middle of the 21st century. As deaths start to exceed births, we will experience the impact of longer lives, fewer workers and more retirees. How societies decide to reorganize and adapt will have a major impact. With the exception of Africa, populations of the world's major regions are expected to decline significantly. The positive impacts include less pressure on resources and reduced burden for women. As with many paradigm shifts, the effects may be barely noticeable initially, only to skyrocket later.

- **Longevity:** Advances in technology and healthcare drive longer and healthier lifespans. These developments will strain existing social security and pension systems as non-working segments grow faster than the working population.

Driver of disruption (viii): Information – instantaneous and ubiquitous

We define disruption's effects on information as 'info-ruption', a pervasive and radical change in worldwide data with cascading effects on how information is interpreted, used and misused. *Through info-ruption, anything can change in an instant.*

As connectivity grows exponentially, the rise of misinformation could be described as an arms race. Now, an undeclared and invisible war is fought entirely through algorithms, narratives and manipulated media. Unlike traditional warfare, information has no rules, is easily distributed and has limited marginal cost. The dangers arising from our information and its effect on truth are surfacing. State and non-state actors have strategies in place to harness information's power.

Cyber and data breaches of some of the world's most sensitive government agencies and infrastructure are so frequent today that they may soon become banal. Organizations that do not build deep cyber capabilities will suffer in this new era of cyber insecurity.

Our ability to address our rapidly expanding information universe could determine the course of history. Those who can effectively deploy information gain incredible power, which has led to a resurgence of authoritarianism across the globe.

We must become familiar with the way media works, to distinguish trusted information sources from malicious content. Media literacy and critical thinking can counter the spread of fake content. Without effective education, info-ruption may lead to disastrous consequences as algorithms reshape society.

For all the benefits of infinite information at everyone's fingertips, its disruptive nature is greater than ever. As information is produced at an accelerating pace, this amplifies its impact by orders of magnitude. When manipulated, personalized information becomes even more convincing, and *truth evades objectivity, morphing into a subjective reality for every individual.*

Metaruption #5: Rapidly approaching new eras

Our *'rapidly approaching new eras'* bring an entirely new meaning to our lives and world order:

- *quantum computing and artificial life*
- *new frontiers, geopolitical and economic reshuffling*

Driver of disruption (ix): Quantum computing and artificial life

We are in the early stages of understanding how quantum computers could be useful:

- **Revolutions across fields:** Quantum could allow infinite simulations, experiments and tests – ushering in new drugs for life-threatening diseases, climate change solutions and breakthroughs in materials technology and engineering.

- **Significant investments:** Despite enormous scientific hurdles to overcome before deployment, more organizations than ever are committing resources to quantum.

- **National security:** Quantum could be an existential geopolitical threat, especially if quantum computers make current cybersecurity protections obsolete.

Beyond quantum computing, other game-changing technologies will define a new era in which technology and humanity fuse. Biotechnology, nanotechnology, AI and robotics will dramatically enhance human capabilities, while gene-editing technologies correct genetic defects and diseases. *Healthcare is shifting from diagnosis to prevention and augmentation, blurring the line between human and technology.*

Driver of disruption (x): New frontiers, geopolitical and economic reshuffling

The space industry is undergoing a significant transformation. As the commercial and geostrategic battles for space take shape, we approach an era where space moves from the *final* frontier to a *financial* frontier.

Meanwhile, on Earth, in addition to the momentum of China and Asia, Africa has pathways to become a future centre of gravity, driven by a demographic surge and innovation. As the aggregate populations of the G7 (Canada, France, Germany, Italy, Japan, the UK and the US) represent less than 10 per cent of the world's eight billion people and a decreasing proportion of GDP,[8] we enter new frontiers of a diminished Western world and an expansion into space.

The rise of China, Russia's invasion of Ukraine and these countries' aligned interests are disrupting globalization. Even the US dollar may lose its reserve currency status as other regions try to decouple from it. These all result in fractures to the global connectivity, technology standards, marketplaces, supply chains and economies that has been prevalent for decades. *Reshoring is replacing offshoring and outsourcing.*

As the United States sanctions Chinese tech companies, China aims to achieve autonomy in critical sectors such as AI, quantum computing and space. This new phase of enhanced tensions between the US and China has widespread geopolitical implications. *How the West reacts to China's rise will be an epoch-defining driver of disruption.*

China's economic growth, technological development, strict governmental control, long-term investments in education and infrastructure projects throughout Asia and Africa make it a viable contender to become the world's economic and political leader. In contrast, the US is mired in short-termism, dysfunctional political governance and polarization, distracting it from longer-term strategies and making it vulnerable, exacerbated by a record-breaking budget deficit.

Furthermore, with global institutions fragmenting, geopolitical tensions rising and protectionism increasing, how can the world find global solutions to systemic challenges like pandemics, climate mitigation and AI regulation? *Regional approaches are inadequate for holistic issues.*

Understanding what remains constant

While the drivers of disruption foster uncertainty and change, we can identify factors that remain constant. What could provide some predictability?

As we exercise our futures intelligence, it is valuable to anticipate what features of the present may continue.

Identifying what is stable over time

Jeff Bezos illustrates the value of identifying stability: 'I very frequently get the question: "What's going to change in the next 10 years?" And that is a very interesting question; it's a very common one. I almost never get the question: "What's not going to change in the next 10 years?" And I submit to you that that second question is actually the more important.'[9]

Identifying constants is not trivial. Every potential constant can be disputed, or unexpectedly take new forms. For instance, even if Moore's Law dies suddenly, increasing computing power could remain a constant if it comes from alternative breakthroughs such as quantum computing. The outcomes may be achieved even outside of Moore's Law.

Despite the unpredictability of our complex world, focusing on constants is still insightful. *Relative to the variabilities of change, the unwavering direction and consistent rhythm of constants stand out.*

We seek to explore possible futures by challenging assumptions while reducing uncertainties. Because our constants are likely to remain relatively static, their outcomes should not be surprising. We can be anticipatory, prepare, monitor and mitigate.

In defining constants, we study the durability and features of the underlying phenomena. *If these constants are subject to an exponential trajectory, the momentum could make them accelerate.*

Exploring 10 constants

As we develop a better understanding of the drivers of disruption, we can now contrast 10 constants:

1 **UN-VICE as a constant environment of the world:** The UN-VICE environment is an inherent constant. It is easier to imagine the world as predictable, but this world does not exist. Reality will continue to display UN-VICE features: unknown, volatile, intersecting, complex, exponential.

2 **Disruption continues as a steady state:** Patterns are increasingly hard to interpret and current paths are certain to be disrupted. Disruption is a constant.

3 **Sustainable is the new digital:** In our transparent and traceable world, extractive economies are challenged. Effective decision-making integrates sustainable futures, minimizing resource usage, extending product life cycles and featuring biodegradable products.

4 Technology's exponential evolution: Technology's evolution leads to cheaper, faster and increasing computer processing power. Miniaturization races towards invisible computing. Amara's Law prevails as we overestimate the short-term consequences of technology but underestimate its long-term impacts. AI, robotics, healthcare and ClimateTech converge to create digital synergies and prices continuously decrease.

5 Machines continue to learn quickly: Machines will continue to learn with increasingly higher-level human functions and understanding. Generative AI systems further amplify creativity and productivity.

6 Information plays key role in decision-making: The world – including humans – is a string of networked data constantly interpreted, decoded, programmed and edited. Unless humanity materially changes its relationship with technology and information, AI will play an increasing role in decision-making.

7 A decentralized, permissionless world emerges: Decentralization emerges from collective intelligence platforms and self-organized networks. These gradually erode dominant centralized control structures. Decentralization will continue to offer society novel ways to interact.

8 Continued paradigm shifts: Technology enables radical transparency and traceability, reinforcing accountability. The evolution from shareholder primacy to stakeholder capitalism will continue, seeking gender, racial, social, generational and environmental balances. Social change will constantly push existing boundaries.

9 The fusion of BioTech and AI: The biological, physical and digital will merge. This fusion could result in hyper-augmented humans, potentially combining human intelligence and cognitive computing. Breakthroughs in drug discovery, genetic engineering and synbio may become magic algorithms playing god and creating inorganic life.

10 Demand driven by whatever solves the 'JTBD': The Jobs to Be Done (JTBD) framework pioneered by Clayton Christensen is a popular method for understanding customer behaviour and possibilities for innovation. JTBD suggests that people buy products and services to get a specific job done. Christensen says that people don't simply buy them, they 'hire' them to help them make progress in some activity or task. Accordingly, they will 'fire' the product or service if another can do the job better.[10]

The difference between constants and change

KEY POINTS
Integrate the 10 constants for futures intelligence

Having reviewed both the drivers of disruption and the constants, we observe that these constants are the other side of the same coin. The mirror image of disruption is a constant (Figure 3.4).

The constancy of these elements allows you to use them to your advantage, reducing uncertainty and increasing agency. We have the latitude to prepare the next-order implications of their continued evolution.

We will always need to navigate our unknown world, but we don't have to do so in ignorance.

As we investigate change, the paradoxes and liminal nature of disruption somehow reflect the constants.

Changing and constant at the same time

Once we establish that disruption is a steady state, is there really a difference between disruptions and constants?

Figure 3.4   Disruptions = constants

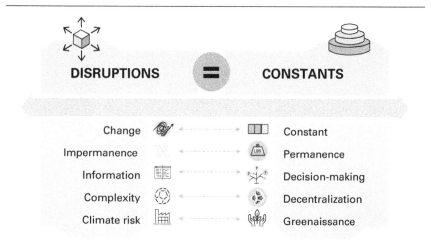

| DISRUPTIONS | = | CONSTANTS |

Change	Constant
Impermanence	Permanence
Information	Decision-making
Complexity	Decentralization
Climate risk	Greenaissance

In Japanese, *mujō* means impermanence: everything and everyone is constantly changing. Impermanence is called *Anicca* in Pali, the sacred language of Theravāda Buddhism. *Anicca* is an essential doctrine shared equally in Buddhism and Hinduism. In the teachings of the Buddha, life itself is comparable to a river that continuously flows, but never holds the same water. The Greek philosopher Heraclitus said that 'no man ever steps in the same river twice, for it is not the same river and he's not the same man'.

Nothing is permanent but impermanence. At the same time, everything is in constant change.

As you dive into life, whether there are changes, or constants, or changing constants, or constant changes, they are one and the same.

Some things will constantly emerge; others may disappear or change at different rates. Ultimately, we have agency to determine our future. We have choices as, above all, we are human.

Notes

1 F J Aguilar (1967) *Scanning the Business Environment*, Macmillan, New York, NY

2 R Spitz and L Zuin (2022) *The Definitive Guide to Thriving on Disruption: Reframing and navigating disruption*, Disruptive Futures Institute, San Francisco, CA

3 R Kurzweil. Kurzweil's Law (aka 'the law of accelerating returns'), The Kurzweil Library, 12 January 2004. www.thekurzweillibrary.com/kurzweils-law-aka-the-law-of-accelerating-returns (archived at https://perma.cc/BR9F-KGAQ)

4 National Human Genome Research Institute. The cost of sequencing a human genome, 2021. www.genome.gov/about-genomics/fact-sheets/Sequencing-Human-Genome-cost (archived at https://perma.cc/LJ3F-HBDM)

5 L Carroll (1871) *Through the Looking-Glass*, Macmillan, London, UK

6 N Bostrom (2014) *Superintelligence: Paths, dangers, strategies*, Oxford University Press, Oxford

7 M Tegmark (2017) *Life 3.0: Being human in the age of artificial intelligence*, Alfred A Knopf, New York, NY

8 F Richter (2022) How representative is the G7 of the world it's trying to lead? Statista, 27 June 2022. www.statista.com/chart/27687/g7-share-of-global-gdp-and-population (archived at https://perma.cc/Q9HG-BJCE)

9 Amazon Web Services (2012) 2012 re:invent day 2: Fireside chat with Jeff Bezos and Werner Vogels, YouTube, 2012. www.youtube.com/watch?v= O4MtQGRIIuA (archived at https://perma.cc/8N36-BRES)

10 C M Christensen, T Hall, K Dillon and D S Duncan. Know your customers' 'jobs to be done', *Harvard Business Review*, September 2016. www.hbr.org/ 2016/09/know-your-customers-jobs-to-be-done (archived at https://perma.cc/ W4TL-9U76)

4

Tools for navigating and anticipating disruption

OBJECTIVES
Navigating disruption to anticipate inflection points

We can proactively prepare for changes and anticipate inflection points. Anticipatory thinking equips us to navigate the ripple effects of disruptions, shape the future by driving change and plan for whatever lies ahead.

Learning to ride cycles and navigate change

Developing early warning systems

The future does not exist today, so we have the opportunity to imagine it, shape it and navigate towards it. However, our current maps of the future are limited, so we need to develop early warning systems:

- **Wider:** Look at a broader scope and dynamic context holistically.

- **Deeper:** Investigate the signals, drivers and interrelationships systemically.

- **Longer:** Study the past and explore different timeframes ahead.

Our navigational toolbox equips us with compasses calibrated for the unpredictable. We learn to assess the patterns of change, look back to see ahead, ride innovation cycles, anticipate inflection points and calibrate the dimensions of uncertainty.

The basic dimensions of change

Fundamental change takes on many forms. The agricultural revolution was different from the birth of the internet. The features of change are constant: replacement with something new, becoming thoroughly different or altering direction.

Peter Bishop and Andy Hines[1] frame change by analysing its four basic dimensions:

1 **Sources and levels:** Where does change come from? STEEPE is a framework for scanning and analysing environments across social, technological, environmental, economic, political and ethical factors, which can interact at different levels.

2 **Time horizons:** Substantive change necessitates longer timeframes. Sectors like consumer electronics and fashion experience rapid shifts, whereas infrastructure and climate operate on extended timelines.

3 **Rates of change:** Is change gradual, sudden or discontinuous? Discontinuity requires navigation without known references – relying on creativity to find our way.

4 **Shapes of change:** Transitions involve exponential, asymptotic or S-curve changes, but none of these continue indefinitely. Change itself is subject to slowdowns and reversals.

Looking back to see ahead

To understand transformational changes, we identify patterns in potential indicators. Historical patterns illuminate sources, timeframes, velocities and shapes of change. While history may not repeat, it can rhyme. When exploring the future, it's often advised to understand at least twice the past time horizon. For Winston Churchill, 'The farther backward you look, the farther forward you can see.'

EXAMPLE

Corporate life cycle and strategic longevity

Companies come and go and their life cycles are shrinking. Disruption fuels new industries and start-ups that replace industry leaders. Companies seek stability, yet profound change is common and can be swift.

In their 'How to thrive in the 2020s' study, Boston Consulting Group estimated that the odds of corporations failing were increasing: one in three public companies may cease to exist in their current form over the next five years, a rate six times higher than 40 years ago.[2] Innovation consulting firm Innosight's 2021 Corporate Longevity Forecast report shows the S&P 500 tenure of companies is growing shorter over time.[3] In the late 1970s, a company was listed on the index for an average of 30–35 years. This decade, that average is forecast to shrink to 15–20 years.

Companies can exit stock market indices like the S&P 500 due to mergers and acquisitions (M&A), going private or reorganization, but technology and innovation also play a role. These factors reshape business models and influence consumer trends.

Compressed supercycles and waves

Innovation life cycles have impacted economies for centuries. The Visual Capitalist illustrated these as five historic waves:[4]

1 **The Industrial Revolution:** Water power was harnessed to manufacture textiles and iron goods. Factories emerged and cities expanded around them.

2 **Industrial expansion:** Advancements in the rail industry enabled many other industries to develop.

3 **Electrification:** Electrification and Ford's modern assembly lines transformed the automotive industry.

4 **Oil and capital:** Aviation revolutionized travel and the global electronics industry emerged.

5 **Digital revolution:** The fifth wave was driven by the internet and digitization.

These waves are occurring more frequently. The Industrial Revolution began in 1785 and lasted 60 years, while the digital revolution began in 1990 and lasted around 30 years, now paving the way for a new transformative era building on the foundation of digitization.

As the energy transition comes to the forefront, we now move into the sixth wave, which we call Greenaissance, addressing climate change's complex challenges. This wave is marked by rapidly evolving and converging technologies including AI, robotics, materials technologies and IoT across agriculture, energy, transportation and construction.

The Perez Technological Surge Cycle

In her Technological Surge Cycle,[5] Carlota Perez defines our current technological revolutions as techno-economic paradigm shifts, drawing parallels between these and financial cycles. Each cycle, or technology surge, can take 50–60 years (e.g. age of railways, to steel and electricity, through mass production and automobiles, to today's information society). These innovations initially disrupted businesses, but ultimately disrupted the world.

Perez distinguishes between the installation phase marked by infrastructure construction and new technologies, and the subsequent deployment phase characterized by widespread adoption. As technological waves condense and supercycles falter, will we still see distinct, long-term cycles of breakthroughs and deployment? Or will these transitions become almost imperceptible shifts unfolding within years?

Disruption's great paradox: Change is slow but inflection points cascade rapidly

Despite technological accelerations, change is generally slow, difficult and unequally distributed. What determines an inflection point? Which changes will achieve widespread adoption?

EXAMPLE

How device transition triggered larger mutations

From vacuum tubes to transistors, from mainframe to personal computers and from handheld devices to smartphones, computing has shifted significantly over time. These transitions seamlessly integrated computers into our daily lives, making them both pervasive and invisible.

While handheld devices were available in the 1990s, mobile computing could not become ubiquitous without greater bandwidth and usability. Everything prior to the iPhone's 2007 launch paved the way for the smartphone explosion. The Palm PDA was first to market, but was not transformational. The current popularity of smartphones was only possible thanks to earlier devices and the internet.

When Apple launched its App Store in 2008, it paved the way for the pervasive mobile platforms we know today, including Instagram, Snapchat, Uber and WhatsApp.

Transformative change can seem deceptively slow. Some developing technologies, like habitable space stations, 4D printing, brain–computer interfaces and flying taxis, provide decades of signals before they materialize. As Silicon Valley forecaster Paul Saffo reminds us, *we should never mistake a clear view for a short distance.*[6]

When drivers such as miniaturization, price and performance converge, technologies can achieve exponential user adoption. Stacked innovations build on existing technologies, which can scale rapidly. The art is to gauge the rhythm of the inflection points driving the transformative shift.

Change may be slow, but the tempo of disruption is fast

Even when we carefully monitor innovations, we may fail to recognize the patterns of change. Inflection points, or tipping points, mark transformative shifts from one stage to another. These pivotal moments emerge when minor changes converge, giving rise to watershed transitions that redefine paradigms.

KEY POINTS
Why we miss inflection points

While the rhythm of change may appear slow, the tempo of disruption is extremely fast.

We miss inflection points for two contradictory reasons. We call this the *'Inflection Paradox'* (Figure 4.1):

- **Amara's Law:** In the early stages, one may be tempted to dismiss overhyped emerging technology. Then, after the prolonged wait, we underestimate its long-term impacts.

Figure 4.1 The Inflection Paradox

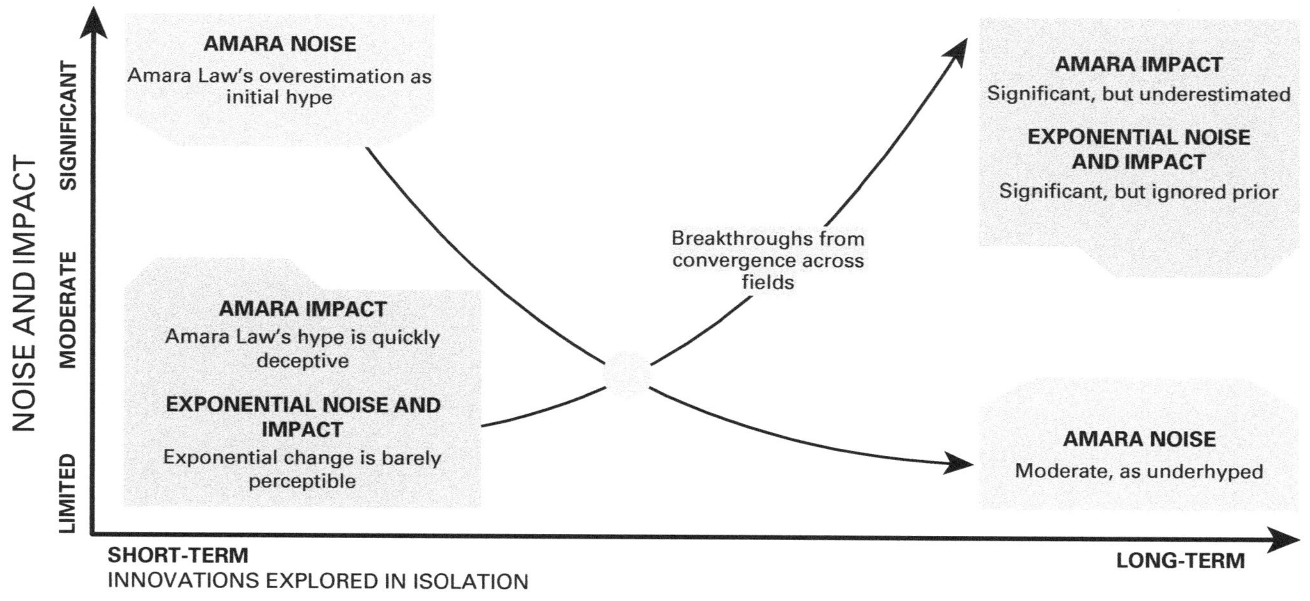

AMARA NOISE
Amara Law's overestimation as initial hype

AMARA IMPACT
Amara Law's hype is quickly deceptive

EXPONENTIAL NOISE AND IMPACT
Exponential change is barely perceptible

Breakthroughs from convergence across fields

AMARA IMPACT
Significant, but underestimated

EXPONENTIAL NOISE AND IMPACT
Significant, but ignored prior

AMARA NOISE
Moderate, as underhyped

LONG-TERM

SHORT-TERM
INNOVATIONS EXPLORED IN ISOLATION

NOISE AND IMPACT

LIMITED   MODERATE   SIGNIFICANT

> • **The shape of exponential change:** Despite the noise, early developments are barely perceptible. Even explosive growth only becomes apparent after some time. Longer-term, we completely underestimate the dramatic effects of exponential change.
>
> The Inflection Paradox describes these conflicting drivers and cognitive biases that contribute to missing inflection points. One issue which exacerbates this is that innovations are siloed, despite breakthroughs often occurring across fields.

Anticipating inflection points

Everett Rogers' work on the diffusion of innovations[7] illustrates the journey of the S-curve, which shows the rate of innovation adoption through phases:

- Nascent innovations start on the fringe, characterized by informal experiments.
- Development of prototypes, used by early adopters.
- After signs of commercial success, innovations are more rapidly adopted, curving upwards and accelerating.
- As innovations follow the S-curve, adoption slows and plateaus. Companies or projects become more structured, gaining greater access to funding.
- An inflection point occurs when small changes are sufficient to drive more transformative changes.

S-curves typically denote a new era. In strategy, declining growth requires companies to make changes to maintain momentum. Detecting nascent signals before their rapid growth can yield opportunities, and failure to do so can be costly.

Reaching critical mass

The challenge lies in understanding how emerging phenomena might reach tipping points. Questions about whether a given innovation will endure or fade become paramount. Identifying the timing of inflection points is crucial for effective decision-making.

Inflection points can be seen in social movements, innovations and business transitions, with technology playing a disproportionate role. Persisting with the same behaviours after any inflection point is a sure-fire way to lose relevance.

Technological breakthroughs typically require years to materialize. Upon reaching inflection points, however, relevance can be short-lived – due either to rapid obsolescence or suboptimal timing.

Netscape once dominated the browser market and Yahoo! was the leading search engine, but neither stood the test of time. General Magic, a 1990 Apple spin-off, offers a compelling case study in the PDA's pre-iPhone evolution.[8] Though ahead of its time for the mid-1990s internet infrastructure, General Magic paved the way for future breakthroughs with innovations like multimedia email, software modems and touchscreens. Some products never achieve critical mass, but pave the way to mass adoption of later technologies.

KEY POINTS
Explorers, pioneers and settlers

The S-curve can help us better imagine what lies ahead. Analogies comparing today's innovators with prospectors in the California Gold Rush abound. Early innovators are often described as explorers, pioneers or settlers.

In Silicon Valley, a common saying is 'pioneers get the arrows while settlers get the land'. Being a first mover is not necessarily an advantage. As noted in Amara's Law, we often overestimate the impact of a technology early on. It was not the explorers who popularized the first commercially successful browsers or smartphones, but pioneers like Google and Apple following in their footsteps.

Appreciating these archetypes can help us navigate disruption:

- **Explorers are inventors:** True adventurers explore unknown environments with no context, taking on the most risk. Examples include Marco Polo (explorer), Nikola Tesla (AC electric system), Xerox PARC (PC), Netscape (browser), General Magic (smartphone), SpaceX (commercial reusable rockets).

- **Pioneers make improvements:** Benefitting from explorers' footprints, explorers apply their own innovation to succeed. Examples include

Robert Noyce and Gordon Moore (Intel, chips), Steve Jobs and Steve Wozniak (Apple, PC), Bill Gates (Microsoft, PC operating system), Peter Thiel (PayPal, online payments), Larry Page and Sergey Brin (Google, browser).

- **Settlers create value by imitating:** Focused on established environments, settlers exploit and develop existing opportunities. Most of the world are settlers, focused on effective execution and harvesting.

For today's complex challenges, we are called to be explorers and pioneers. Simply executing established ideas holds less promise, especially considering that compressed life cycles can leave you imitating outdated strategies. But modern pioneering doesn't necessarily mean being first or going it alone; it arises from the synthesis of fresh combinations, perspectives and collaborations.

The value creation trade-off lies between innovation and invention: are you offering an incremental improvement, or something entirely new?

Monitor inflection points before they flex

The challenge with inflection points is that they only become obvious in hindsight. Below are filters to take the pulse of inflection points before they arrive:

- **Frameworks:** Continuously assessing and monitoring new ideas, technologies and trends.
- **Human, intellectual and financial capital:** Drivers for new values, fields and money.
- **External and macro perspectives:** These play a significant role, crossing thresholds through new times, rules and politics.

Frameworks

Monitor signals of change using frameworks to continuously evaluate:

- **New ideas:** The S-curve and innovation life cycle frameworks can be applied to any novel phenomena, including nascent ideas, patents and product launches.
- **New technology:** NASA's Technology Readiness Level (TRL) can help evaluate and monitor emerging technologies over time. The metric quantifies

a technology's maturity on a scale from 1 (idea) to 9 (fully commercialized). Monitoring the move from concept to prototype provides insights well before actual products are incorporated into daily life.

- **New trends:** Gartner Hype Cycles visualize the evolution of emerging technologies through five key phases: innovation trigger, peak of inflated expectations, trough of disillusionment, slope of enlightenment and plateau of productivity. Emerging technologies often have disruptive potential, but may never achieve critical mass. If adopted, most reach the plateau of productivity (mainstream usage) between five and ten years.

The changing technological landscape of the past decades can shed light on future inflection points. *But no exploration of the past should be confused with a prediction.*

Mark Mine, a technologist, analysed 25 years of Gartner's Hype Cycles. He found that one-third of the 300 technologies featured appeared only once before disappearing.[9] Venture capitalist Michael Mullany also analysed decades of Hype Cycles, finding that many technologies are flashes in the pan.[10] The challenges lie in implementation. Certain technologies, such as quantum computing and brain-computer interfaces, keep receding into the future. Other technologies, including natural language processing and computer vision, make key breakthroughs in stealth mode.

While change often happens in slow motion, neglecting to monitor its progress can lead to sudden disruption. *Breakthroughs are even more abrupt and turbulent when we are not paying attention.*

Human, intellectual and financial capital

The value of intangibles is increasing. Drivers, triggers and inflection points to look for include:

- **New values – societal or generational shifts:** Changing consumer and generational behaviour, expectations and values. Examples include Millennials and Gen Z representing two-thirds of the workforce by 2030 and California banning new petrol car sales by 2035.

- **New fields – cross-pollination:** Frontier breakthroughs combine technologies from different fields. Examples include 3D-printed meat alternatives, bioprinted organs and implantable devices.

- **New value generation – cost competitiveness, user experience, functionality:** Constantly smaller, faster, cheaper computing power. Cost curve inflection points are critical for consumer products like mixed-reality headsets, but also for sectors like space. Examples include India-based Jio developing affordable smartphones, SpaceX and Blue Origin's reusable launchers, deep learning graphics processing units (GPUs) and human genome sequencing.

- **New money – follow the investments:** Venture capital (VC) money, acquisitions and partnerships can signal future inflection points transforming entire industries. For instance, Microsoft invested in OpenAI for generative AI and L'Oreal acquired ModiFace for virtual try-ons. However, beware of herd mentality and noise. Magic Leap's augmented reality projects attracted billions in investments, but were then forced to pivot, as the technology was overhyped. Even though these conflicting signals result in setbacks, given the Inflection Paradox, they could still pave the way for future tipping points.

External and macro

External and macro factors play a significant role in reaching critical mass:

- **New times – non-linear shocks:** External shocks that drive turbulent times catalyse transformational change. Examples include climate (venture and infrastructure investments, subsidies, R&D), Covid (drug discovery, future of work and travel) and the 2008 financial meltdown (bitcoin, blockchain).

- **New rules – regulations:** Sectors including healthcare, finance and energy have strong regulatory drivers. Monitor the timing, nature and next-order implications of such regulatory changes that drive future inflection points. Open banking standards enabled banking APIs, allowing software companies to make payments, circumventing bank infrastructure.

- **New politics – geopolitical:** Supranational interests and geopolitical sensitivities drive investments in some sectors; protectionism also triggers inflection points. Examples include AI, space, semiconductors, quantum and cybersecurity.

Futures intelligence for constant change

Themes of anticipation

The term 'anticipatory' is intimately related to the foresight field. The objective of exploring the possible futures and drivers of change systemically is to inform actionable short-term decision-making.

Anticipatory frameworks allow us to develop our capacities and mindsets to prepare for, imagine and build longer-term futures. To paraphrase the inventor Charles Kettering, we should all be concerned about the future because we are destined to spend the rest of our lives there. Exploring possible futures can reveal opportunities and enable timely responses to changes.

At the root of being anticipatory is the characterization of 'anticipation'. In philosophy, Heidegger uses the German term *Dasein* (literally meaning 'to be there') existentially, to describe the experience and temporality of being. In that context, Heidegger sees *anticipation* as a projection towards the future, where one looks forward to a possible way of being.[11]

Anticipation is also fundamental in natural sciences, from physics to biology, and in human sciences, including anthropology, psychology and economics. In nature, animals anticipate winter by storing food, migrating and growing thicker fur. Plants also anticipate winter.

Being anticipatory does not require formal tools. Often, common sense, mindfulness and critical thinking will beat any tools. Being in the world is being anticipatory.

EXAMPLE

Anticipatory Agassi

Tennis is largely about problem solving. With a fresh perspective Andre Agassi solved a problem posed by Boris Becker, an opponent who had defeated him three times using a serve the game had never seen before. Although Becker's serve was revolutionary, there was a chink in his armour. Agassi reviewed videos of previous matches. He made a specific observation and interpreted the signal: 'When Boris serves, he sticks out his tongue. If it is in the left of his mouth, he serves down the tramlines. If it sticks out to the front, he will serve down the centre.'[12]

After making this observation, Agassi defined his options and planned. He now had a valuable piece of information, but would lose his advantage if he revealed it by overusing it. Thus, Agassi didn't react perfectly to every serve, deliberately losing some points to keep his information a secret.

This led Agassi to win nine of their next eleven matches. After Becker retired, they had a beer together and Agassi finally revealed the secret. Becker was floored. According to Agassi, Becker said: 'It's like you read my mind. Little did I know you were just reading my tongue.'

Being anticipatory involves thinking deeply about the future, which may also entail a detailed assessment of the past.

Preparation and visioning

As we prepare for the future to unfold, we leverage anticipatory mindsets for two key objectives. First, preparation: we consciously build our capacity to adapt to any potential scenarios. Second, visioning: we ignite our imagination with an engaging vision, articulating our desired future for ourselves and others.

Both objectives are intrinsically linked as we seek to anticipate disruption. Whether proactively preparing for any future eventualities or seeking clarity to direct our vision, being anticipatory empowers us to respond to and even shape many disruptions ahead.

Futures Cone: Visioning aspirational futures

Visioning involves mapping out possible futures, with the agency to develop, communicate and realize our preferred future.

The Futures Cone allows the mapping of a range of possible futures, divided into four categories (Figure 4.2):[13]

- **Possible futures:** The widest range of events that could unfold, including Black Swans and Wild Cards.
- **Plausible futures:** Scenarios that may happen, given the bounds of uncertainty.
- **Probable futures:** What we believe is most likely, based on current trends.
- **Preferable futures:** What we actually want to happen.

Figure 4.2   The Futures Cone: Choose your own future

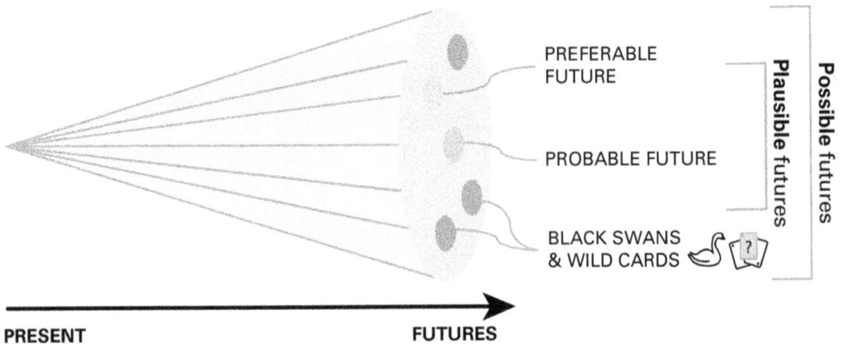

NOTE Adapted from T Hancock and C Bezold. Possible futures, preferable futures, *The Healthcare Forum Journal*, 1994, 37 (2), 23–29

Visioning is different from strategy

Bruce Sterling, the American science fiction writer, said, 'When you can't imagine how things are going to change, that doesn't mean that nothing will change. It means that things will change in ways that are unimaginable.'[14]

So how is visioning different from a strategic plan? Visioning goes further. It's more aspirational, pushing beyond the perceived limits of reality, putting us on the other side of the boundaries of change. In perpetually evolving environments, there is an inherent need to act and respond with novel options. Today's wicked problems cannot afford failure of imagination.

The danger in decision-making is paralysis by analysis because ever-changing environments require creating something new, often in real-time. Deeply uncertain situations require continuous learning, constant assumption challenging and responding to dynamic change. Here, analysis can be limiting.

Limitations of traditional planning

Traditional planning approaches utilize techniques that assume the world's predictability. These are becoming increasingly ineffective in our UN-VICE global systems (Figure 4.3).

Seeking to predict an answer is reasonable when addressing clearly defined questions and reliable historical data in stable environments. However, when uncertainties and elusive answers abound, focus must shift to formulating insightful questions before searching for answers.

Figure 4.3 Strategic plan versus futures

Strategic plan vs futures

Shorter-term	Longer-term
Milestones	Emergent
Answer	Question
Controllable, linear, stable, contained	Systemic, non-linear, complex, spillover
Model uncertainties to deliver certainty	Explore and prepare for any change
A strategic plan	Multiple futures
Reductionist and deterministic	Agency and indeterminacy
Data and noise	Scanning and signals
Predictions and assumptions	Plurality and uncertainty

Figure 4.4 Certainty is in the past

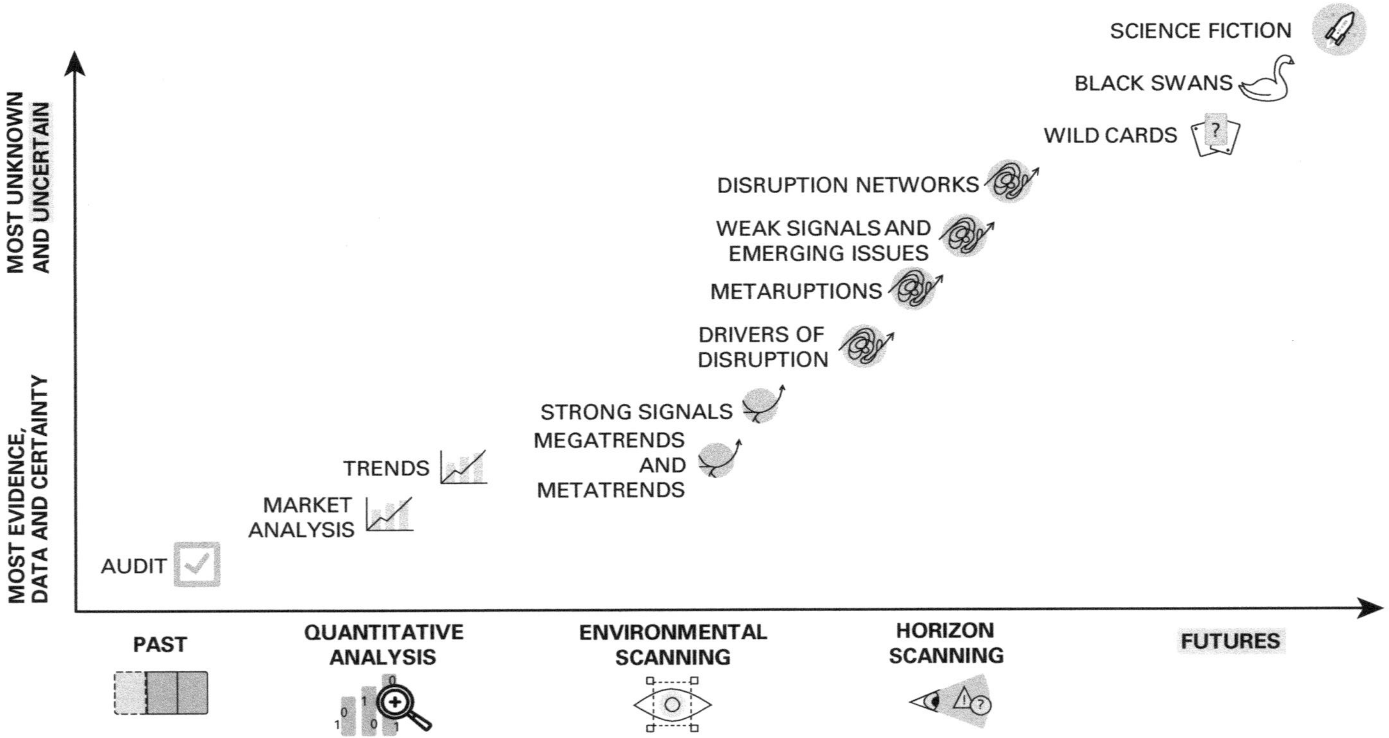

When variables and their interactions are more volatile, relying solely on predictions can be detrimental, especially when decisions hinge on their accuracy. The future is unmapped; you can't rely on modelling uncertainties to deliver certainty.

Examples highlighting the limitations of predictions are everywhere. For instance, in 2023, the CEO of JPMorgan Chase pointed out that central bank inflation forecasting had been '100 per cent dead wrong'.[15] Experts face challenges in predicting complex future outlooks, underscoring the need for humility.

Certainty is in the past

Quantitative analysis offers us evidence which can support our understanding of current and past situations. We typically feel more certain that we understand past events in retrospect. But that doesn't mean our data is complete, or that our models are accurate. Trends are also based on the past and are visible in hindsight.

Meanwhile, strong signals give us indications of possible futures. As disruption is constant, we should seek to understand the dynamics of underlying change to enhance our capacities. Science fiction can help us peer even farther into the futures, as these quickly become science fact (Figure 4.4).

Wild card events – low-probability, high-impact surprises – are imaginable, but their effects are unpredictable. Today, wild cards appear with greater frequency (extreme climate events, high inflation, Brexit, global pandemic, food and energy insecurity, war, erosion of major democracies). *Rare is becoming less rare.*

As uncertainty multiplies over time, it becomes more costly to assume the world is predictable. The greater the extent of unknown variables, the less predictable the environment. For those intent on business as usual, the scope of value destruction is growing.

EXAMPLE

Consultants rely on certainty

The world's consultants spend their time advising on restructuring, optimizing and finding every possible source of cost savings. But these strategies ignore the greatest cost of all: the cost of relying on assumptions, which is going through the roof.

Many perceived cost savings actually make organizations more fragile, like 'optimizing' supply chains. Think how much companies could save if they were more thoughtful about the assumptions they relied on. The cost of being anticipatory pales in comparison with the costs of lacking resilience. Broadening and reimagining assumptions offers more effective cost savings than skimping on food subsidies, employee benefits or Post-it notes.

Alternatives to assumptions

While there are no outright alternatives to making assumptions, we can consider how we rely on them. First, acknowledge the limitations and increasing cost of relying on assumptions. Second, imagine what the open futures could become; outcomes are not predetermined. Third, appreciate that static assumptions need constant updating because the world is in endless flux. Finally, integrate that non-linearity amplifies assumptions over time.

For these reasons, the Bank of England may integrate extreme weather scenarios into its financial stability assessments (for instance, imagining if Westminster were plunged under water).

Scenario development: Asking questions

Futures mindsets do not preclude the use of assumptions. However, with foresight, we are not looking for a predetermined answer. Foresight is the capacity to explore the possible futures systemically, as well as drivers of change, to inform short-term decision-making. We ask questions, challenge views and explore what we may not be thinking about – what lies below the surface. We ask: Why? Why not? What if? What if not? So what? For these questions focused on the futures, there is no data.

In foresight, insights from historic analysis and trends are helpful for sense making, but only to provide a snapshot of the existing world as a base. Our imagination helps build out different scenarios, outcomes and possible futures. Some of these are more probable; others may be our vision of the preferable futures; we also integrate outliers. Black Swans (unpredictable, rare and extremely impactful events) and Butterfly Effects (small causes with outsized spillover effects) are possible.

After the first atomic bomb was dropped during World War II, the world was confronted with the unprecedented possibility of nuclear annihilation.

There were previously no comparable ways of ending civilization. The use of scenarios for highly uncertain situations was originally developed by Herman Kahn for military and nuclear strategy in the 1950s (RAND Corporation) and by Pierre Wack for business strategy in the 1970s (Royal Dutch Shell).[16]

Scenario planning builds on linear strategic planning, but the fundamental departure is that the futures are different from the past, longer timeframes matter and next-order impacts need to be captured. *Scenarios help solve problems differently because they can illuminate new possibilities and ignite hope.*

Good scenarios offer both plausible and challenging narratives for a handful of alternative futures. Some, we may wish to create; others, we need to prepare for. By looking a decade ahead, we can depart from the world we know, investigate unknowns and acknowledge deep uncertainties we cannot ignore. We integrate the trends we observe as a baseline while also imagining the cascading impacts of emerging issues.

In co-creating scenarios, we take ownership of uncertainty, consider what could be at stake and explore a diverse range of possibilities not captured by quantitative analysis. Scenarios are dynamic living narratives that require updating as the world evolves.

Start with the future

Most organizations and leaders take a present–forward approach. They look at the world, their business, product pipeline and projects from their current state and project how the future may be developed from here. A 'backcasting' (or future–back) approach provides a framework to reset assumptions, acknowledging that yesterday's assumptions may no longer be valid.

Like chess masters who imagine the endgame as opposed to the next few moves, companies that stay relevant imagine their options from a 'future–back' and 'today–forward' perspective. Backcasting starts with an aspirational future, then works back to identify pathways, including key challenges, toward that preferred future today.

Backcasting identifies an aspirational future rather than being constrained by present limitations. The objective is to dream bold futures, addressing our most complex problems.

Backcasting addresses some of the limitations of present–forward strategies, including status quo inertia, relying on historical trend extrapolation and short-term thinking (typically two to five years), which can limit reimagining transformative new paradigms. Additionally, assumptions are often defined by today's starting point.

The 2×2 Double Uncertainty method

The 2×2 technique was formalized in the 1990s by foresight practitioners who had developed leading scenario practices within Shell and the Global Business Network.[17] This extensive experience helped define and refine the technique. The 2×2 is known by many names, including Double Uncertainty and Axes of Uncertainty.

Two aspects of this technique are particularly beneficial:

- **Highest importance and greatest uncertainty:** For a given topic, practitioners choose the two drivers considered to be of the greatest uncertainty and the highest importance, then plot each on an axis.

- **Scenario generation:** The resulting 2×2 matrix forms the basis for potential scenarios.

The scenarios flesh out both risks and opportunities, useful for prioritizing and implementing. There are four steps to the 2×2 method: (i) identify the question to be answered; (ii) distinguish the macro-drivers of that topic's future, identifiable through scanning techniques such as STEEPE; (iii) choose the two most fundamental drivers to be the critical uncertainties; and (iv) build scenarios from them.

The 2×2 matrix is particularly insightful when you select the two most important drivers with the most uncertain outcomes, then plot axes that illustrate extreme opposite outcomes. Practitioners can make their resulting scenarios 'come to life' through narrative storytelling and discussion of deeper implications. Additionally, they can switch out critical drivers and compare scenarios.

Though the 2×2 is popular for its simplicity, it is inherently limited because it only explores two main drivers. Practitioners can also add a third dimension to increase the complexity of the framework.

CHECKLIST
Bridging the futures readiness gap

Explore the following eight considerations to gauge your organization's future readiness:

- **Language:** The degree to which the leadership teams use future-focused language, or, in contrast, language such as 'This is impossible', 'It has never happened before', 'This is the way it is done.'

- **Capabilities and mindset**: An organization's awareness of futures thinking and depth of foresight capacity within leadership teams.

- **Timeframes**: The frequency of exploring multiple futures with longer timeframes (beyond five, even ten, years).

- **Investigating change**: The processes in place to scan, monitor and evaluate weak signals, emerging issues and next-order implications.

- **Decision-making**: The leadership team's ability for sense-making and decision-making in deeply uncertain environments.

- **Predictability**: Understanding that the planning tools used by leadership, finance and risk management teams do not translate into predictability about the future.

- **Quantitative and qualitative filters**: Thoughtful use of data insights and financial projections, rather than unwavering reliance to the exclusion of qualitative approaches.

- **Organizational structure**: Decision-making processes are fluid and agile instead of centralized and hierarchical.

Levels of uncertainty

Today, surprise is often the result of not listening well enough. Beyond scanning for discernable signals and scenario development, there are additional ways to better prepare for the surprises ahead. We constantly need to assess what is knowable (what you could know, but don't) and what is unknowable (what you cannot actually know).

Nassim Nicholas Taleb uses the famous example of *Black Swans*[18] to describe unforeseeable events with extreme impacts. This term originates from the old European belief that all swans were white until the first encounter with a black swan challenged that. However, in the cases of Kodak, Nokia, Blockbuster, Sears and Toys 'R' Us, where poor strategic decision-making led to foreseeable corporate demise, a better metaphor is the *Gray Rhino*.[19]

Michele Wucker defines Gray Rhino events as highly probable and obvious yet, despite clear warning signs, we still fail to respond. We may diagnose the danger half-heartedly, deny that it exists or pass the buck. Then, we panic when it's too late, as the Gray Rhino is already charging our way.

At its simplest level, a Black Swan is something we can't even imagine, things we thought impossible. A Gray Rhino is obvious – even likely. But with our heads in the sand, we decide to ignore the charging rhino.

Know your Black Swans from your Gray Rhinos to avoid being trampled.

Unaccountability breeds Gray Rhinos

The scale of the crisis resulting from the Covid pandemic was in part due to a Gray Rhino.

With Covid, the lack of preparation globally was just the tip of the iceberg in our failures to respond. The warnings were multiple: US intelligence; Bill Gates' now infamous 2015 TED Talk; World Health Organization warnings; the World Economic Forum listing infectious diseases amongst the greatest risks; and Merck stating in 2018 that infectious disease outbreaks with potential devastating consequences were a 'certainty'.

The eventuality of a global pandemic was certain, leaving uncertain only the timing and impact.

Contact tracing, masks, respirators and other equipment would not have prevented the pandemic, but reasonable anticipatory steps would have had a beneficial impact if leaders had integrated the possibility of a pandemic (a Gray Rhino). Instead, few asked themselves how they would respond to what was evidently a likely event. Short-term thinking often leads to exponentially higher costs. In this case, beyond the lives lost, the world saved billions to waste trillions.

In 2021, millions of Texans were without electricity for prolonged periods because of extreme weather. Power outages were just the start, as antiquated policies and infrastructure exposed drinking water to freezing temperatures. During the same week that NASA's Johnson Space Center in Houston saw its *Perseverance* rover land on Mars, Texans were without water or electricity.

The companies responsible for ensuring reliable power deliberately skimped on investments, over-optimized and relied on flawed assessments of future weather variations and capacity. Meanwhile, over the years, their shareholders were delighted to extract maximum value, ignoring regulators' recommendations that utilities use more insulation, heated pipes and other steps to winterize plants. With no one accountable to broader stakeholders or incentivized to make changes, the fragile power suppliers did not deem it necessary to anticipate anything beyond what their statistical models estimated as short-term requirements for an assumed normal, predictable world.

Climate change means extreme weather is becoming frequent. With unprepared, unaccountable leaderships, blackouts during arctic blasts will also become normal. Never mind that the reckless short-termism of these energy companies, shareholders and regulators ignored the broader set of stakeholders in the first place; they made themselves too fragile to deliver the one thing their customers are paying them for – energy and water. When capitalism and politics are unchecked, the results are potentially catastrophic.

'It has never happened before' and 'We have never seen this' are not reasons to dismiss possibilities. 'Very unlikely' is evolving into 'unlikely', and sometimes even 'likely'.

The Complex Five of disruption: Know your unknowns

Our UN-VICE environment is not as binary as either Black Swans appearing out of nowhere, or predictable Gray Rhinos. We must appreciate the variability, nuances and textures within the spectrum of these two extremes.

The most famous quote of former US Secretary of Defense Donald Rumsfeld during the Bush Administration is 'there are known knowns; there are things we know we know. We also know there are known unknowns; that is to say we know there are some things we do not know. But there are also unknown unknowns – the ones we don't know we don't know.'[20] This 2002 quote was in relation to uncertain evidence regarding Saddam Hussein's alleged weapons of mass destruction.

Recognizing the different types of uncertainty is a prerequisite to better anticipate for unknown futures:

- **Known knowns:** Things we know that we know, as evident as 'the sun rises in the morning and sets at night'. For these, we use author Michele Wucker's definition of 'Gray Rhino'. There is no *un*certainty with Gray Rhinos; we might treat them as contingent or unknown, but they are outright certain.

- **Unknown knowns:** Things that we think that we know, but it transpires that we may not actually understand them when they manifest. For example, increasing ocean temperatures and acidity levels prompted perfect conditions for jellyfish population growth.[21] This increase then forced shutdowns from jellyfish clogs in the cooling systems of nuclear reactors around the world. Here, situations that we believe we initially understand and might even expect can become far more complex, as small changes drive larger and less predictable impacts. To describe such unknown knowns, Postnormal Times uses the term 'Black Jellyfish'.[22]

- **Known unknowns:** Things we know we don't know, including new diseases, the unfolding impacts of climate change and geopolitical events triggering mass migration. These are obvious, highly likely threats, but with few willing to acknowledge or see them. We call these known unknowns 'Black Elephants', based on a term attributed to the Institute for Collapsonomics.[23]

- **Unknown unknowns:** Things that we don't know that we don't know. For these unpredictable 'outliers' we use Taleb's 'Black Swans'.

All these degrees of uncertainty share a common trait: absence of evidence is not evidence of absence.

Ripple effects from our majestic butterfly

We might be tempted to look at these animals in isolation, but there is one beautiful and brightly coloured flying insect whose flapping wings can bring them together. Many changes seem insignificant at first, then mushroom into something much larger. In our dynamic, complex world, there are numerous cause-and-effect relationships that can't be identified or understood. *A single triggering phenomenon can generate an avalanche of disproportionate – and seemingly disparate – impacts when the simultaneous ripple effects collide.*

The *Butterfly Effect*, defined by meteorologist Edward Lorenz, describes how small changes can have significant and unpredictable consequences. To illustrate, Lorenz described a butterfly flapping its wings in one location influencing a tornado formation elsewhere.

A famous historical example of a ripple effect is the assassination of Archduke Franz Ferdinand, seen as a catalyst to both World Wars. A communication failure with the driver regarding a change in route resulted in the Archduke's assassination after a failed attempt. What would have happened (or not happened) if the route had been changed and he had not been assassinated?

Responding to the Complex Five

Our Complex Five[24] refer to the five most important animals in our 'hunting' for big disruptors – rhinos, jellyfish, swans, elephants and butterflies (Figure 4.5).

The Big Five in safaris (buffalo, leopards, lions, elephants and rhinos) are dangerous because of their strength and size. *In our disruptive world, the smallest changes can cause large impacts.*

The swans, jellyfish and butterflies can be more dangerous than elephants and rhinos. And while certain Big Five safari animals are endangered, our

Figure 4.5   The Complex Five

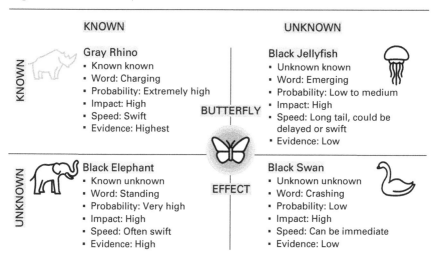

Complex Five of disruption are increasingly prevalent, spreading and grow-ing. Paradoxically, this does not always make them easier to spot.

Gray Rhino – known known

The Gray Rhino is high-impact, extremely probable and obvious. Unlike the 'invisible' Black Elephant, which for now may be sitting quietly, it is difficult *not* to see the Gray Rhino, as it is already charging towards us. While we have the choice to respond – or not – to the Gray Rhino, inaction comes at a cost. Examples include the Covid pandemic, Greek credit crisis, Argentina credit crisis and Challenger Space Shuttle accident. Issues with Gray Rhinos include denial, ignorance and hidden agendas.

Despite knowledge of the risks and clarity of the situation, responses often fall short because decisions are made too late. The rhino charges in plain sight, yet we turn a blind eye to it. Be the first to point out its existence (don't assume someone else will). When taking action before getting tram-pled, consider the speed of development, the degree of consensus on root causes and possible solutions and the size and complexity of the problems. As Wucker points out, Rhinos can be anticipated, rather than denied, mud-dling along and panicking when it is too late.

Black Jellyfish – unknown known

Seemingly insignificant initial ad hoc observations can have knock-on ef-fects. What we believe we understand and control manifests in complex systems, cascading into interwoven, disproportionate, unexpected, uncontrollable and often cumulative effects. Examples include social media, artificial intelligence and CRISPR gene editing. It is difficult to anticipate how benign or small changes will mutate into large-scale impacts over time, even scaling into irreversibility.

While the normalcy of the known initial situation may display a degree of predictability, Black Jellyfish grow into something far less predictable, often contradictory. To respond, consider second-order effects by asking 'What if this expanded larger than expected?' and 'What else might this impact?'

Black Elephant – known unknown

Black Elephants are similar to Gray Rhinos, but the elephant is standing, versus a charging rhino. Black Elephants are highly likely and widely anticipated, but end up ignored, as no one wants to deal with them. When they materialize, they are dismissed as a Black Swan. Examples include ocean acidification, the effects of climate change, Brexit, the European migration crisis, Russia's expansion strategy, cyber threats and terrorism. The term 'Black Elephant' aptly captures known unknowns: risks we may be aware of, but fail to confront as we ignore the 'elephant in the room'. We may not fully understand the scope of the risks, or they may not be completely integrated. When Black Elephants are discussed by experts and non-experts alike, too many divergent views can translate into a 'low credibility' situation, reinforcing the status quo.

Responses to the Black Elephant, at a societal level, require finding alignment and understanding the changes throughout the system to take appropriate initiatives. In more specific situations, own the response and mobilize action. Don't let the Black Elephant blindside you, or those threats we choose not to see will morph into a Gray Rhino and head straight for us.

Black Swan – unknown unknown

A by-product of complex adaptive systems, Black Swans are game changers with monumental impacts, only explainable retrospectively. Black Swans are unlikely and unpredictable. Examples include the Spanish flu pandemic, the spectacular rise of the internet and smartphones as invisible computers, the 9/11 attacks, World War I, the 'Arab Spring', and the Fukushima nuclear disaster. The greatest challenge with a Black Swan is that we don't know what we don't know. The odds of these rare events and their runaway chain reactions are not computable.

Responses to Black Swans include building resilient foundations and paying attention to the outsized 'fat tail', where consequential rare events have profound impacts. However unpredictable Black Swan outliers are, you can still be anticipatory. Look for the nonobvious. Accept randomness. Be aware of cognitive bias and understand that the modern world is dominated by very rare events. When Black Swans arise, integrate that they are game changers and rise up from the devastation. However, Black Swans aren't only adverse; take the miraculous discovery of a cure for an incurable disease. It is wise to seek exposure to positive Black Swans, which can act as a hedge against negative ones.

Perspectives and preparation can change classifications

Examples of the Complex Five are subjective. Depending on perspectives and filters used for evaluating events, they could be classified into multiple categories.

Views are often divided in distinguishing Black Swans from the other animals. Events that arose 'unexpectedly' without any prior signals could be deemed Black Swans by some, but others believe the possibilities of these events were known, even expected. Covid is not a Black Swan because experts warned us about the possibility of a pandemic for some time.

The difference between a Black Swan and another Complex Five lies in the extent of our preparation, assumptions and imagination. Many considered the 9/11 attacks to be a Black Swan. Others contend that there were visible warning signs: the 1993 World Trade Center bombing, extremists seeking to avenge US interference in the Arab world and failed coordination between US intelligence agencies.

We could argue that none of 2022–23's macroeconomic events were Black Swans, as they all had sufficient warning signs. For instance, stock market and technology valuations oscillated from bear to bull and back, high inflation followed extended periods of central banks 'printing' money and weather volatility was forewarned by countless climate reports.

None of these were Black Swans, which is the 'go to' taxonomy for C-suites and policymakers justifying their surprise in the face of the assumptions they made, signals they ignored and preparation they skimped on.

> **KEY POINTS**
> Track the Complex Five without getting stung or trampled
>
> - **Study zoology:** Examine the natural habitat, evolutionary process and system interactions of the rhinos, jellyfish, swans, elephants and butterflies.
>
> - **Read paw prints:** Draw inspiration from safari's Big Five by learning valuable lessons in awe while remaining highly alert. Like elephants communicating across large distances with low frequencies, pick up, interpret and act on weak signals as they evolve. Like spotting the secretive leopard hiding during the day, learn to find what is concealed.
>
> - **Explore the natural contradictions:** Swiftness and leisure, abruptness with poise, power and agility, alone and in packs.
>
> - **Mutations are not extinctions:** The nature of uncertainty evolves over time. Our Complex Five are not disappearing; they are blooming and expanding their reach. The fact that you don't see them doesn't mean they are absent. Just like the caterpillar, our animals can transform. The Butterfly Effect may trigger a Black Elephant to metamorphose into a charging Gray Rhino if it feels energized.
>
> - **Climbing into irreversibility:** Pay particular attention to escalations and tipping points, as trivial signals snowball into uncontrollable issues before action is taken. Once the predator is climbing with its prey, it might be too late.
>
> - **Anticipation does not provide certainty:** Our safari demands continuous alertness and emergence.

Predictability (and unpredictability)

Uncertainty is the only certainty

As our world grows more complex, so does our uncertainty. The farther we peer into the future, the greater the uncertainty. Therefore, thinking in longer timeframes early on provides the greatest value. *Uncertainty is an inherent trait of the future.*

Deep uncertainty hinders predictability

Two dynamics define deep uncertainty.

First, we do not know the nature and probability for individual possible future events. What are the direct and spillover effects of climate change?

What are the ramifications of advancements in genomics, longevity and syn-bio? What is the probability of rare yet high-impact events, such the collapse of the internet? And so on.

Secondly, if these events occur, how will they interplay with other dynamic scenarios? The resulting impact cascades create deeper uncertainties as they interact in unexpected ways and lead to chaotic outcomes. How do the complexities of energy turmoil, food insecurity, pandemics, China's ascendance, Russia's conflict in Ukraine, polarization, emerging technologies and extreme weather conditions intertwine? What unfolds when advancing AI systems, the Space Race and audacious cyberattacks on vital networked infrastructure converge?

Our objective is to understand the features that enable predictability. When parameters are known and stable, we can venture into predictions. In deep uncertainty, countless unknown variables hinder predictability. *Given the inverse relationship between predictability and uncertainty, the cost of maintaining business as usual rises significantly.*

Reframing predictability, risk and uncertainty

Prediction is inherently speculative. Evaluating predictability requires an understanding of the degrees of certainty (Figure 4.6):

- **Risk – most predictable:** All parameters are known, such as the outcomes and the likelihood of occurrences. For example, the risk of a smoker dying from lung cancer.

- **Uncertainty – some predictability:** The likelihood of future events are incalculable. A decision-maker has a broad sense of the possibilities but

Figure 4.6   Risk, uncertainty and deep uncertainty

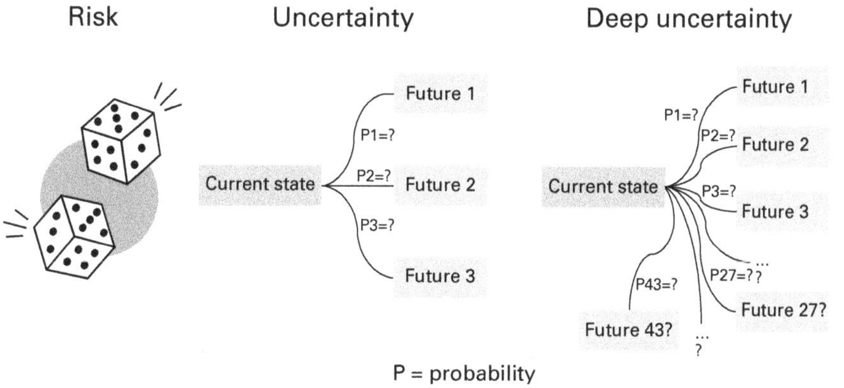

P = probability

difficulty in measuring their likelihoods. For instance, the chances of a recession, of China becoming the world's #1 economy or of a pandemic. Each of these specific events are known, but their probabilities are not.

- **Deep uncertainty – least predictable:** Stakeholders cannot agree on the nature of potential future states. Possible outcomes are numerous and unknown. One may be able to enumerate many plausible futures, but won't be able to rank them in terms of likelihood or importance. The relationships among actions, outcomes, consequences and probabilities are difficult to comprehend and agree upon. Examples would include the extent of sea level rise, the singularity, biowarfare or living on Mars.

Uncertainty thwarts predictability

The most challenging aspect of prognostication is that our complex world is deeply uncertain and becoming increasingly so.

Constraints of predictions

Answering narrow, probability-based questions, such as the Good Judgment Project's 'Will North Korea launch a new multistage missile in the next year?', is different from answering questions about the possible future states of deeply uncertain environments.

To explore the unknown, we can combine forecasts with broader approaches from the foresight field, like scenario development. Combining tools can be helpful in anticipating possible futures and preparing responses.

Relying on predictions alone is dangerous. Any predictions about the future should be scrutinized. No one knows how the future will unfold. There are too many unknown knowns and unknown unknowns (Figure 4.7).

Expert consultants, economists, investment bankers, analysts, forecasters and algorithms that claim to have data-driven predictive capabilities somehow extrapolate the past. Even if some prognostics seem likely to materialize, complex systems display unpredictable dynamics. Intersections determine outcomes, so how do any of the individual prognostics interact?

Table 4.1 compares the features that drive predictability and unpredictability.

Figure 4.7   Prediction versus foresight

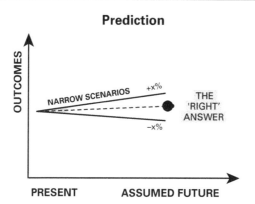

Prediction

OUTCOMES

NARROW SCENARIOS +x%

THE 'RIGHT' ANSWER

−x%

PRESENT   ASSUMED FUTURE

Features allowing prediction
- All parameters known
- Specific question
- Prediction is a right answer

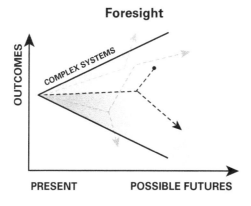

Foresight

OUTCOMES

COMPLEX SYSTEMS

PRESENT   POSSIBLE FUTURES

Uncertainties prevent prediction

- Multiple unknowns
- Broad possibilities
- No right answer

The six degrees of (un)predictability

Our UN-VICE for predictions combines data, expert advice, non-expert advice, forecasting, diverse perspectives and extensive imagination. But none of these individually is the panacea.

Table 4.1 Comparing predictability

Prediction – features supporting predictability	Foresight – uncertainties prevent predictability
Parameters and variables are all known	Multiple unknowns
Narrow scenarios	Multilayered, multidimensional, non-linear and complex
Most probable	Probable, plausible, possible, wild cards and 'What if?'
A specific answer to a precise question	Uncertain, broad possibilities, no right answer
Well-defined, contained, discrete, linear situations	Signals, emergence, next-order impacts, dynamic, intersecting, spillover
Typical actors: industry experts, economists, consultancies, Good Judgment Project	Typical actors: interdisciplinary, futurists, strategic and government foresight, science fiction

When exploring the futures, critically evaluate any assumptions and stakeholder incentives, appreciating the broader systems. We call this anticipatory foresight approach the *Six Degrees of (Un)Predictability* (Figure 4.8):

1 **Know your knowns:** Assess the drivers of the predictions to ascertain the ratio of assumptions to knowledge. Separate fact from unknown.

2 **Qualify your unknowns:** Challenge the validity of what you assume is not certain. Examine diverse and opposing views and imagine alternatives.

3 **Consider impact cascades:** Ripple effects could include scenarios that run counter to deeply ingrained assumptions. These 'impact cascades' help us visualize how initial developments create more changes – and in turn, reverberate further.

4 **Imagine possibilities:** Adopt the beginner's mind (*shoshin*) by asking questions instead of relying on answers. Be imaginative and open new doors.

5 **Ascertain incentives, biases and track records:** Stakeholders invariably have values, interests, objectives and relationships. They are often incentivized to form a point of view that can influence the prognostications.

Figure 4.8 The six degrees of (un)predictability

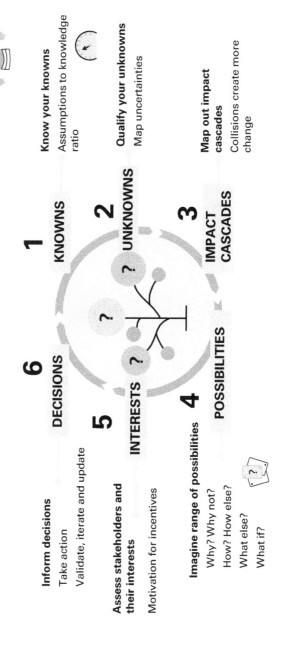

Know your knowns
Assumptions to knowledge ratio

Qualify your unknowns
Map uncertainties

Map out impact cascades
Collisions create more change

1 KNOWNS

2 UNKNOWNS

3 IMPACT CASCADES

6 DECISIONS

5 INTERESTS

4 POSSIBILITIES

Inform decisions
Take action
Validate, iterate and update

Assess stakeholders and their interests
Motivation for incentives

Imagine range of possibilities
Why? Why not?
How? How else?
What else?
What if?

6 Inform decisions: Be agile in decision-making – there may be no right answers. The environment is constantly updating, offering novel opportunities. Iterate in this dynamic world. Disconfirm what is no longer valid.

Notes

1   P C Bishop and A Hines (2012) *Teaching about the Future*, Palgrave Macmillan, Basingstoke

2   Boston Consulting Group. How to thrive in the 2020s, Boston Consulting Group, 2021

3   Innosight. 2021 Corporate Longevity Forecast, Innosight, 2021. www. innosight.com/insight/creative-destruction (archived at https://perma.cc/ L846-RC59)

4   D Neufeld. Long waves: The history of innovation cycles, Visual Capitalist, 30 June 2021. www.visualcapitalist.com/the-history-of-innovation-cycles (archived at https://perma.cc/NS3T-5Y5T)

5   C Perez (2002) *Technological Revolutions and Financial Capital: The dynamics of bubbles and golden ages*, Edward Elgar, Cheltenham

6   P Saffo. Six rules for effective forecasting, *Harvard Business Review*, July–August 2007. www.hbr.org/2007/07/six-rules-for-effective-forecasting (archived at https://perma.cc/D7XR-47YK)

7   E Rogers (2003) *Diffusion of Innovations*, 5th edn, Free Press, New York, NY

8   M Stern, S Kerruish and M Maude. *General Magic*, Spellbound Productions, 2018

9   M Mine. A quarter century of hype: 25 years of the Gartner hype cycle, Vimeo, 2020. www.vimeo.com/464835556 (archived at https://perma.cc/ TAP9-PUJF)

10 M Mullany. 8 lessons from 20 years of hype cycles, LinkedIn, 7 December 2016. www.linkedin.com/pulse/8-lessons-from-20-years-hype-cycles-michael-mullany (archived at https://perma.cc/2MVN-79JX)

11 M Heidegger (1927) *Sein und Zeit* [Being and Time], Max Niemeyer Verlag, Tübingen

12 The Players' Tribune Football (2017) Andre Agassi: How I beat Boris Becker, Facebook. www.facebook.com/watch/?v=1249137535168463 (archived at https://perma.cc/V7EA-ZYUW)

13 T Hancock and C Bezold. Possible futures, preferable futures, *The Healthcare Forum Journal*, 1994, 37 (2), 23–29

14 B Sterling. Bruce Sterling: State of the world, 2009, The Well, 2 January 2009. people.well.com/conf/inkwell.vue/topics/343/Bruce-Sterling-State-of-the-World-page01.html#post14 (archived at https://perma.cc/AC2C-QNQM)

15 J Cox. Jamie Dimon rips central banks for being '100 per cent dead wrong' on economic forecasts, CNBC, 24 October 2023. www.cnbc.com/2023/10/24/jamie-dimon-rips-central-banks-for-being-100percent-dead-wrong-on-economic-forecasts.html (archived at https://perma.cc/RDY4-C3SM)

16 T J Chermack, S A Lynham and W E A Ruona. A review of scenario planning literature, *Futures Research Quarterly*, 2001, 17 (2), 7–32

17 P Schwartz (1996) *The Art of the Long View: Paths to strategic insight for yourself and your company*, Doubleday, Toronto, ON

18 N N Taleb (2007) *The Black Swan: The impact of the highly improbable*, Random House, New York, NY

19 M Wucker (2016) *The Gray Rhino: How to recognize and act on the obvious dangers we ignore*, St Martin's Press, New York, NY

20 D H Rumsfeld. DoD news briefing – Secretary Rumsfeld and Gen. Myers, US Department of Defense [Internet Archive], 12 February 2002. web.archive.org/web/20160406235718/http://archive.defense.gov/Transcripts/Transcript.aspx?TranscriptID=2636 (archived at https://perma.cc/2B7E-284M)

21 L Gershwin (2013) *Stung! On jellyfish blooms and the future of the ocean*, University of Chicago Press, Chicago, IL

22 Z Sardar and J A Sweeney. The three tomorrows of postnormal times, *Futures*, 2016, 75. www.doi.org/10.1016/j.futures.2015.10.004 (archived at https://perma.cc/6GN5-W42B)

23 D Hind and V Gupta. Black Elephants and skull jackets: A conversation with Vinay Gupta, *Dark Mountain*, Scribd, 2010. www.scribd.com/document/30711287/Dougald-Hine-Black-Elephants-and-Skull-Jackets-A-Conversation-with-Vinay-Gupta (archived at https://perma.cc/4VTS-MAYM)

24 R Spitz and L Zuin (2022) *The Definitive Guide to Thriving on Disruption: Essential frameworks for disruption and uncertainty*, Disruptive Futures Institute, San Francisco, CA

Part Two
How to drive systems innovation and transformational change

5

Disruption as a springboard for creating impact and value

OBJECTIVES

Antifragile value creation across time horizons

Disruption presents both opportunities for value creation and risks of value erosion. Relevance is the key driver of impact. To achieve and sustain relevance, we must invest in human capital, 'beta test' ideas, establish antifragile foundations for resilience and think across varying time horizons.

Relevance drives impact

Anything that can be automated, cognified, decentralized, digitized, disintermediated or virtualized will be. This will radically transform every aspect of the economy, including industries and professions. Those who understand this will start seeing new opportunities for products, services and business models.

Intangibles are the next battlefield: human capital, intellectual capital, augmented services, new business-models-as-a-system, the metaverse, Web 3.0, digital and virtual assets. Intangibles create optionality, drive innovation and reduce environmental impacts compared to physical alternatives. AI, cloud computing and digital collaboration tools pave the way for this transformational journey.

Developing human capital

Human and intellectual capital may be the most important intangible assets.

Talent is no longer a formal full-time employee in a fixed location. Human capital is connected globally. Decentralization and flexible work are here to stay, expanding talent access digitally. Across fields, regions and hierarchies, organizations and their offerings are dematerialized.

Developing intellectual capital requires shared visions, investment in education and a culture of nurturing effective employees. Collective know-how, skills and experiences make an organization's employees so valuable.

Slack: Achieving relevance through a beginner's mind

Founded in 2009, Slack, the popular instant-messaging platform, was acquired by Salesforce in 2020 for nearly $30 billion, marking one of the largest software acquisitions ever.

How did Slack achieve relevance?

- **Relevance is defined by stakeholders:** Slack constantly leveraged user feedback to form relevant perspectives, showcasing both *shoshin* (beginner's mind) and *mujō* (impermanence).
- **Learning in loops:** In 2011, Slack co-founder Stewart Butterfield launched a multiplayer online video game named Glitch that failed. Butterfield saw the value in the messaging apps they created for the game and adapted these tools for enterprise software, driving a massive shift in team collaboration.
- **Addressing a problem to be solved:** Slack addressed communication pain points (email overload, user-friendly interface, seamless integration).
- **Defining a new software category:** Slack's technology was not groundbreaking, but enabled a fundamental change in workplace communication.

Once achieved, maintaining relevance requires constant listening, questioning, prototyping and testing.

CASE STUDY   Monitor relevance or become a case study
for irrelevance

Monitor Group, a counterexample to Slack, rose to prominence during the 1980s, becoming one of the world's most respected strategy consultancies. Monitor's founders included Michael Porter, creator of the Five Forces of Competitive Analysis.

Porter's Five Forces was a key underpinning of the consultancy's work in the more predictable environments of the 1980s and 1990s. However, for Monitor's clients, relying on barriers to entry as a source of competitive advantage proved irrelevant for the 21st century's swings.

As the competitive advantage of their advice decayed, Monitor's demise (acquired by Deloitte in 2013) became a notable case study on how a once-mighty consultancy failed to bring sustained relevance to its clients.

The consulting industry, valued in the hundreds of billions, confronts significant challenges amid economic uncertainty and widely publicized controversies. However, the true peril may arise from its dependence on pre-packaged solutions. Clinging to formulaic playbooks ensures irrelevance in UN-VICE environments.

Beta test for relevance

During a 'beta test', software is tested in real-world situations before its official release. Here, the software's essential features are complete, but may contain bugs. Safe experimentation during the 'beta phase' can increase understanding before the final sign-offs.

These six software strategies can help you beta test your projects and ideas:[1]

Create stacked models and suites

Think of software like a digital Swiss Army knife: a single platform, packed with diverse tools. Stacked models seamlessly interconnect software components to create a powerhouse of functionality. While users typically don't take advantage of every single function, these suites naturally provide increased optionality at a negligible incremental cost.

How can you build stacks into strategies, ecosystems and ideas to tackle diverse challenges and create a whole greater than the sum of its parts?

Incorporate slack, even if unnecessary today

Operating at full capacity is a fragile strategy. The technology industry typically builds extra capacity into their systems. This slack offers protection when unforeseen circumstances arise and accelerates adoption should the technology demand rapid growth at short notice.

Slack is inexpensive when you don't need it but exorbitantly costly when you don't have it. Incorporate buffer space to enhance agility.

Develop flexible formats and distribution

Software is the paragon of flexible revenue and distribution. It can be sold, licensed or offered as a subscription service to businesses, consumers or both. It can be provided on-premise or through the cloud.

How can you offer valuable solutions in new formats and models?

Explore in safe sandboxes

A 'sandbox' is a safe environment that allows developers to test new software without risking the rest of the system. New ideas come from experimentation, which is best done without the risk of ruin.

Can you create protected spaces to experiment, tinker and answer important questions with no current answers?

Dance with wicked problems

Wicked problems feel like a complex labyrinth. Their solutions and requirements only become clear in hindsight, making traditional approaches ineffective. In our world of unknown unknowns, adaptive problem-finding is a crucial weapon.

The smarter you iterate, the faster you'll unravel the maze. Each attempt, even if they fail, reveals insights and narrows the ambiguity. Success emerges in retrospect.

Upgrade your intangibles

Intellectual property differentiates software companies. Similarly, soft skills and human capital separate you from your peers. While intangibles may be susceptible to viruses or obsolescence, updating them keeps you ahead of the curve.

Erase outdated elements and rewrite programs: learn, unlearn and relearn to constantly adapt.

Measuring intellectual capital

Employee expertise, critical thinking and relationships are difficult to measure but very valuable.

Intellectual property can be a proxy for intellectual capital. What are the designs, patents, rights and trademarks of an organization? The competitive advantage, quantity and uniqueness of intellectual property all play into the value of intellectual capital.

The world's most valuable companies develop intellectual capital by investing smartly in their employees.

CASE STUDY   Google's most valuable intangible assets

In *How Google Works*, Eric Schmidt and Jonathan Rosenberg outline how the group drove value creation by harnessing key human factors:[2]

- **Learners for constant change:** Hire 'learning animals' over specialists. In dynamic fields, conditions change frequently, so experience is not as important as creativity and natural learning ability. Resourceful learners can adapt to new roles; specialists may not.

- **Small teams, huge impact:** Lengthy, costly R&D cycles are replaced by faster, iterative and flexible product development. Small teams can create products that reach the world in an instant.

- **Freedom:** Ideas come from anywhere. Empower smart creatives to work on what they want without interference from an imperial manager.

- **Hiring defines a company:** Changing group culture from within is hard. Hiring the right employees makes it easier. Reward your best interviewers, as great people attract more great people.

- **Relationships over processes:** In successful organizations, business always outruns process. If you don't have chaos, something is wrong. In the turbulence, depend on relationships as much as the process to get things done. Your best insights come from these relationships, not from formal processes.

- **Imagine the unimaginable.** Ask what could be true in five years. What thing that is unimaginable when abiding by conventional wisdom is, in fact, imaginable?

Since Schmidt and Rosenberg wrote the book in 2015, Google has evolved and may not still have the same superpowers in managing its human capital. Their lessons are no less valuable.

The (in)tangibility of innovation

Innovation is one of the most intangible investments. According to Adam Grant's research of original thinkers, the more prolific you are, the more your new ideas will feed on innovation.[3]

To drive innovation, it's a good idea to have bad ideas, and many of them.

In our distributed world, tangible assets such as offices, factories, hardware, machinery and inventory are diminishing in value. They are less relevant in our networked, data-driven world.

In *Zero to One*, Peter Thiel maintains that 'proprietary technology' requires creating something new. For Thiel, true proprietary technology has a tenfold advantage over any competitors.[4]

Technology, services and brands are 'intangible' innovations. They are made up of ideas, patents and algorithms. They also rely on human and intellectual capital, such as employee skills, know-how and resourcefulness.

The rising intangible business models and economies

As the world's economies dematerialize and virtualize, the value being created is intangible. Trillion-dollar companies, including Apple, Microsoft and Alphabet/Google, are experiencing extraordinary scaling driven by their massive intellectual capital.

The value of intangibles derived from intellectual property rights and trademarks has never been higher. According to Ocean Tomo (JS Held),[5] a firm specializing in intangible asset valuation, intangible asset market value comprised 90 per cent of the S&P 500 in 2020. This means that 90 per cent of the value of S&P 500 companies was represented by intangible assets. Tangible assets like real estate, factories, equipment and stock made up only 10 per cent.

In 1985, the percentage of intangibles was 32 per cent, then 68 per cent in 1995, 80 per cent in 2005 and over 90 per cent in 2020. *Over the past 35 years, the percentage of intangible assets almost tripled.*

KEY POINTS

No escape from intangibles, but beware of risks

This shift from industrial companies to services, technology and knowledge economies has important ramifications:

- **No alternatives:** From skills to services, know-how, expertise and technology, tomorrow's value will be driven by digitized, dematerialized and virtualized intangible assets.

- **The fugacity of intangibles:** While investing in intangibles is indispensable, you must constantly evaluate the risk of obsolescence and value erosion. At any point, someone can develop better programs, algorithms and user experience. Furthermore, impairment, regulation, market adjustments and meltdowns can have a significant and sudden impact on technology valuations.

- **Nurture human capital:** Values, impact and development matter more than anything. Invest in your human capital – they walk through the door every day and can leave at any time.

- **Protect your reputation:** The scrutiny of every aspect of a business will increase in our radically transparent, traceable and accountable world. Survival will depend on maintaining trust, which takes a long time to build but is shattered in an instant.

- **Cybersecurity:** Global threats are a daily occurrence. With the rise of digital connectivity, cyberattacks are becoming common.

Pursuing intangible assets does not mean developing low-margin loss-making businesses. Commoditized, unprofitable e-commerce companies with low barriers to entry will never be a sustainable driver for value creation as they bleed cash to 'grow at any cost'.

While indispensable for value creation, the potential speed of obsolescence can dampen the resilience of intangible assets.

Antifragile foundations for value creation

We prize resilience and robustness for their ability to adapt to change. While fragile entities may crumble, resilient ones emerge unaffected. Antifragility goes beyond both of these to thrive in the face of disruption, fuelling innovation and value creation (Figure 5.1).

New opportunities for the antifragile

In a couple of books from his Incerto series, Nassim Nicholas Taleb develops the concept of antifragility: 'Antifragility is beyond resilience or robustness. The resilient resists shocks and stays the same; the antifragile gets better.'[6]

Figure 5.1   Antifragile value creation

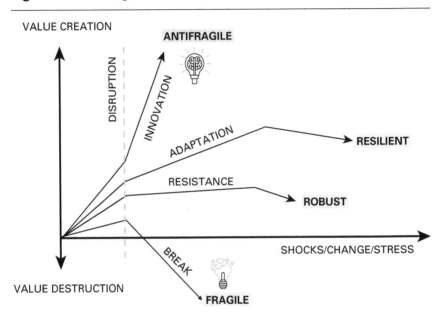

NOTE Adapted from N N Taleb (2012) *Antifragile: Things that gain from disorder*, Random House, New York, NY

Where foundations are weak, structures collapse. With antifragility, new nodes emerge across the edges and live laboratories open to allow tinkering, challenging and prototyping. The information learned from experimentations and failures blossoms into inspiration.

In our UN-VICE world, building antifragile foundations is a prerequisite to leverage disruption for value creation. We must develop mindsets and systems that strengthen from stress and disorder.

Optimization relies on stable and predictable environments. Many of the world's brittle features come from the belief that efficiency is best. Businesses, their shareholders and their consultants design systems to squeeze out any waste. As antifragile foundations thrive through random events and shocks, efficacy beats efficiency (Figure 5.2).

The trade-off between efficiency and resiliency is a trade-off between fragile and antifragile.

Figure 5.2 Fragile, resilient, antifragile

Nothing to gain | Loss | Penalize

Fragile

↗

DAMAGED
BY DISORDER

- Breaks
- Asymmetric:
  more downside from shocks
- Cannot sense or respond to shocks
- Hates errors as large, irreversible
  (but rare)
- Seeks order
- **Complicated**
- Fewer interdependencies
- Causality

Robust | Resilient

→

UNAFFECTED
BY DISORDER

- Resists shocks
- Adapts
- Remains the same
- Prerequisite to antifragile
- Errors are just information
- Suppressed randomness
  and volatility (stressors)
- Redundancy
- Slack

Nothing to lose | Gain | Benefit

Antifragile

↗

BENEFITS
FROM DISORDER

- Innovates, evolves
- More upside from random
  events or shocks
- Thrives with uncertainty,
  randomness and stressors
- Likes errors
  (frequent and small)
- Embraces adventure and risk
- **Complex systems**
- Many interdependencies
- Causal opacity

NOTE Adapted from N N Taleb (2012) *Antifragile: Things that gain from disorder*, Random House, New York, NY

Antifragility is adapted to our world's many interdependencies. The complex systems we create must be resilient to swerves. Shocks allow antifragile systems to evolve, strengthening through the natural selection-like pressure. Fragile systems are damaged by disorder because they experience more downside from shocks than upside.

EXAMPLE

The fragility of share buybacks

Popular financial theory champions efficient capital deployment, which includes using spare cash to buy back the company's own shares. Every year, global share buybacks consistently exceed $500 billion. Because share buybacks can increase stock prices, they pacify stakeholders and hit short-term market targets. However, this short-lived boost comes along with the lasting disappearance of cash reserves. Companies that are inclined toward share buybacks find themselves more vulnerable.

Cash-rich companies exhibit a different narrative during crises. Past market upheavals (such as the 2008 crash, Covid pandemic or interest rate hikes in 2022–23) have shown that holding cash, seemingly inefficient in a stable world, provides crucial optionality when reality bites. Armed with substantial cash reserves and liquidity, these antifragile giants thrive and can invest, while fragile, over-leveraged companies may require bailouts or fail altogether. This clash between financial theory and reality challenges assumptions about capital allocation. Resilience in a volatile world necessitates strategic cash reserves to weather 'What if?' shocks.

Omnipresent disruption is a constant, in which entirely new paradigms are forged and reshaped. Here, systemic disruptive effects are compounded, as both hazards and opportunities interact multiplicatively. We define this era as Disruption 3.0.

While Disruption 3.0 invites novel approaches, antifragile foundations are required to weather the turbulence and leverage the opportunities. *Building antifragile foundations is like building an immune system.*

Asymmetry: The reason you need antifragility

Evaluating risk and uncertainty is necessary to develop antifragility, as the focus shifts from probabilities to potential outcomes.

The fragile has an asymmetric relationship when it comes to adverse changes. *This asymmetry means that the fragile suffers a disproportionate amount of downside from shocks.*

We often discount the dangers of low-likelihood events, even when their magnitude would be catastrophic. We might disregard these activities because they don't appear near the centre of the 'bell curve', but their abnormally high impact makes them more dangerous than we account for. They might be rare, but they can be big.

Organizational resilience and existential risk management

Given the asymmetry of low-probability but very high-consequence risks, organizations and their governance bodies must put forth a greater effort to define and manage existential risks. In addition to climate, organizations can no longer ignore cybersecurity and infrastructure risks (like energy and data centres), as well as geopolitical tensions and even space risks (such as satellites and communications). Bad actors regularly test the limits of our systems – a prolonged breakdown of our infrastructure is conceivable.

Enter the Chief Existential Officer

With an increasing number of asymmetric risks and opportunities, organizations need a Chief Existential Officer (CEO^2) more than a chief risk officer. While the chief risk officer focuses on conventional regulatory, compliance and technology risks, the CEO^2 acknowledges and acts upon a new set of extreme risks that stretch past typical planning cycles.

Existential risks go beyond day-to-day business risks. They include AI, biosecurity, climate, cybersecurity, geopolitical and societal paradigm shift risks, which display asymmetric outcomes that could jeopardize the future of humanity altogether. Despite this, outsized opportunities often accompany the risks: Greenaissance is an era of renewal with massive investment opportunities in environment, social justice and systems innovation.

The fragility of assumptions

Despite fragility's undesirable consequences, its pervasive nature persists. The root cause? Flawed assumptions (Figure 5.3). These not only render our world fragile but also impede breakthroughs. Paul Graham believes that new ideas are often concealed behind misguided assumptions and ideas that contradict flawed assumptions are suppressed.

Figure 5.3 Assumptions value chain

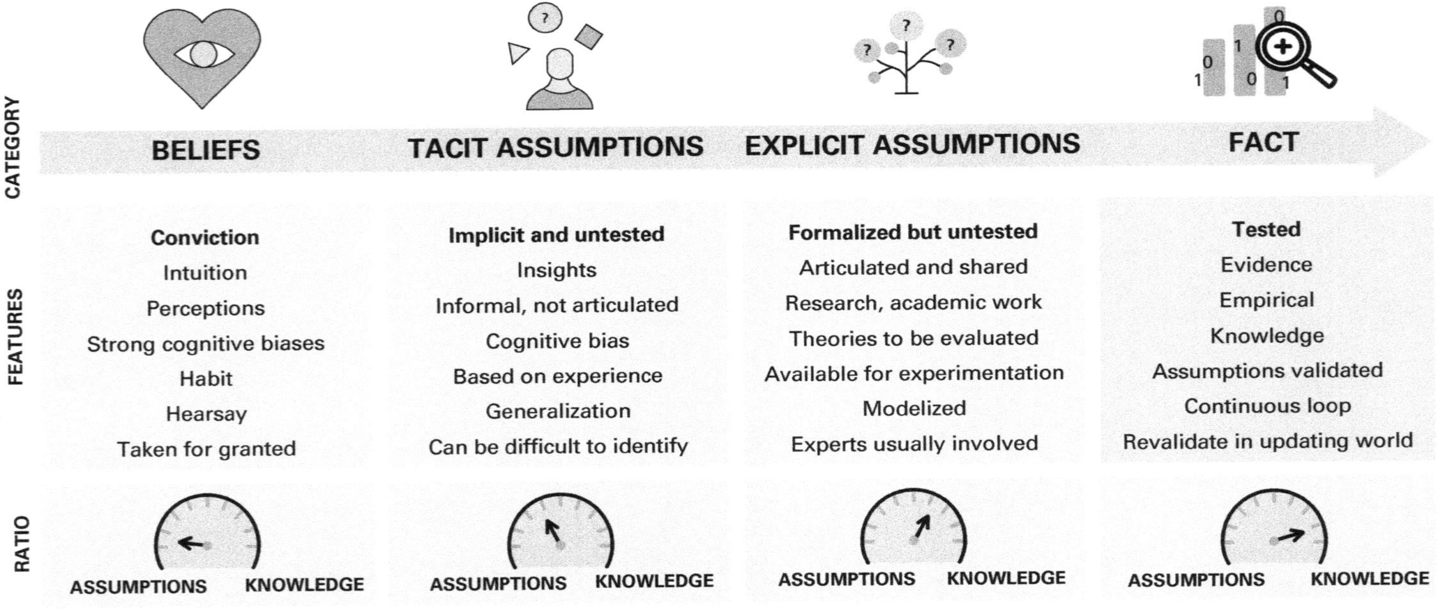

CATEGORY	BELIEFS	TACIT ASSUMPTIONS	EXPLICIT ASSUMPTIONS	FACT
FEATURES	**Conviction** Intuition Perceptions Strong cognitive biases Habit Hearsay Taken for granted	**Implicit and untested** Insights Informal, not articulated Cognitive bias Based on experience Generalization Can be difficult to identify	**Formalized but untested** Articulated and shared Research, academic work Theories to be evaluated Available for experimentation Modelized Experts usually involved	**Tested** Evidence Empirical Knowledge Assumptions validated Continuous loop Revalidate in updating world
RATIO	ASSUMPTIONS KNOWLEDGE	ASSUMPTIONS KNOWLEDGE	ASSUMPTIONS KNOWLEDGE	ASSUMPTIONS KNOWLEDGE

Unlike facts, for which there is empirical evidence, assumptions are untested. Fixed assumptions are like betting on a specific future. The fragility lies in relying on the completeness of what is known and the implications if assumptions prove to be flawed.

Insights from data can be invaluable as feedback for decision-making, but should never be confused with being a proxy for the future, a predictor of the future, nor the future itself.

The future is unknown and we all constantly make assumptions. But to rely on assumptions as if they are facts is often costly and sometimes dangerous.

Fixed assumptions versus malleable futures

In the 1980s, IBM made a series of binary assumptions about the future of the PC industry. They failed to anticipate the wide adoption of PCs and hugely underestimated the potential of Microsoft and Apple as competitors. Examples like this arise every day, everywhere in the world. Decision-makers who cannot imagine evolving futures follow fragile sets of fixed assumptions, relying on incorrect views of the world, with noteworthy consequences.

Nokia assumed it would remain the king of mobile phones. However, smartphones are miniature computers and processing power increased exponentially while size and costs declined. Nokia missed the fact that an emerging computer manufacturer (Apple) could provide breakthrough innovation more relevant than basic replicable voice communication.

In 2016, Porsche's CEO Oliver Blume sought to justify his partnership strategy with technology companies. Taking aim at Tesla, Blume confidently claimed that 'An iPhone belongs in your pocket, not on the road.' Subsequently, many original equipment manufacturers (OEMs) have acknowledged that technology partnerships are the way forward for tomorrow's automotive 'operating system'.

Over the past decades, Germany's energy policy, military strategy and defence budgets assumed that interdependence with Russia would produce stability. This assumption proved to be a disaster. In 2022, Germany found itself extremely reliant on Russian supplies and realized that it had determined its strategies on assumptions of stability.

Surfacing and challenging assumptions is important because they can shape the way we think and decide. One objective is to avoid having a high assumptions-to-knowledge ratio. Another objective is to spur imagination and not be limited to restrictive views.

The issue with uncompromising reliance on flawed assumptions is not being wrong, but being unprepared for alternative outcomes.

Eight concepts characterizing antifragile

Eight guiding concepts characterize antifragile:

1 Disorder follows the next order.

2 Non-prediction allows emergence.

3 Trial and error spurs discovery.

4 Imperfection beats perfection.

5 'What if?' builds optionality.

6 Tinkering supports decision-making.

7 Decentralization eliminates a single point of failure.

8 Commitment ensures alignment.

1. Disorder follows the next order

Taleb highlights the human body as nature's finest testimony of antifragility. The immune system strengthens with persistent exposure to threats and exercised muscles become powerful over time. Health, strength and energy improve to better address future stresses.

Antifragile foundations thrive on uncertainty, unpredictability and variability. *Stressors, incoherence and even mistakes strengthen antifragile systems, rather than breaking them.*

2. Non-prediction allows emergence

New ideas are fluid and emerge constantly. Where uncertainty is omnipresent, we only understand the results of our actions in retrospect. Opacity, incompleteness and the erratic dance of chance are not burdens on our emergent existence, but the very fabric of it.

Reminiscent of a quote by George Bernard Shaw, Joe MacMillan, the lead character in *Halt and Catch Fire,* said, 'I thought that maybe we could do this precisely because we're all unreasonable people and progress depends on our changing the world to fit us. Not the other way around.'[7]

> **KEY POINTS**
> The thing that gets you to the thing
>
> Visionaries create a malleable, emergent future instead of adapting to a predetermined future. Bill Gates and Steve Jobs understood that the future was not about predicting the demand for PCs, but imagining the power the technology yields. As MacMillan also said: 'Computers aren't the thing. They're the thing that gets us to the thing.'

3. Trial and error spurs discovery

You want foundations that experience more upside from shocks that might arise, even if those shocks are from errors or failures. Antifragile foundations flourish on mistakes. The testing mode enables experimentation, discovery and learning. Similar to Darwin's natural selection, trial and error triages and retains the surviving ideas.

We call 'failovation' the sort of failure that generates innovation (potentially prompting a standing ovation). A surprising number of successful inventions were created through an initial failure:

- **Pacemakers:** While trying to record heart rhythms, inventor Wilson Greatbatch accidentally used the wrong size resistor. This resistor emitted electrical pulses that Greatbatch later used to stimulate heart circuitry.

- **Post-it notes:** While attempting to create a super-strong adhesive for aerospace, 3M scientist Spencer Silver accidentally created an incredibly weak, pressure-sensitive adhesive we use today.

- **Microwave:** When a radar engineer accidentally melted the chocolate bar in his pocket, he didn't advance his assigned task at all... but he did discover a new way to heat food.

4. Imperfection beats perfection

While Western culture chases perfection, Eastern philosophy thrives on *wabi sabi*, an appreciation of imperfection. The roughness, asymmetries and incompleteness of *wabi sabi* allows us to appreciate the impermanence all around us. *The antifragile perfects being imperfect.*

In *Jugaad Innovation: Think frugal, be flexible, generate breakthrough growth*, Professors Navi Radjou, Jaideep Prabhu and Simone Ahuja looked at a more democratic way of carrying out R&D: frugal innovation.[8] *Jugaad* is the Hindi word for an ingenious solution in the face of adversity. The bottom-up *Jugaad* innovation contrasts with the Western R&D strategy which tends to be structured top-down. *Jugaad* innovation, a more informal, improvised approach to antifragile value creation, relies on six principles: 'seek opportunity in adversity, do more with less, think and act flexibly, keep it simple, include the margin... follow your heart'.

In India, creating, adapting and repairing objects is a way of life. Designed for scarcity, rapid change and new challenges, frugal innovation addresses societal and generational shifts that seek alternatives to globalization.

CASE STUDY   The Indian telecoms market

Thriving on constraints and limited investment provides optionality. *Jugaad* offers alignment in our multi-stakeholder world by 'including the margin'. It seeks eco-friendliness, challenging hyper-consumerism's impact on our finite planet.

In India, telecom operator Reliance Jio is a potent example of frugal innovation. A segment of India's internet user base had been historically priced out of access. Jio's model undercuts competitors by serving a new market. Although individually small, the cities, towns and villages that comprise Jio's market represent a large portion of India's growing population.

Instead of creating any new technology, Jio offers cheap data and useful apps, providing voice and data services to hundreds of millions at unprecedentedly low prices. Jio is also capitalizing on India's smartphone market through its convergence of physical devices, low-cost digital services and an entire ecosystem of apps (gaming, streaming, shopping, banking).

5. 'What if?' builds optionality

Instead of fearing failure, embrace it as a stepping stone for exploration. Be bold, experiment frequently and see each misstep as a piece of the puzzle. Like informal sketches on an artist's canvas, these seemingly insignificant tests build a wealth of potential paths you might not have stumbled upon otherwise. If something doesn't click, pivot lightly – the investment isn't significant. But if a spark ignites, the uncovered possibilities could be game-changers.

EXAMPLE

What if all meetings shifted to video?

Antifragile organizations constantly conduct small tests to allow optionality. They may be slightly inefficient, but that redundancy allows experimentation. Much of the corporate world rewards efficiency, even hyper-optimization. When anything goes wrong, the system buckles.

Intentional redundancy drives strategic resilience. Extra capacity in Zoom's software architecture allowed them to quickly scale at the start of the Covid pandemic, capturing extreme market share. This is the equivalent of holding excess cash on the balance sheet, or having supply chains that are not overly stretched in case any link in the chain fails. *This adaptive strategy shifts from 'just in time' to 'just in case'.*

6. Tinkering supports decision-making

Stochastic approaches waltz with chance, intentionally half-hearted, even superficial. 'Tinkering' is a wonderfully representative word for this casual way of experimenting. Often without any immediately obvious benefit, tinkering has the potential to yield original ideas. This contrasts more burdensome research methods, which may not capture the full potential of serendipitous discovery and adaptive problem-solving.

Wandering allows for exploration, constant trial-and-error and imperfection. But this pragmatic experimentation can strike discoveries to build synergies across businesses.

EXAMPLE

Amazon, the accidental global leader in the cloud market

Jeff Bezos calls failure and invention 'inseparable twins'. It was partly due to entangled, inefficient and messy knots during Amazon's early days of significant growth that they stumbled upon ideas that eventually became Amazon Web Services (AWS). Today, AWS is still ahead of Microsoft Azure and Google Cloud in cloud infrastructure, benefiting from its early leadership position in the market. The Synergy Research Group estimated the 2023 cloud infrastructure market to be worth around $250 billion; AWS led with over 30 per cent market share.[9]

7. Decentralization eliminates a single point of failure

Decentralization is the process of transferring control, power or decision-making abilities from a singular (centralized) authority to a distributed set of entities. In decentralized organizations, decisions are made at all levels, reducing formal structures into an agile, permissionless environment.

At the onset of Russia's invasion of Ukraine, Moscow's cyberattacks knocked out communications infrastructure and satellite networks owned by US Viasat. In contrast, Starlink's network of low Earth orbit (LEO) satellites demonstrated antifragility, remaining operational and delivering internet access within Ukraine amidst the ongoing conflict. Unbounded by centralized infrastructure, Starlink's distributed system eliminates critical dependencies, making it difficult to completely shut down the overall service.[10]

Building distributed architecture and overlaps can prevent a key vulnerability from creating devastation. *Decentralized systems can offer more resilience and antifragility, as this single point of failure does not exist.*

8. Commitment ensures alignment

Beware of the unaccountable: those who have the authority to make decisions but benefit only from upsides. Have 'skin in the game'[11] and expect others to be similarly aligned. Make potential losses for adverse outcomes as relevant as the incentives. Be as committed as if you owned the business and expect others to have the same philosophy.

The unaccountable are often rewarded, or at least not penalized, for building and operating fragile systems.

The US healthcare industry is the symptom of a question Goldman Sachs asked in one of its BioTech research reports: 'Is curing patients a sustainable business model?'[12] How much profit would the healthcare industry lose if people were healthier? Chronic treatments, continuous drugs and frequent hospitalizations are recurring revenues for the pharmaceutical industry, more valuable than effective therapies. Therefore, curing patients may not be sustainable for the healthcare industry. As the healthcare industry seeks to maximize its economic value, there is an endemic lack of alignment between the interests of its shareholders, and the well-being of its patients and of society at large.

CASE STUDY   US healthcare, the epitome of the unaccountable

By downplaying the potential for addiction, the Food and Drug Administration (FDA) contributed to the opioid epidemic, which killed hundreds of thousands from overdoses and destroyed many more lives.

- **Maximizing sales at all costs:** The maker of OxyContin, Purdue Pharma and its owners, the Sackler family, battled for bankruptcy protection following a multibillion dollar settlement for fuelling the US opioid epidemic. Despite knowing the high risk of dependence and addiction, there was too much money to be made, so all parties promoted the drug to maximize sales while ignoring the human devastation.

- **Money talks, duty walks:** The FDA did not fulfil its duties in approving and regulating OxyContin due to watered-down labelling, which promoted the drug for common conditions for which opioids should not be given. Many of the committees, advisors and experts consulted by the FDA had financial ties to the pharmaceutical companies, including Purdue. They knew how addictive these opioids are, but ignored this fact in order to build their bank accounts.

- **The most trusted strategic adviser in the world:** Despite a tarnished track record, McKinsey & Company recruits the best, pays the highest, advises the world and positions its alumni to run the world's largest companies, who then retain McKinsey for consulting projects.[13] In April 2022, the FDA said it may not issue new contracts to McKinsey due to its failure to disclose possible conflicts of interest with both the FDA and opioid manufacturers. In 2021, McKinsey paid nearly $600 million to settle allegations over its role in the opioid epidemic.

Learn the language of antifragility

Disruptive times deeply affect the shared language we use. The antifragile thrives on friction, uncertainty and systems thinking, while the fragile relies on prediction, individual pieces, certainty and a lack of friction.

The antifragile nurtures critical thinking and heuristic mindsets. The fragile is dogmatic, seeking probability-based decision-making.

When it comes to governance, the antifragile experiments in the emergent, decentralized, non-hierarchical and self-organized, whereas the fragile seeks refuge in planned, centralized, hierarchical structures.

Antifragile business is driven by innovation, agility and tinkering, while the fragile business feels protected by experts, structures and academic validation.

Antifragile ownership focuses on accountability, commitment, entrepreneurs and stakeholders, while the fragile owner is unaccountable, relying on authority, bureaucrats and shareholders.

KEY POINTS
Nothing to lose, may even gain

An organization or individual cannot be antifragile without being exceptionally resilient. For Taleb, resilience is like rubber; it can deform to adapt to the impact, then reshape. If you rely only on robustness or resilience, you may see breakage over time as conditions change.

When you are antifragile, you have nothing to lose from random events or shocks and can actually gain despite the chaos.

Developing antifragility means focusing on the amplitude of potential consequences, not the probability.

Thinking in different time horizons

Thinking across different time horizons is a crucial skill for driving impact and sustainable value creation. We can choose our own perception of time to exercise our long-term thinking muscles, to bring our future vision into focus and to spot opportunities.

Our expanding liminal present

Neither the past nor the future exist. Zen Buddhism is helpful in reclaiming nowness. This contrasts the Western mindset, which obsesses with past regrets.

Paradoxically, truly experiencing the present is compatible with the future. Embracing nowness allows one to emerge with more clarity for the future. But technology is blurring the lines of real and unreal and maybe also the past, present and future.

With incursions such as AI negotiating legal contracts, bioprinted organs and flying cars, is the present spilling prematurely into the future? Or is the future encroaching on the present with dystopian pandemics, climate-driven wildfires and bad actors hacking military infrastructure?

In our UN-VICE world, the line between the present and future is becoming blurred. The liminal states between time periods are themselves growing, as present and future realities intersect.

The choices we make today about how we will engage with the future intimately affect the present.

The antidote to short-termism

Keynes famously wrote that in the long run we are all dead, in the context that 'economists set themselves too easy, too useless a task if in tempestuous seasons they can only tell us that when the storm is past the ocean is flat again'.[14]

The debate on the nature of time and how one conceives the flow of time is rich and open. Change is slow, but disruption has an increasing tempo of accelerating appearances, with ripple effects occurring further in the continuum of time.

The present is the only thing that exists. It matters greatly, but not to the exclusion of the future ahead and the weight of history.

Futures thinking provides a blank canvas. As the world will be radically transformed over the coming years, there is no alternative but to understand what key features to look out for, what fragments of the future are emerging today – sometimes prematurely and unannounced.

Today, few can focus beyond the next news cycle. But looking farther into the future is necessary for our planet's regeneration and sustainability. To realize the futures we want, we should learn to identify the more tumultuous storms ahead, to tame the ocean for smoother sailing.

Multiple timeframes offer multiple levers for change

Thinking in terms of multiple timeframes involves alternating our focus between short-, medium- and long-term periods, applying levers to identify and drive change through time.

'We always overestimate the change that will occur in the short term and underestimate the change that will occur in the long term.' There are numerous versions of this quote and the idea has been attributed to Roy Amara, Arthur C Clarke and Ray Kurzweil, but the powerful message is the same.

Bill Gates framed it as: 'People overestimate what can be done in one year and underestimate what can be done in ten years.'

An attempt to revolutionize capitalism?

Based on his 2011 book *The Lean Startup*, Eric Ries launched the Long-Term Stock Exchange (LTSE) in 2020.[15]

Ries felt that despite the momentum of environmental, social and governance (ESG) practices, there was a need for a different type of stock exchange. Current CEOs report to their boards of directors and boards are accountable to shareholders who seek to maximize value. As long as company valuations and fund performance are based on short-term earnings, ESG indexes can be incentivized to greenwash, social wash and even future wash – without accountability to long-term environmental and social impacts.

Companies that join the LTSE are accountable for their long-term value creation. This includes a broad group of stakeholders, not just shareholders. Ries sees the LTSE's long-term focus as the way to move beyond 'conventional exchange incentives that benefit from volatility and speculation'.

LTSE's five policies – LTSE is governed by five policies:

1 **Longer time horizons:** Decision-making based on years to decades, not quarters.

2 **Board involvement:** Explicit oversight of long-term planning, strategy and success metrics.

3 **Diverse stakeholders:** Requires justifying how the business's long-term success will be guided by stakeholders.

4 **Accountability:** Executive and board compensation aligned with long-term results.

5 **Engagement:** Commitment to engage with long-term shareholders.

LTSE's vision is to establish a public market for companies that actively contribute to the sustainable creation and preservation of value for all its stakeholders.

Distinct timescales and paces of change to sustain shocks

Reconciling shareholder primacy with stakeholder capitalism requires a system that is capable of adopting different timescales. To gain strength from disruption is to have a system that can operate at different rates of change. Thinking in different timeframes allows an interplay between change and constant, stable and unstable, while sustaining through shocks.

Pace layers

Stewart Brand, founder of The Long Now Foundation and Global Business Network, developed the Pace Layer model to provide different levels of corrective feedback. The idea is an actionable framework for thinking about the future, where some phenomena change more swiftly than others.

Brand proposes six layers, from slowest to fastest:

- *nature* (planet)
- *culture* (social, religion)
- *governance* (rule of law, government, public sector)
- *infrastructure* (transportation, communication systems, education, science)
- *commerce* (business, industry, private sector)
- *fashion* (clothing, art, creative, experimental, frothy, self-preoccupied)

In a durable and healthy society, each layer operates at its own pace while respecting the different speeds of the other levels:

- Fast layers learn; slow layers remember.
- Fast layers propose; slow layers dispose.
- Fast layers absorb shocks; slow layers integrate shocks and ensure they don't reoccur.
- Fast layers are discontinuous; slow layers are continuous.
- Fast layers innovate; slow layers constrain.

A combination of fast and slow is required when thinking in different time horizons. In times of major change, people focus on the short term, when the long term is vastly more important.

The dynamics between layers drive disruption

The first moon landing in 1969 coincided with the first generation of microprocessors that enabled the use of computers in space – an example of the intersection between infrastructure and governance. *Innovation is a dialogue between layers.*

When evaluating disruption, consider the interrelationships between layers. What seems slow to some may seem fast to others. Perceived speed depends on how observers position themselves. Conflicts arise when timeframes are not explicit and therefore not understood.

Fast, slow and unintended consequences

Successful innovation is a conversation across layers – some fast, some slower. Ideally, the conversation also includes unintended consequences that could appear later, once our sometimes rushed innovations are revealed.

Innovation typically moves downwards to lower layers and today's innovations often create tomorrow's challenges. Thomas Midgley Jr, one of the most respected engineers of his time, solved the problem of premature combustion in engines by adding lead to gasoline. He was also the father of modern refrigeration, inventing the freon gas used in fluorocarbon refrigerants. Both inventions were harmful to humans and the environment and were later banned.

Fast-moving projects that solve immediate problems are exciting, but we need to think about the consequences. Proceeding slowly and thoughtfully can be more powerful and reduce the chances of unintended consequences.

When there is rapid change, it is helpful to step back and see what is causing the disruptions. Even in Silicon Valley, it can take 20 years to achieve overnight success. *Poised, patient innovation has extraordinary power.*

Never let a good crisis go to waste

In today's disruptive times, we note that opportunities are found in the turbulence at the boundaries of fast and slow layers. Winston Churchill is credited with saying: 'Never let a good crisis go to waste.'

Some of the greatest businesses are born during periods of major shocks. Around the time of the 2000 dot-com bubble, Google, Netflix and Salesforce emerged. Airbnb and Uber were founded during the 2008 global financial crisis.

Long-term thinking for short-term opportunities

Most people – including most CEOs – tend to see the future only months or, at best, years ahead. Visionaries think decades or even centuries into the future, while simultaneously checking in with the past. This permits visionaries to make bets that will only pay off decades down the line – but when they do, they cause massive transformations. For instance, Jeff Bezos' vision for asteroid mining may take a hundred years, but could it help solve tomorrow's energy crisis?

Sam Altman, founder of OpenAI and former President of Y Combinator, argues that long-term thinking is 'one of the few arbitrage opportunities left in the market',[16] a perspective shared by both Warren Buffet and Elon Musk.

There are many benefits to living and breathing with longer time horizons in our UN-VICE world. *Long-term thinking fleshes out short-term opportunities.*

KEY POINTS
Advantages of long-term thinking

- **Less competition:** As most of the world tends to focus on the short term, the longer-term horizons allow a multiplier effect of small initial initiatives that grow over time.

- **Easier to prioritize:** The ability to focus on relevant innovation and initiatives needed for the real transformations ahead, as opposed to short-term hype.

- **Visioning and working towards our preferred futures:** Imagining impossible futures with the audacity to make them possible.

Three Horizons for transformative change

Bill Sharpe,[17] together with Andrew Curry and Anthony Hodgson,[18] created a version of the Three Horizons as a tool to help anticipate and drive transformational change (Figure 5.4). Their Three Horizons framework is powerful because all horizons exist in the present, as early signals of the future are visible today.

The roles we play today – an explorer, pioneer or settler – affect all the horizons.

To understand the dynamic changes over time, we begin with H1 to establish a baseline as the status quo; then move to H3 to envision the more distant future possibilities; and finally analyse how to bridge the longer-term vision by assessing the transition zone of H2:

- **Horizon 1 – current status:** The first horizon represents currently accepted ways of doing things and typically spans the next five years. This primarily

Figure 5.4 Three Horizons

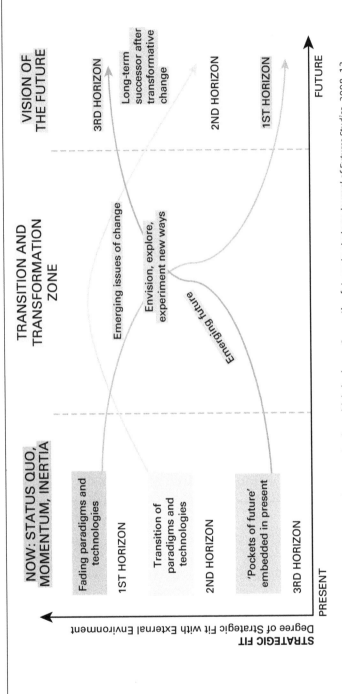

NOTE Adapted from B Sharpe, A Curry and A Hodgson. Seeing in multiple horizons: Connecting futures to strategy. *Journal of Futures Studies,* 2008, 13

includes our current 'business as usual' plans. Here, we may choose to ignore future risks, especially if our core business is stable and profitable. In H1, there should be a sense of ephemerality due to our changing environment. Opportunities may be missed and emerging conditions require us to seek initiatives when our current paradigms no longer fit. We need to ask ourselves what alternatives to the status quo are already perceptible. Which concerns may warrant or drive changes in the future?

- **Horizon 3 – vision of the future:** Long-term successor, probably beyond 10 years from today. H3 pushes the boundaries, requiring the vision of explorers for what may seem improbable, even impossible. The ideas that shape H3 may today be fringe, but they are a response to a radically changing environment. Some H3 features may be entirely new, while others may endure from the present. Understanding what futures could develop in H3 helps imagine which alternatives to explore in H2.

- **Horizon 2 – transition period:** Emerging issues driving change towards H3 as a transitional phase, over the next five to ten years. The fundamental question of H2 is how to reach H3. The transformational zone is a response to the shortcomings of H1 and anticipates the possibilities of H3. H2 requires an entrepreneurial and creative mindset and it tends to be unstable as H1 and H3 invariably collide. Embracing H2's messy disruptions is a prerequisite to reach the future visions of H3. Avoiding this tumultuous phase altogether can be more dangerous than embracing it. H2 is a turbulent transition phase, but a necessary one.

Chronos versus Kairos: Choosing your future today

The power of the Three Horizons is the ability to explore all three modes of awareness simultaneously, instead of pushing more radical research or pilot programmes into H3. The journey to the transformative opportunities of H3 starts now, in H1.

For Curry and Hodgson, an important component of the Three Horizon model is the compatibility between *Chronos* and *Kairos*, different concepts of time in ancient Greece. Chronos is the objective understanding of time passing; the sequential, continuous, chronological idea of time. Kairos is a non-linear, dynamic and subjective orientation of time; this represents a specific opportunity.

By using both Chronos and Kairos to position yourself in H3, you are presented with windows of opportunity along the way. Imagining these futures with curiosity will help you see windows as they emerge. These windows may not last long, but Kairos offers the opportunity to anticipate the future at any point in time.

Inside Intel: From chips to algorithms

The chips are down: The semiconductor industry's paradigm shifts

The semiconductor market, in which Intel is a global leader, is undergoing major shifts that will transform the industry. First, chip demand from China will evaporate because national security concerns and trade restrictions have driven China to accelerate its own semiconductor development. Second, value chain shifts require different chips. The value of many industries will be driven by their 'operating systems', powered by AI chips. With its acquisition of Mobileye, Intel is exposed to driverless technology. The automotive industry's primary value creator will be the AI system that powers automated driving and safety features. Third, clients compete rather than outsource. Not surprisingly, Apple, Google, Amazon and Meta develop their own AI chips, because today's deep learning breakthroughs are increasingly achieved through hardware. These companies compete head-on with their former suppliers, including Intel.

Intel's possible vision of the futures

The ongoing challenges to Intel's strategy provide an illustration of transformational change over time.

Intel intends to remain a leader in semiconductor manufacturing, but with the flexibility to control AI chip design. Intel will move from relying on its legacy to focus on the next generation of AI chips that support mobility shifts, breakthrough R&D and energy-efficient data centres. Furthermore, Intel understands that its next competitors are not semiconductor players in legacy markets, like PCs or servers. Instead, Intel looks to the future of AI, including sentient tools, intelligent machines and smart cities. As Intel frees itself from the constraints of its vertically integrated outsourced PC chip manufacturer model, it gains design flexibility to enter new markets.

Intel's competitors are investing heavily in becoming software players and tomorrow's semiconductor leaders. Software is only one piece of Intel's vision, as AI moves from the edge to the centre in a world of intelligent, aware and social machines.[19]

Transformation is turbulent: Intel's three horizons

Let's analyse Intel with the perspectives of the Three Horizons:

- **Horizon 1 – current status:** For decades, Intel benefited from Moore's Law as the leading manufacturer of central processing units for PCs and data centres. As Intel had invested less in new production capacity, the stock market penalized them for losing market share and chip shortages. How worried is the stock market about radical and permanent shifts in the semiconductor industry? What would happen to Intel if it ignored emerging changes and continued to operate a legacy business focused on capacity-building to fulfil short-term supply chains for yesterday's segments?

- **Horizon 3 – vision of the future:** Intel sees the need to reinvent itself and drive the longer-term future of AI, autonomous systems and smart mobility. In H3, Intel may leave behind many of the pure-play, volume-driven semiconductor players as paradigms shift.

- **Horizon 2 – transition:** Intel explores deploying its long-term future vision in H2. Intel understands that change is turbulent and unpredictable. The company has not always wanted to compete in all product lines – even if this meant breaking with market expectations. Radical transformation is sometimes chaotic, evidenced by the highly vocal challenges Intel faces as it navigates short-term market expectations. By disrupting itself, Intel is moving from a leading volume chip company to reimagining its relevance as an industry leader in the future of mobility and intelligent machines.

Convergence creates new fields beyond chips

In Intel's case study, we see legacy verticals blur and new fields emerge. Turning towards H3, the company moves on from its legacy into an unsettling transition phase. Intel nearly missed the mobile shift of the 2000s and still has its challenges. In 2022, Intel IPO'd Mobileye's activities, with the intention of retaining control.

Intel offers a thought-provoking example of H3 strategy. It no longer seeks to control 80 per cent of the computer processor market, but to move forward to something new.

Transitions and change are difficult for everyone because systemic disruption can be existential. Even for NVIDIA, the AI chip global market leader that reached a $2 trillion valuation in 2024, its CEO and co-founder Jensen Huang acknowledges that the company is always in peril.

In comes the Chief Bridging Officer

The present is ephemeral – it is here now, then dissipates. While strategic plans are the future, they will never exist because we are only ever in the present. With a constantly accelerating present, the C-suites of hierarchical, top-down organizations risk getting absorbed in the day-to-day, never able to translate today into the longer-term vision. Additionally, those tasked with longer-term vision may not be living and breathing what is required in the present to sail to the future. *This requires the agility to glide across chasms where bridges have yet to be built.*

Poor coordination throughout organizations can cause strategies to falter. Complexity can be counterintuitive when compared to well-established, linear ways of thinking.

We imagine the chief bridging officer (CBO),[20] whose role is to bridge the vision of the future with constantly updating complex environments.

CBO job specification

The CBO builds and crosses these bridges:

- **Present and future:** A bridge connecting present strategic imperatives and bets with long-term futures. Seize the evolutionary potential of today's emergence, with the foresight of aspirational and alternative futures.

- **Legacy and disruption:** Anticipate industry shifts to bridge legacy models with disruptive ventures. Empower diverse teams to probe new ideas, experiment, iterate and develop insights for future growth opportunities. This exploration can involve testing new markets, teaming up with start-ups and venturing with innovative accelerators.

- **Assumptions and possibilities:** A bridge between what a company assumes it is (or has to be) today versus what the world could be tomorrow. Banish being a prisoner of assumptions, legacy and history. Build a bridge between uncertainties and what is knowable. Anticipate existential risks to unlock opportunities. Climate risk is a good example of this, opening the door to the enormous opportunities of Greenaissance.

- **Incentives and alignment:** Align the vision of stakeholders and broader society. Banish narrow shareholder incentives, which drive inadequate and short-term outcomes. Work with policymakers to seek broader alignment and incentivize our systems.

The CBO should have the agility to constantly respond to changes in the external environment and initiate adjustments with anticipatory vision, consistent with long-term aspirations. *This 'outside in' thinking requires anticipating the 'What if?' questions, rather than reacting to them.* Strategies become sketched outlines which are changing, tested, validated and iterated. A fixed long-term strategic plan is simply an envisioned trajectory; this direction may evolve as it is ideated and prototyped to reconcile the vision with the tangible.

KEY POINTS

Thinking in multiple timeframes for today's decisions

One of the most deeply ingrained misconceptions about long-term thinking is that it does not concern the present.

- **The present matters:** It is the only thing that exists, but not to the exclusion of the future.
- **Long-term thinking informs action today:** Changing the present often results in a broad set of self-reinforcing benefits across time horizons.

Respecting time for all its richness, nuances and liminality allows us to develop a healthy relationship with unknowability. We have the agency to seize opportunities and adapt our perceptions by zooming out to the future and zooming back in to the present.

Only by respecting the holistic nature of systems and interrelationships between their parts do we enable transformational change. The decisions we make today – as well as choices we ignore today – are not disconnected from the past or the future. Enacting shifts at the levels of structures and models are the most effective leverage points to trigger change.

Notes

1 R Spitz and L Zuin (2023) *The Definitive Guide to Thriving on Disruption: Beta your life: Existence in a disruptive world*, Disruptive Futures Institute, San Francisco, CA

2 E Schmidt and J Rosenberg (2015) *How Google Works*, John Murray, London

3 A Grant (2016) *Originals: How non-conformists move the world*, Viking, New York, NY

4   P A Thiel and B Masters (2014) *Zero to One: Notes on startups, or how to build the future*, Crown Business, New York, NY

5   Ocean Tomo. Intangible asset market value study, Ocean Tomo, 2020. www.oceantomo.com/intangible-asset-market-value-study (archived at https://perma.cc/34GS-J85Z)

6   N N Taleb (2012) *Antifragile: Things that gain from disorder*, Random House, New York, NY

7   J J Campanella (Director). I/O (season 1, episode 1) *Halt and Catch Fire*, AMC Studios, 1 January 2015

8   N Radjou and J Prabhu (2017) *Jugaad Innovation: Think frugal, be flexible, generate breakthrough growth*, trans Dr Simone Ahuja, Penguin Random House, Delhi

9   F Richter. Amazon maintains cloud lead as Microsoft edges closer, Statista, 5 February 2024. www.statista.com/chart/18819/worldwide-market-share-of-leading-cloud-infrastructure-service-providers (archived at https://perma.cc/NMC5-MBTM)

10 C Miller, M Scott and B Bender. UkraineX: How Elon Musk's space satellites changed the war on the ground, Politico, 8 June 2022. www.politico.eu/article/elon-musk-ukraine-starlink (archived at https://perma.cc/Y2ZT-NZ3X)

11 N N Taleb (2018) *Skin in the Game: Hidden asymmetries in daily life*, Random House, New York, NY

12 T Kim. Goldman Sachs asks in biotech research report: 'Is curing patients a sustainable business model?', CNBC, 11 April 2018. www.cnbc.com/2018/04/11/goldman-asks-is-curing-patients-a-sustainable-business-model.html (archived at https://perma.cc/84FK-DXRR)

13 W Bogdanich and M Forsythe (2022) *When McKinsey Comes to Town: The hidden influence of the world's most powerful consulting firm*, Random House, New York, NY

14 J M Keynes (1923) *A Tract on Monetary Reform*, Macmillan, London

15 E Ries (2011) *The Lean Startup*, Portfolio Penguin, London

16 Y Combinator. Sam Altman: How to build the future, YouTube, 27 September 2016. www.youtube.com/watch?v=sYMqVwsewSg (archived at https://perma.cc/WC2R-CZAZ)

17 B Sharpe (2013) *Three Horizons 2020: The patterning of hope*, Triarchy Press, Charmouth, Dorset

18 A Curry and A Hodgson. Seeing in multiple horizons: Connecting futures to strategy, *Journal of Futures Studies*, 2008, 13 (1), 1–20

19 R Spitz and L Zuin (2023) *The Definitive Guide to Thriving on Disruption: Disruption as a springboard to value creation*, Disruptive Futures Institute, San Francisco, CA

20 R Spitz and L Zuin (2022) *The Definitive Guide to Thriving on Disruption: Essential frameworks for disruption and uncertainty*, Disruptive Futures Institute, San Francisco, CA

6
Harnessing systems innovation to solve our complex challenges

OBJECTIVES
Driving transformation with systems innovation

Climate change, societal paradigm shifts, emerging technologies; the world's most critical challenges are complex. Addressing these requires systems-level change, not isolated fixes. Systems innovation is instrumental to identifying and harnessing effective levers to enable widespread change across complex systems.

Beyond strategy: Levers for transformative change

Wicked problems exist in dynamic, non-linear environments. Solutions emerge not from pre-established answers but through critical thinking, experimentation and sound judgement. These complex environments lack clear definition and display conflicting stakeholder interests. Respondents must use active sense-making for situational awareness, acknowledging the emergent properties and interconnectedness. Different response options must be tested based on the perceived features of each situation.

Only bold actions and strategic choices can solve our most complex risks. In *Thinking in Systems*, environmental scientist Donella Meadows outlined how applying shifts at the appropriate levels is the most effective way to trigger paradigm changes, where small interventions can result in large changes throughout the entire system.[1]

Opportunities arise by moving from silos to systems and rethinking the structures that incentivize our actions.

Resistance to change: Discarding inertia

In the decade ahead, we will face choices related to climate, society and emerging technologies that have unprecedented ramifications. We have the agency to make those choices, but agency alone will not suffice. One challenge is that timeframes stretch beyond traditional horizons. Business and political cycles are too short to be impacted by these challenges, so there are no incentives to address them.

Inaction may lead to the decimation of entire industries, economies and humanity itself. Our society can transform itself, but this requires discarding the inertia of the status quo.

We need a coordinated reset of our systems to prepare for these risks, averting unthinkable outcomes and capturing opportunities that arise through change. There is still time to align policymakers, technology leaders, society and our planet, but the window of opportunity is narrowing.

Beware of 'futurewashing', where empty promises about future actions replace taking actual steps today.

Change faces powerful resistance, fuelled by those who benefit from the status quo. Inertia also stems from a lack of understanding about how to effectively transform complex systems that are locked into established patterns.

Aligning effective actions for complex challenges

This chapter outlines tools for driving change in complex systems, accounting for the path dependencies of wicked problems.

These problems require us to look at how systems are interconnected from social, economic, political and technological perspectives. Addressing these depends on awareness of the dynamics of the many drivers through a systemic lens. Solutions need to be applied to high-leverage points to be effective, where subtle interventions can result in large changes. Applying Meadows' framework, incentives are strong leverage points because they represent the rules of the system and its boundaries.

Anticipatory governance plays a key role in formulating, aligning and executing responses. How do we move from instant gratification to accountability for our choices?

With complex, systemic challenges, there are no individual winners. *Collectively addressing these means we all win; failure means we all lose.*

Innovating with business-models-as-a-system

Trusted partnerships can help address complex challenges by co-designing business models as adaptable, evolving pieces in larger ecosystems.

Digital infrastructure paves the way for systemic models

Social media platforms (Facebook, Twitter/X, Instagram, YouTube) and marketplaces (Amazon, Google, Shopify, Uber, Airbnb, Mercado Libre) permit fast scaling and disintermediation.

Platforms allow business models to reach hundreds of millions (if not billions) of users without owning any of the underlying assets being exchanged. Amazon, Meta and Google (or in China, Alibaba, Tencent and Baidu) are amongst the world's most valuable platforms due to their skill in matching suppliers or producers with consumers and information.

Despite the success, these platforms have many limitations. First, they are extractive, ignoring broader systemic effects. Social media is a prime example, maximizing revenue growth and monetizing attention at the cost of user addiction, misinformation, polarization and privacy. Second, there is limited loyalty, as customers can switch to competing platforms with better user experience. Third, there are low barriers to entry. Platforms rely on available technology, limiting opportunities to create anything new.

Like rails or banking infrastructure, platforms offer a narrow transactional solution. Nonetheless, this relatively mature digital infrastructure paves the way to emergent models that can address the world's challenges and opportunities systemically.

Systems-level innovation

Systems-level innovation acknowledges how everything is interconnected. In perpetually evolving environments, there is an inherent need to act and respond with novel options.

Hardwired models only change periodically – if at all. To be relevant in today's UN-VICE world, business models must adapt to paradigm shifts with agility. Dynamic business models support experimentation, catalyse innovation and create shared value for the entire ecosystem, providing deeper complementarities between participants.

Ecosystems and business-models-as-a-system

We define these ecosystems as business-models-as-a-system (BMaaS),[2] which emerge thanks to three key elements: eco, co and ecosystems.

- **'Eco' is eco-friendly:** New opportunities, jobs and industries for those creative enough to shift to more sustainable ecosystems across agriculture, energy, transportation, real estate, retail and more.
- **'Co' refers to collaboration:** *Co*-created, *co*-evolving, *c*onnected and *c*onsumers.
- **'Ecosystems' live and breathe dynamic changes:** They are systemic, in flux, interdependent and generate feedback loops to emerge with something new.

Business models as systems are needed to respond to the deeply complex challenges of today's world. Traditional business models don't tend to change – or only do so periodically. BMaaS are constantly adapting to surrounding ecosystem shifts. Collaborative ecosystems support novel explorations and synthesize innovation. BMaaS are interconnected and constantly evolving – it's alive, it's eco, it's co, it's an ecosystem and it's a system (Figure 6.1).

Similar to living organisms, these living BMaaS change creatively within their ecosystems as they unfold.

The idea of thinking about business in terms of an ecosystem is not new. In the 1990s, James F Moore wrote about the co-evolution of business, social and economic systems. Today, the difference is the number of factors that are fundamentally increasing uncertainty and unpredictability. In a hyperconnected age of compressed life cycles, both the disruption drivers and the cost of business as usual are far greater. With this complex, technological and systemic context in mind, we update the co-creation opportunities for driving change in intermingled ecosystems.

Figure 6.1 Business-models-as-a-system

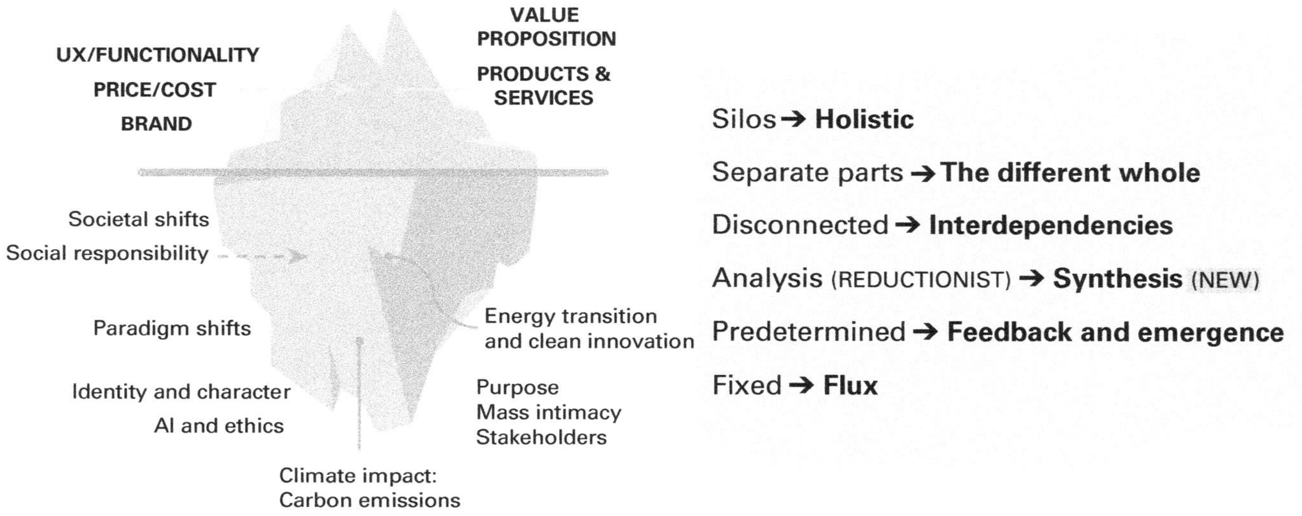

VALUE
PROPOSITION

PRODUCTS &
SERVICES

UX/FUNCTIONALITY

PRICE/COST

BRAND

Societal shifts

Social responsibility

Paradigm shifts

Identity and character

AI and ethics

Energy transition
and clean innovation

Purpose
Mass intimacy
Stakeholders

Climate impact:
Carbon emissions

Silos → **Holistic**

Separate parts → **The different whole**

Disconnected → **Interdependencies**

Analysis (REDUCTIONIST) → **Synthesis** (NEW)

Predetermined → **Feedback and emergence**

Fixed → **Flux**

Complexity demands systems innovation, not point solutions

The industrial and mechanical world often relies on specific expertise and technological fixes. Conversely, our updated UN-VICE environment cannot rely on predetermined solutions.

There are few straightforward relationships in these complex environments, and spillovers complicate any siloed solutions. Embracing tomorrow's challenges requires a collaborative and adaptive approach that harnesses the levers for change to drive systems innovation.

BMaaS are particularly suited to systems innovation, as they nurture the creation of new markets and ecosystems – even if that means disrupting themselves.

Today's global issues require system-wide innovation.

The six core features of BMaaS

Let's now explore the six core features of BMaaS:

1 Alive: Evolving models allow experimentation.

2 Liminal blurs boundaries.

3 Diverse perspectives enable emergence.

4 Harness sustainable change.

5 Co-create, deliver and capture new value.

6 Leverage network effects and technology.

1. Alive: Evolving models allow experimentation

BMaaS are fluid and dynamic, constantly evolving and interconnected – with interdependencies, feedback loops, synthesis and constant co-emergence.

Curiosity and creativity allow instructive patterns to emerge, as these can be perceived but not predicted. Relying on analysis alone may not work. Experimentation in a safe-to-fail environment provides a direction towards the next moves. It also offers the opportunity to test counterintuitive ideas that can yield surprising results.

By monitoring feedback, you can evaluate what is effective or not. Imagine you are a musician improvising a live performance. As you play, you gauge the reactions of the audience. You seek to reinforce what is working and perform less of what does not receive enthusiastic reactions. But you need to monitor this feedback to decide on your next move.

EXAMPLE
Living cities and green urbanization

Cities developed after the advent of the automobile have infrastructure centred around cars. However, the need for individual vehicle ownership may be reduced by viable alternatives such as cycling, autonomous commercial vehicles and passenger shuttles. Thus, the urban landscape may be reinvented. Adaptive infrastructure and smart cities that incentivize a symbiotic human–environment relationship could drastically change the appearance of our urban structure. Greener and smarter cities can be designed with the environment in mind, including cycling lanes, high-speed rail and green buildings.

Living cities could drive sustainable futures, with opportunities for dynamic innovations between the public and private sectors. City-level initiatives such as smart street lamps, self-cooling buildings, connected electric smart cars and chargers support green transportation and adaptive infrastructure.

As humanity invests billions of dollars to enable regenerative transformation, there are new opportunities to support climate mitigation and adaptation with innovative solutions.

2. Liminal blurs boundaries

BMaaS blur boundaries between industries and players. They deliver value across stakeholders, working collaboratively to address systemic challenges.

In open ecosystems, partners are customers, suppliers and even competitors. You can collaborate closely within your ecosystem to identify strengths you didn't know you had. Even competitors influence and interact with each other and the broader ecosystems virtuously, without clear delimitations. Competitors can also collaborate, known as 'coopetition', where cooperation trumps competition. All partners have a specific role to play within an ecosystem.

CASE STUDY   Tesla: Driving-as-a-system

While it may appear as though Tesla's main assets are their sleek electric vehicles, battery technology and status-oriented branding, the company's most impactful assets lie beneath the surface.

Tesla's advantage may have emerged because the company leverages its ecosystems better than its peers. Tesla vertically integrates more parts of its wider production supply chain. It has a hand in designing the vehicle, manufacturing the battery and developing its software (which are key to the underlying value of a car today). This allows Tesla to then partner smartly, relying on other parties for the components they are better suited to complete. Additionally, Tesla emulates a collaborative open-source strategy regarding intellectual property within its ecosystem. According to Musk, 'Our true competition is not the small trickle of non-Tesla electric cars being produced, but rather the enormous flood of gasoline cars pouring out of the world's factories every day.'[3]

Could Tesla's BMaaS be the chief factor in its success? As Honda, Ford, General Motors and others adopted Tesla's electric vehicle charging technology, Tesla may have reached a virtuous inflection point in scaling it across software, hardware, infrastructure and energy.

There are still ecological and human rights concerns surrounding the sourcing of heavy materials for electric vehicle batteries, but Tesla claims to be working towards more world-friendly supply chain solutions. Tesla batteries boast high potential for reuse and recycling; they claim around 90 per cent of a Tesla battery is recyclable and even after the battery is no longer usable in a vehicle, it can still be used for household electricity storage.

The sustainable energy transition requires a systems approach. For instance, improved electric vehicle batteries may not solve energy transition challenges if these cannot be scaled to meet supply, if ethical raw materials are not available, if charging networks aren't resilient and reliable, if the cost of electric vehicles and batteries are prohibitive and if the life cycle of electric vehicles creates greater pollution. To address these challenges, Tesla continues to partner closely across fields.

Batteries are a key part of Tesla's vehicles, but the group's focus on batteries is much broader than cars. For over 15 years, Tesla has built integrated high-performance battery systems designed to store grid and solar energy for businesses as well as individuals.

Tesla's Powerwall, a home battery system that stores solar energy, allows Tesla owners to receive compensation for providing grid services. Distributed energy storage systems, known as virtual power plants, offer a glimpse into a future where expensive and polluting power plants are circumvented.

Tesla's system-oriented strategy doesn't stop at the environment. Instead of building a car as a car, Tesla has essentially built a vehicle *around* a computer and *as* a computer. The company uses wireless updates to upgrade the software and battery of the vehicle, even after purchase. For example, Tesla released an update that scans ahead for potholes, automatically adjusting the vehicle's suspension to prevent damage. Tesla vehicles also gather data to constantly improve the vehicle experience, using its customer base to help the company create value for the user. The more data Tesla gathers from its vehicles, the better its traffic visualization software becomes. This data ecosystem creates value for everyone: users, suppliers, partners, even competitors.

3. Diverse perspectives enable emergence

Ecosystems create value by combining and harnessing the unique perspectives, capabilities and knowledge of each participant. Diversity requires multiple fields – each offering different expertise. The intersection of these drives co-innovation. The synthesis of these broad perspectives creates newness that a self-sufficient, ignorant or optimized organization could not achieve alone. In BMaaS, collaboration is broader and deeper, with more diverse participants than a bilateral alliance.

Tapping into collective intelligence provides unparalleled perspectives from broad sets of participants. This can include customers, prospects, suppliers, partners, investors and future talent (who often seek a sense of belonging). Involvement and crowdsourcing are effective, but require agile structures to empower decision-making at the periphery.

Complexity and diversity: Compounding forces for creativity – Various cultures, experiences, environments and fields pick up different signals before the future emerges. *The importance of diversity cannot be overstated because it enables a richer set of signals.* These in turn allow flawed or stale assumptions to be challenged.

Had IBM not relied on uniform decision-makers, they may have seen beyond the narrow legacy enterprise mainframe markets, which influenced their dismissal of the nascent personal computer market (benefitting Apple and Microsoft). At that time, IBM was not diverse enough to imagine anything different from their flawed assumptions.

In fluid environments, innovation arises when fresh perspectives make new combinations. As we develop multiple hypotheses, our experiments reveal whether they move us in the right direction. We need 'safe-to-fail' experiments when there are no straightforward answers, and diversity drives the curiosity to conceptualize these.

Professor Scott Page considers different types of community compositions and varying interaction structures. This diversity is critical in complex systems, allowing different responses to shocks. By encouraging diverse perspectives and participation, we can generate emergent thinking.[4]

Page establishes that diversity provides the seeds for novelty by creating outliers able to fuel tipping points for major breakthroughs.

4. Harness sustainable change

One of the objectives of BMaaS is to address challenges together, with broader benefits for society at large. These could include any of the United Nations' 17 Sustainable Development Goals (SDGs), which individual actors would be unable to address alone. XPRIZE is a good example of an organization addressing complex challenges in this way, by offering prizes for successful achievement of important societal aims.

Complex systems display multiple relationships and interconnections. Financial systems, markets, energy supply and social networks exhibit a strong degree of 'tight coupling'. *In tight coupling, small ripples in quiet waters become tidal waves.*

Tight coupling is a form of fragility. This contagion arises when the margins for error are slim (versus allowing for slack or buffers). Examples of contagions abound: the 2008 financial crisis, extensive global supply chain disruptions during the Covid pandemic or Europe's 2021 energy crisis.

Cascading failures are more likely to happen with tight coupling, often characterized by highly structured interactions, centralized control and optimized processes. The possibilities range from supply chain dependencies to cyberattacks that knock out power or internet. Such fragility is not conducive to system innovations.

KEY POINTS
Loose coupling reduces dependencies

With dependencies, a change in one aspect of a system immediately creates unanticipated changes across many other components. Loose coupling decreases this risk of cross-contamination.

Central to loose coupling are flexibility, decentralization and distribution, empowering systems to adapt, self-organize and operate with built-in redundancy. This provides greater agility and room to manoeuvre, allowing some degree of containment of the impacts. Rather than succumbing to the smallest change, flexibility offers enhanced ability to anticipate and respond to the disruptions ahead.

Loosely coupled systems enable experimentation and learning, benefitting from feedback loops. When things go wrong, we can learn lessons and iterate for improvements. Conversely, in tight coupling, the contagion can spread quickly, reducing the opportunity to respond effectively.

In the same way that diverse perspectives facilitate emergence, a diversity of views also helps identify the potential problems which could result from tight coupling and excessive interdependencies. These outside perspectives may challenge assumptions and enable us to see things differently rather than continue with what may have worked in the past or what seems to be the best approach. New perspectives increase the chance of probing questions to explore *'What if?'*

5. Co-create, deliver and capture new value

Different players in these ecosystems generate, deliver and capture value for one another as well as customers. This value incentivizes actors to solve systemic problems together in the process. In contrast, linear business models focus on binary value creation – for shareholders and end customers.

One of the main value drivers of ecosystems is to co-stumble upon new ideas, but this value does not have to be traditional or financial. Contributions are often non-monetary and take on many forms.

Ecosystems are partially fluid networks of multiple types of organizations. No one party controls the ecosystem, although there can be an orchestrator with a greater role. An orchestrator may have a deeper appreciation of the ecosystem's value propositions and purpose, as well as the means to make things happen.

KEY POINTS
Understanding motives and values

Ecosystem development requires alignment of shared values and objectives, with an understanding of the role and unique value of each participant. The value contributed by participants varies and can include financing, technology, know-how, data, customers, market access or R&D.

When the ecosystem does well, the individual actors also win. For ecosystem business models such as BMaaS to work, they must be virtuous for every actor. Such ecosystems are 'win–win', the opposite of zero-sum games.

Thoughtful economics and incentives can attract participants, customers, investments and talent. *Understanding the motives and values of involved organizations helps achieve alignment and manage ecosystem dynamics.*

6. Leverage network effects and technology

Network effects can be leveraged to reach a critical mass of participants. This creates a fertile, self-sustaining ecosystem where innovation and social entrepreneurship thrive. While this may take the form of platforms, it often does not rely on established global technology giants. Instead, BMaaS will offer the benefits of a platform without depending on an Amazon or Google.

No company or technology can operate in isolation. Tomorrow's futures are shaped by co-developed and cross-fertilized R&D, technologies and standards. Complex challenges, such as mitigating climate change, require the support of frontier technologies. These nascent technologies may not have clear financial returns at the onset, but are critical for driving new (and necessary) breakthroughs. Technology is an enabler, not the end result.

CASE STUDY   John Deere: Agriculture-as-a-system

Above the surface, John Deere produces and sells agricultural, forestry and construction machinery. They compete on price, technology and the effectiveness of aftermarket parts and maintenance. John Deere works closely with dealers and parts suppliers worldwide for product distribution.

Below the surface, John Deere harnesses the three constituents of BMaaS:

- **Eco:** Eco-friendly with a sustainable ecosystem strategy. Precision agriculture reduces chemical and herbicide use, improves soil health and optimizes irrigation for water efficiency.

- **Co:** John Deere is constantly involved in collaborative open ecosystems. The group excels at co-creating and co-evolving connected consumers, partners and suppliers.
- **Ecosystems breathe dynamic changes:** John Deere's strategy is always in flux, generating feedback loops that open new pathways.

John Deere's open ecosystems evolve through constant engagement with clients, dealers, suppliers and developers. This networked exchange of information provides significant data and insights, where machinery becomes as effective as a computer. Interactions within the network are as valuable as new sales.

Despite serving traditional industries, John Deere is one of the most innovative and technology-savvy groups. Combining 5G, IoT-based sensors, geolocation and telematics with computer vision and lidar technology, the group has also developed autonomous-driving tractors. John Deere University is available to company employees, dealers and other stakeholders to build shared values and upskill.

John Deere invests in its ecosystem, gaining access to dynamic information from any device. With AI and machine learning, the group created a powerful 'Big Ag' data platform. Their software can distinguish weeds from plants, anticipate breakdowns and allow real-time decisions by evaluating the soil, crop and weather. This real-time data is more effective than delayed observations from flying drones. As the platform gains users, John Deere offers more value and data that can be shared with participants.

Despite successes, companies must constantly monitor emerging signals of change, both for opportunities and threats. John Deere's employees have followed the company's value creation, wanting to get a greater share of the pie. John Deere improved employment terms to ensure that their greatest asset – their employees – found their ecosystem relationship virtuous. As is the case across industries, many of John Deere's loyal customers have pushed for the right to repair – to allow the independent repair of existing equipment rather than forcing new purchases or manufacturer repairs. In 2023, the American Farm Bureau Federation and Deere & Co signed a memorandum of understanding, allowing their US customers to repair their own equipment with more economical independent options for parts and service.

Beginner's mind, especially when everything is going well

Even when everything seems settled, there will be both new opportunities and challenges because disruption is a constant. The emergent and fluid nature of BMaaS provides the agility to build resilience, adapt and thrive on changes. By testing novel ideas and innovating, the entire ecosystem can benefit.

Four drivers for systems-level change

Achieving sustainable futures requires humanity to solve our most complex, systemic and existential risks. This demands a deep understanding of systems-level change – deeper than surface-level point solutions. To achieve transformations, organizations must consider a broad set of stakeholders, partners and complex ecosystem interactions.[5]

There are four related mindsets and actions that can lead to systems-level transformative change (Figure 6.2):

- **Strategic foresight for adaptive and resilient futures:** Anticipatory thinking and adaptive decision-making for resilient and sustainable futures.

- **Virtuous inflection points:** Understanding beneficial tipping points to offer pathways for desired changes.

Figure 6.2 Systems-level change for sustainable futures

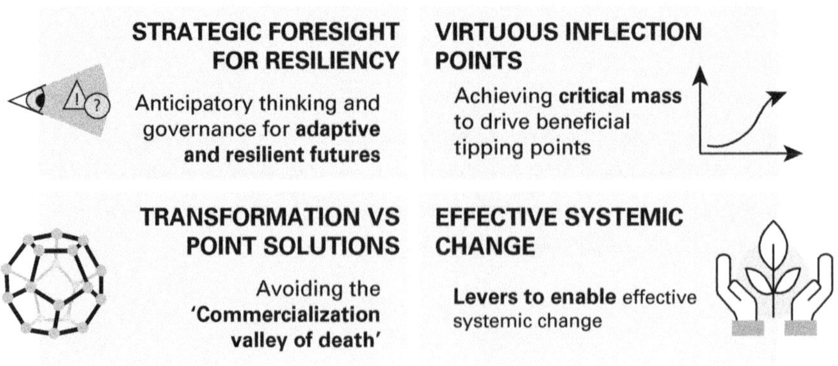

STRATEGIC FORESIGHT FOR RESILIENCY

Anticipatory thinking and governance for **adaptive and resilient futures**

VIRTUOUS INFLECTION POINTS

Achieving **critical mass** to drive beneficial tipping points

TRANSFORMATION VS POINT SOLUTIONS

Avoiding the **'Commercialization valley of death'**

EFFECTIVE SYSTEMIC CHANGE

Levers to enable effective systemic change

- **Transformational innovation versus point solutions:** Beyond controlled environments, we must determine which innovations can scale cost-effectively to become commercially viable and interact seamlessly in our world.
- **Levers for effective systemic change:** Identify and harness effective levers to enable change across emerging complex systems.

Strategic foresight for adaptive and resilient futures

The year 2023 became known as the hottest on record. Thousands died across Europe when temperatures soared and wildfires raged. China, elsewhere in Asia, the US, North Africa and the Middle East also experienced record-breaking heat. For much of the world, this unprecedented heat confronted unprepared infrastructure. This caused transport system breakdowns, melting airport runways and server outages.

The economy, technology and infrastructure are directly impacted by extreme heat. Cooling systems are put under intense pressure, as are the materials of buildings. Transportation systems, business productivity, global supply chains and food systems are also seriously impacted.

The frequency and severity of extreme weather events driven by climate change could mean longer heatwaves, worse droughts and stronger storms, all of which also impact financial stability.

Climate risk can affect any organization in a multitude of ways: financial risks and business models (transition risks); impairment of assets, damaged property and supply chain issues (physical risks); and claims made by parties suffering losses or damage (liability risks). Every person, asset and business is exposed to climate risk, from critical infrastructure to homes and hotels. These risks threaten the livelihood of billions of people – and trillions of dollars in physical assets.

Current environmental initiatives often focus on mitigation, which is insufficient. We must also prepare for change through climate adaptation and strategic resilience. Adaptation entails making adjustments in systems, whether in anticipation of or in response to evolving environments, to minimize negative outcomes and facilitate beneficial changes. Resilience is the ability for a system to absorb shocks and respond effectively by virtue of effective anticipation, preparation and adaptation.

Foresight supports adaptation strategies by adjusting systems in anticipation of evolving environments. This informs climate-aligned decision-making in advance of many climate eventualities (versus responding after the fact).

EXAMPLE
Climate-aligned decision-making

By combining strategic foresight with climate intelligence, anticipatory decision-makers can develop adaptive resilience for business models, assets and supply chains by integrating the possible next-order implications of shocks.

Many start-ups operate in climate intelligence, including ClimateAI, Jupiter Intelligence and Mitiga Solutions. These organizations enable climate-aligned decisions to identify emerging opportunities while building resilient adaptation to absorb shocks – instead of just mitigating the risks.

Organizations can harness climate adaptation in a number of ways: first, by incorporating physical risk into decision-making (to avoid increasing exposure to climate hazards and manage existing challenges); second, by designing for changing climate conditions (infrastructure such as bridges, water systems and communications networks); and third, by identifying dependencies (understanding vulnerabilities to enable contingency plans that protect supply chains and day-to-day operations).

Virtuous inflection points to achieve critical mass

Understanding what triggers beneficial tipping points in the adoption of system innovations can offer pathways to supporting transformational changes.

Malcolm Gladwell's *The Tipping Point*[6] is famous for illustrating how rapidly phenomena can spread. Gladwell imagines that widespread social phenomena are akin to epidemics. Ideas, actions and styles can 'spread just like viruses do'.

Inflection points arise when small changes interact and enable the emergence of watershed changes that replace past paradigms. The initial stages can seem slow... until they aren't. Self-reinforcing technologies and collective actions can significantly boost the adoption of low-carbon solutions, eventually reaching a virtuous inflection point.

Younger generations care deeply about how climate change will affect them and future generations. They will increasingly scrutinize how governments and corporations implement sustainability, from clean supply chains to how brands address the environment's different layers. Regulators, investors and customers alike now expect these structural transformations.

Despite green- and bluewashing, the world is watching and it is harder to hide in today's hyperconnected traceable society. A number of initiatives announced in the early 2020s provide initial signs that we may be reaching key enabling conditions for more sustainable futures.

EXAMPLE

A once-in-a-generation virtuous tipping point?

Unprecedented momentum supports the energy transition. The US Inflation Reduction Act provides hundreds of billions of dollars to support clean energy, manufacturing and R&D. In Europe and the UK, powerful legislation pushes for fossil phaseouts, laws on greenlabelling and against greenwashing, bans on imports linked to deforestation, and extensive funding and subsidies. We could be approaching a virtuous inflection point for structural transformations to deliver on environmental responsibilities.

Renewable is also reaching a tipping point. Renewable energy (solar, wind, hydro and bioenergy) is expected to become the largest source of global electricity by 2025.[7] Wind and solar are the fastest-growing sources and combined are expected to produce around one-third of global power by 2030.[8]

Additionally, consider electrification. The more electric vehicles are produced, the cheaper production becomes as automakers travel up the innovation learning curve. By banning gasoline cars in multiple jurisdictions, policymakers contribute to a virtuous tipping point for the automotive sector, eventually reaching a world where electric vehicles are cheaper than petrol cars.

There are headwinds on the pathways to positive inflection points, including the reversal of climate commitments and unproven technologies. However, numerous green technologies are maturing. If system innovations accelerate as they combine with effective policies, changemakers embracing decarbonization can marginalize players dependent on traditional energy sources.

We can achieve virtuous tipping points as initiatives align and accelerate. Decarbonization will become more cost-effective, with the benefits eventually exceeding the transition costs.

Figure 6.3 TRL and beyond: Green tech critical challenge

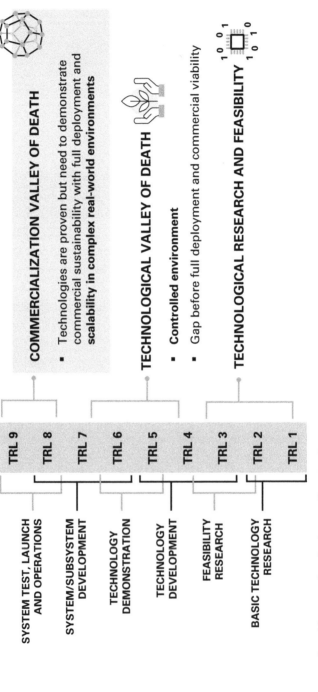

COMMERCIALIZATION VALLEY OF DEATH

- Technologies are proven but need to demonstrate commercial sustainability with full deployment and scalability in complex real-world environments

TECHNOLOGICAL VALLEY OF DEATH

- Controlled environment
- Gap before full deployment and commercial viability

TECHNOLOGICAL RESEARCH AND FEASIBILITY

TRL 9
TRL 8
TRL 7
TRL 6
TRL 5
TRL 4
TRL 3
TRL 2
TRL 1

SYSTEM TEST, LAUNCH AND OPERATIONS

SYSTEM/SUBSYSTEM DEVELOPMENT

TECHNOLOGY DEMONSTRATION

TECHNOLOGY DEVELOPMENT

FEASIBILITY RESEARCH

BASIC TECHNOLOGY RESEARCH

NOTE Adapted from NASA'S Technology Readiness Level

Transformational innovation versus point solutions

NASA's Technology Readiness Level (TRL) was originally created in the 1960s to evaluate space technologies. Today, it is used to quantify the maturity of a technology's development from 1 to 9. The higher a technology ranks, the more technically developed and qualified it is (Figure 6.3).[9]

For new technologies to scale, they must survive the so-called 'valleys of death'. Traditionally, the term refers to the 'technological valley of death', where a new innovation faces significant challenges in moving from the controlled lab environment to a working prototype. TRL guides scaling technologies through the technological valley of death by outlining the stages required for an idea to transition from basic research to proof of concept.

However, the system test, launch and initial operation is the highest level of NASA's TRL. While this is a critical part of demonstrating technological viability to secure funding, it is just the beginning.

The 'commercialization valley of death' is between the phases of demonstration and commercialization – when technologies are proven but require more capital to scale. This valley is particularly difficult for green tech, which must effect change in a dynamic, complex, real-world environment to prove its worth to investors. At this high-risk stage, funding is most critical – and most difficult to secure.[10]

Complex real-world deployment

For ClimateTech, overcoming the commercialization valley of death is much more difficult than for discrete technologies:

- **Mastering hardware, software and infrastructure:** Tomorrow's green champions need to harness breakthrough innovations in energy storage, renewables, green hydrogen and carbon capture, which often combine software, hardware and infrastructure to produce and operate physical products.

- **Different capital requirements:** Transformational green technologies often require new innovative infrastructure, which carries costly, longer-term and riskier initial capital.

- **Alignment:** Public–private partnerships and collaboration are required for the successful commercialization of transformational ClimateTech. These diverse ecosystems and interrelationships must be aligned for deployments to achieve mass adoption.

Commercial viability amidst complex emergent ecosystems

ClimateTech has to provide solutions that address more than specific customer pain points. A start-up offering consumer or enterprise applications, software or technology is often simply relying on customers to purchase and use their applications, which can be relatively self-contained. Our greatest challenges require systemic transformative change, not isolated linear solutions.

For the energy transition and decarbonization, founders, businesses and investors must consider a broad set of stakeholders, partners and complex ecosystem interactions, raising the bar for viability. Achieving commercial viability is critical for effecting change at a systems level. Climate problems are complex. The broad set of possibilities multiply that complexity and the solutions themselves are uncertain.

To avoid the commercialization valley of death, ClimateTech has to problem-solve, then deploy, interact and scale emergently in the context of a hyperconnected systemic real world.

Levers for effective systemic change

Donella Meadows[11] taught us that applying shifts at the appropriate levels is the most effective way to trigger change in systems. Leverage will be strongest where the lever is highest – which often correlates with the challenge of implementation.

If we are to address our world's most critical challenges, effective responses need to prioritize high leverage points, where small interventions can result in large changes throughout the entire system.

Systems change is a multifaceted approach across many different points of leverage. Our responses must focus on changing the fundamental structures, culture and mental models below the surface:

- **Mental models:** The worldviews that sustain our beliefs, values or assumptions are the highest leverage points to drive systems change, but also the most difficult to achieve. True education begins on the playground, but is equally important in the boardroom.

- **Structures** produce adverse behaviours such as ineffective (even counterproductive) incentivization. Altering structures can establish which change arises. Aligned policymaking can drive relevant standards, bans, subsidies and investments.

Figure 6.4   Leverage points for effective change

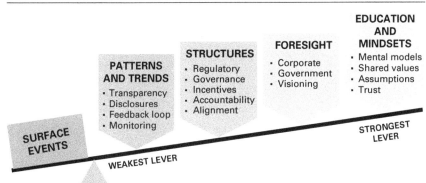

NOTE Inspired by D Meadows. Leverage points: Places to intervene in a system, Academy for Systems Change, The Donella Meadows Project, 1999. www.donellameadows.org/archives/leverage-points-places-to-intervene-in-a-system

- **Patterns and trends** can be monitored over time, with responses evaluated via feedback loops.
- **Surface-level interventions** offer the lowest leverage as they are less integrated in the system. These superficial initiatives are often devoid of enablers for any meaningful change.

Futures studies and systems thinking are instrumental to anticipating, identifying and pulling levers to enable widespread change across complex systems (Figure 6.4).

The initial levers are the strongest, but hardest to implement (mindset, vision, structures). Then, we move towards the weakest levers (observed trends and surface events).

Lever 1: Education and mindsets to transform mental models

Deeply held assumptions and generalizations are formed as children, then carried along when adults enter the workforce. Building resilience into society starts with education. Schooling needs to reframe failure, success and achievement. We must change our mindsets from instant gratification and conventional measures of success to more impactful and systemic mental models.

Trust is foundational to transformational change, but it is eroding quickly. Trust in each other, trust in science, trust yourself and trust that your actions can have an impact on the futures.

Lever 2: Foresight to build shared visions

A number of governments and organizations embrace foresight, which offers a collaborative framework and mindset. They understand how long-term orientation can build shared visions and challenge self-serving, short-term and misaligned governance.

Collective purpose plays an important role in building shared values with passion. This sense of purpose transforms mental models into action-oriented initiatives. *Culture change can forge shared expectations among a broader set of stakeholders as we break down silos.*

Some governments have developed an effective tradition of a structured approach to foresight. What countries like Canada, Finland and Singapore have in common is a longer timeframe and wider systemic lens compared to typical government mandates. They scan decades ahead to identify potential challenges and opportunities, experiment with innovative technologies and new methods, constantly explore emerging ideas and cultivate knowledge for society's benefit. These governments rank highly in education, healthcare, welfare and the environment. To be effective, government foresight must rely on an adaptive network approach, federating centres of excellence while avoiding the stifling effects of an overly centralized agency.

CASE STUDY   Corporate foresight – longitudinal analysis

Certain organizations use corporate foresight to actively explore, shape and manage longer-term futures. The process involves investigating the key drivers of change and next-order implications of potential decisions.

It is often difficult to establish the causal links between using corporate foresight and an organization's ultimate performance. In a study pioneered by Rohrbeck and the Aarhus School of Business and Social Sciences,[12] researchers developed a model to investigate the impact of corporate foresight on performance. Using data on corporate foresight maturity from 2008 and firm performance data from 2015, the researchers could investigate the impact of foresight strategy with a seven-year time lag.

The findings of this longitudinal study showed that participating firms classified as 'vigilant' in terms of future preparedness fared well compared to their peers:

- Vigilant firms were 33 per cent more profitable at EBITDA (earnings before interest, taxes, depreciation and amortization) level than the industry average.

- Additionally, these firms had more than 200 per cent higher average market capitalization growth than participating firms in general.

The seven-year time lag – which is a longer timeframe than many CEO tenures or the immediate concerns of boards – allowed long-term thinking strategies to take effect.

Lever 3: Design the underlying structures to incentivize the system

After rewiring mental models through education and shared visions, the next most powerful lever is to change the structure of incentives. Several initiatives can transform existing power structures that favour short-term fixes into incentive systems that encourage long-term thinking:

- **Sustainable innovation:** Consumers and stakeholders alike may be unforgiving to organizations that deplete resources and plunder the planet, so green practices could increasingly drive revenues. Green technologies, clean energy and smart resource usage will eventually reduce production and operation costs. Tomorrow, long-term thinking will attract and retain the most innovative employees.

- **Regulatory – government and tax policies:** Prototyping and testing breakthrough technologies with actual use cases can lay the groundwork for future regulatory frameworks. Supportive tax policies for capital gains, dividends and income can incentivize the reinvestment of funds into longer-term innovations, technology and employment – as opposed to dividend pay-outs, or the house-of-cards option of excessive share buy-backs.

- **Governance – mandatory formal metrics to measure and monitor:** The survival of society, humanity and our planet depends on anticipatory governance. Thoughtful metrics that measure and monitor the longer-term impacts are useful levers.

- **Compensation and incentives:** Organizations should design compensation with transparent performance metrics to justify how incentivization aligns with longer-term outcomes.

Note that subsidies can work both ways. They can incentivize environmentally friendly initiatives or drive adverse changes. For instance, the International Monetary Fund found that fossil fuel subsidies were a record $7 trillion in 2022 (7.1 per cent of GDP), a $2 trillion increase from 2020 due to government support amid rising energy prices.[13]

KEY POINTS
Incentives determine outcomes

CEO tenures often last less than five years, yet CEO pay is at an all-time high. This system prioritizes short-term gains, with incentives tied to immediate results. Decision-makers focused on the next few quarters may overlook longer-term consequences that don't impact their rewards.

Today, the entire reward system is built on short-term victories. Rewards include re-election, donations, new contracts, bonuses or promotions.

Revamping incentives to foster systems thinking is imperative. Present structures drive short-term and irresponsible actions, favouring choices that yield the most profitable options for decision-makers, not their broader stakeholders.

Lever 4: Disclosure to recognize patterns

Despite offering less leverage than changes at the levels of mental models or structures, disclosures are still helpful.

Whether they are financial, scientific, governmental or environmental, the most effective disclosures are consistent, comparable, reliable, clear, efficient and transparent. Continued progress is being made with climate-related disclosure requirements. More jurisdictions are requiring mandatory disclosures for large companies, including on their vulnerabilities to climate change.

Transparent disclosure and authentic communication can help anticipate what might arise and show stakeholders how an organization prioritizes longer-term strategic decision-making for effective success in our unpredictable world.

Dealing with wicked problems involves exploring interactions and feedback loops for positive leverage. Systems can self-regulate through feedback. Output from one interaction influences the next. It is difficult, if not impossible, to fully anticipate the possible outcomes from structural changes made to the system. *Feedback loops allow change monitoring over time, to recognize patterns and evaluate responses to achieve the desired effects.*

Anticipatory governance for complex challenges

Some considerations for organizations to build anticipatory governance capabilities to address our complex challenges:

- **Futures intelligence:** Diversify the scanning and signals. Interpret next-order impacts and connect the shifting dots with effective action triggers across systems. Challenge assumptions, especially given non-linearity and timeframes of complex systems.

- **Incentivizing the system:** Align leadership and decision-making among stakeholders, values and actions to unleash impactful changes. Governance systems and underlying incentives must be restructured to foster systems-level change. Organizations and their governance bodies need to better define, monitor and address extreme risks and opportunities.

- **Organizational resilience:** To survive and thrive through turbulence, build strategic resilience for climate change, cybersecurity, technological, infrastructure, health, space and geopolitical risks.

- **Business models:** Every aspect of business will require reconsideration to satisfy evolving requirements from a broad set of stakeholders, including employees, customers, investors and regulators.

- **Disclosure:** Radical transparency means information becomes available to everyone, offering a transparent picture on climate risk. Boards will have greater responsibilities in evaluating physical, liability and transition risks, as well as other disruptive paradigm shifts.

- **Evolving ESG landscapes and curbing greenwashing:** Stakeholders start focusing on substantiated ESG data instead of green marketing material. With climate disclosures, detailed evaluations of decarbonization strategies and climate policy become possible. Public markets may transition from focusing on portfolio allocations (as ESG inputs) to integrating impacts from the actual outcomes (as ESG outputs). The burden of proof, a new regulatory environment and climate litigation, will make it more difficult to mislead the public with false or unsubstantiated claims such as 'sustainable', 'net-zero', 'green', 'circular' or 'clean energy'.

Notes

1   D Meadows (2008) *Thinking in Systems: A primer*, Chelsea Green Publishing, White River Junction, VT

2   R Spitz and L Zuin (2023) *The Definitive Guide to Thriving on Disruption: Disruption as a springboard to value creation*, Disruptive Futures Institute, San Francisco, CA

3   E Musk. All our patent are belong to you, Tesla, 12 June 2014. www.tesla. com/blog/all-our-patent-are-belong-you (archived at https://perma.cc/L5ZG-K72V)

4   S E Page (2010) *Diversity and Complexity*, Princeton University Press, Princeton, NJ

5   R Spitz. 4 drivers to achieve systems-level change for sustainable futures, World Economic Forum, 31 October 2023. www.weforum.org/agenda/ 2023/10/systems-level-change-for-sustainable-futures/ (archived at https://perma.cc/CKD3-TQ7V)

6   M Gladwell (2019) *The Tipping Point: How little things can make a big difference*, Back Bay Books, Boston, MA

7   International Energy Agency. Renewables 2022, IEA, 2022. https://iea.blob. core.windows.net/assets/ada7af90-e280-46c4-a577-df2e4fb44254/ Renewables2022.pdf (archived at https://perma.cc/39CG-42PU)

8   Rocky Mountain Institute. X-change: Electricity, RMI, 2023. www.rmi.org/ wp-content/uploads/dlm_uploads/2023/07/rmi_x_change_electricity_2023.pdf (archived at https://perma.cc/3UMQ-Q4FH)

9   J C Mankins. Technology readiness levels, Artemis Innovation, 1995/2004. www.artemisinnovation.com/images/TRL_White_Paper_2004-Edited.pdf (archived at https://perma.cc/6RAH-XDGG)

10 J Jenkins and S Mansur. Bridging the clean energy valleys of death, Breakthrough Institute, November 2011. s3.us-east-2.amazonaws.com/ uploads.thebreakthrough.org/legacy/blog/Valleys_of_Death.pdf (archived at https://perma.cc/RMC3-RA4X)

11 D Meadows. Leverage points: Places to intervene in a system, Academy for Systems Change, The Donella Meadows Project, 1999. www.donellameadows. org/archives/leverage-points-places-to-intervene-in-a-system (archived at https://perma.cc/JP67-E32F)

12 R Rohrbeck, M E Kum, T Jissink and A V Gordon. Corporate foresight benchmarking report 2018: How leading firms build a superior position in markets of the future, SSRN Electronic Journal, 2018. dx.doi.org/10.2139/ ssrn.3178562 (archived at https://perma.cc/649T-6V86)

13 S Black, A A Liu, I Parry and N Vernon. IMF fossil fuels subsidies data: 2023 Update, IMF, 2023. www.imf.org/-/media/Files/Publications/WP/2023/English/ wpiea2023169-print-pdf.ashx (archived at https://perma.cc/6NTV-9NPB)

7
Greenaissance
Value creation for sustainable futures

OBJECTIVES
Greenaissance as a path to sustainable futures

In the face of climate risks, mitigation and building resilience are essential. Greenaissance, a green revolution fuelled by momentous innovation and investment across fields, offers a path towards a sustainable energy future.

Climate risks as the ultimate catalysts

The Anthropocene arrives faster than its ratification

The ultimate disruption would be an existential event so catastrophic that it leads to the extinction of humanity. We may not be able to prevent certain catastrophes; however, many are well within our society's control.

The term 'Anthropocene' describes a new geological epoch in which human beings and their profound impacts are the dominant forces on Earth. In this age, human activity is the most powerful influence, driving irreversible changes to the Earth's climate and environment while transforming humanity itself in the process. The most striking aspect of the Anthropocene is that the responsibility lies squarely with humanity.

Officially, we are still in the Holocene Epoch – the relatively warm period after the last glacial period, which ended around 11,700 years ago. Following the ice age, human species rapidly expanded worldwide, developing major civilizations.

While the ratification process to officially validate the Anthropocene Epoch is ongoing, our geological epoch seems distinct from Holocene. The formal timing still needs to be determined, but compelling arguments suggest the mid-twentieth century is a possible beginning to the Anthropocene (coinciding with the first atomic bomb in 1945 and subsequent Great Acceleration after World War II).

As we destabilize the planetary systems we rely on for survival, the strain on our planet mirrors that in societies. These imbalances reinforce each other.

Transformation is required, changing how we live, work and cooperate. We need new social norms, new values, more effective incentives, new measures of human development and cooperation with – not against – nature.

Sustainability and stewardship

It can feel like the world is behaving as if the climate challenge is too big to solve. Hope should come from the agency we have in relation to humanity's future, as it is firmly within our control (as long as we respond systemically to the interconnected challenges). Our obligation to the future is rooted in intergenerational stewardship; sustainability is the key expression of this responsibility.

The duality of climate change

The Renaissance was a period of philosophical, literary, artistic, cultural and economic 'rebirth' after the Middle Ages. We define Greenaissance as an era of renewal with momentous innovation and investment opportunities, aligned across fields with the common objective of sustainable energy transition.

This emerging Greenaissance era is an unprecedented opportunity to develop innovative solutions to the climate crisis.[1] Sustainable structural transformations are now expected by regulators, many investors and the next generation of customers. As decarbonization scales, it can reach a virtuous inflection point, becoming more cost-effective. The economic benefits could then exceed the transition costs.

Like many disruptions, the duality reveals contradictions. On the one hand, humanity faces many existential risks. On the other hand, we have the agency and necessity to seize emerging opportunities in this context.

The mitigation of and adaptation to the environmental crisis provides historic innovation opportunities for R&D, venture and institutional capital. Entrepreneurs globally must reinvent businesses with more sustainable models and lower resource usage. During the next decades, every organization will need to become an energy company as we regenerate our governance systems and priorities.

Every product, service and offering will come under scrutiny. Those companies that understand the radical changes ahead can adapt, innovate and prosper. Those who do not take a genuine, fundamental and systemic new approach will fail.

A Greenaissance era for sustainable futures

Below are six features of the Greenaissance era:

- **Accountability:** In a world of radical transparency and traceability, digressions from climate goals will stand out. Objective, measurable and comparable climate disclosure norms are emerging.

- **Acceleration and shifts:** Sustainability is the new digital. This is accelerating sectors like electric vehicles, renewable energy and plant-based alternatives. Adapting to evolving consumer preferences is no longer optional. Buckle up, because transitions are tough – but the journey can be rewarding as these shifts reach virtuous tipping points.

- **Resetting profit pools and assets:** Sustainability is a watershed phase for business models and returns. Leadership teams across all industries need to prepare for the rising frequency of extreme weather events, which pose a real threat to business continuity. The Greenaissance reset will leave laggards stranded and their assets written down, while others capture the emerging opportunities.

- **Reinvention and sandboxes:** Products, services and logistics need reinvention. Developing innovation 'sandboxes' to test emerging technologies in the real world will raise the rate of success. Operations need a rethink in a world where efficiency is measured by greenhouse emissions, circularity and regeneration.

- **Complex adaptive systems and cross-fertilization:** Tackling climate demands embracing complexity. Addressing climate challenges means weaving together converging technologies, where external changes in infrastructure, transport, supply chains and cities work in concert with strategic initiatives. BMaaS harness these interconnected ecosystems, fostering collaboration with partners who break down silos.

- **Distributed climate valleys:** The technological innovations that have shaped Silicon Valley – internet infrastructure, mobile applications and platforms – define its legacy. As we transition towards a greener future, climate opportunities will be more evenly distributed throughout the world. These new 'climate valleys' will drive breakthrough innovations across systems, leveraging on their natural resources, while combining software with physical products and infrastructure.

EXAMPLE
Brazil emerging as a Greenaissance leader

Supported by the right investments and policies, Brazil can emerge as a natural leader in ecological transformation. With its vast scale, robust industrial base, abundant natural resources and expertise in biofuels (such as biomethane), Brazil is well positioned to lead the climate transition. As a global leader in sustainable agriculture (top producer of coffee, sugarcane, ethanol, soybeans) and renewable energy sources (hydropower, wind, solar), Brazil could become a frontrunner in addressing climate change, all while respecting the rights of indigenous people to their ancestral land. However, it's crucial for Brazil to calibrate the balance between biofuel production and food security, as the former may not currently be a sustainable way to use fertile land.

Circular strategy and closed-loop business models

Companies aren't currently held responsible for the waste, pollution, resource scarcity, biodiversity loss and other externalities that they create and export. Future models could rectify these issues – and future regulation could penalize them.

The shift from heavy extraction to less resource-intensive business models births many opportunities. Zero-waste strategies design waste out of operations, repairing, reusing and recycling instead of relying on landfills. These business models have many different names and arrangements, but they all share a basis of circularity.

A circular basis for innovation

Economic circularity, or 'the circular economy', provides a framework to minimize resource use, extend product life cycles and proliferate regeneration opportunities across the globe.

We establish three principles to begin achieving these goals. First, design waste out of the system – consume fewer resources initially and create less waste after the product's life cycle. Waste itself becomes a design flaw. Second, create products that last longer and enable easier recycling and up-cycling through careful design. Third, commit to using renewable resources, which reduces environmental externalities.

These principles result in an economy that doesn't merely provide a product to an end consumer. Here, producers, consumers, reusers and even competitors work together to reduce our systems' waste, increase our products' longevity and revitalize the natural landscapes that envelop us.

EXAMPLE
KPIs for circular business models

Circular business models use specific key performance indicators (KPIs) that point to the sustainability and circularity of the company. A circular-oriented company can focus on KPIs such as:

- percentage of energy consumed from renewable sources
- percentage of recycled material used in production
- number of users who share products
- percentage of products that are repaired rather than discarded
- volume of products recollected through recycling programmes
- average lifetime of products

The doughnut economic model

Economist Kate Raworth conceptualized the doughnut economy as a response to humanity's ecological devastation. The model from *Doughnut Economics*[2] has two rings, an outer and an inner, similar to the profile of a doughnut when viewed from above.

The *outer* ring signifies our planet's tolerance threshold across nine different ceilings (climate change, ocean acidification, chemical pollution, nitrogen and phosphorus loading, freshwater withdrawals, land conversion, biodiversity loss, air pollution and ozone layer depletion). If this outer line is crossed, devastating ecological effects occur.

The *inner* ring represents the minimum essential safe and just space for humanity. Inspired by the UN's 17 Sustainable Development Goals, Raworth includes food, health, education, income and work, peace and justice, political voice, social equity, gender equality, housing, networks, energy and water. If this inner line is crossed, society descends into resource crises, lacking the basic necessities required to sustain life or social bases.

Rather than a general guideline for companies to follow, Raworth's model suggests that our world system is constantly teetering between ecological overshoot and shortfall. A balancing act between the two is required for humanity to survive and thrive.

By living circularly within this doughnut, bounded by the rings of overextension and shortfall, humanity can thrive without disasters.

EXAMPLE

Cities as a doughnut

Amsterdam was the birthplace of the stock market. Now, the city is rethinking how capitalism can be changed for the better through the doughnut economy. Amsterdam launched a series of initiatives, including the creation of sustainable artificial islands for housing, slightly higher prices to account for fair wages and carbon emission offsets and sustainability standards for the construction of buildings. Berlin, Brussels and other cities globally are also experimenting with the doughnut economic model.

The doughnut's boundaries provide an opportunity for organizations to recognize where they are operating within the model and how they might improve. Holistic models are required to tackle our immensely complex challenges and applying them to a city offers real-world use cases to learn from.

The MacArthur Butterfly offers a systems approach

A systems perspective is the only way to create effective circular and regenerative economic models.

The MacArthur Butterfly brings the circular model into great detail, using wing-like arrays of interconnections to illustrate the resource flows of a circular and regenerative economy.[3] However, the Butterfly model does more than just illustrate the circular economy. Its arrows depict solutions to many issues that plague circularity, emphasizing the importance of reintegrating materials back into the system before they are externalized as waste.

In circularity, resources that leave the system before being adequately reused and recycled are known as 'leakage'. The MacArthur model illustrates how to best avoid leakage with its dual-sided, cascading stock and resource flows, clearly marking paths they can follow before exiting the system. These include sharing, maintaining/prolonging, reusing/redistributing, refurbishing/remanufacturing and recycling.

EXAMPLE
Biosphere-aligned products

Imagine clothes woven from seaweed, packaging that sprouts from bamboo and fuel generated from algae. Renewable and abundant resources can integrate natural circularity into our economy. The Butterfly model touts the importance of using biosphere-oriented renewable products in the production process. However, these innovations can't take hold unless adequate synergies and ecosystems facilitate them. Without a business and regulatory ecosystem that promotes these regenerative products, the status quo will remain the norm.

Drawbacks of basic circular models

Limitations of the circular economy include returning of products, heavy resource extraction, transition costs, product cannibalization and systemic leakages. The criticism of basic circular models does not deflect from the need to eliminate the waste from harmful extractive and single-use economies. Rather, it reinforces the need to understand current structural challenges and how to address them.

One of circularity's biggest challenges relates to the practicalities, costs and logistics of returning and sharing products. Effective logistics and altering habits are essential to nearly every circularity model, but can be difficult due to friction in the processes and the stubborn momentum of current behaviours. Studies have found that renting clothes can be worse for the environment than throwing them away, given transportation and dry cleaning.[4] *Buying fewer items and using them longer is still the greenest approach – better for the environment than recycling or renting.*

Finally, the pervasive use of modern technology like smartphones, computers and lithium-ion batteries makes it difficult to omit them. This threatens the impact of circular systems that would normally reduce or eliminate such resource-intensive products. Instead, strategies of extended lifespans, effective recycling and responsible sourcing can contribute to a more impactful circular approach.

Segmenting the Greenaissance opportunities

Some people believe that we can change the climate to combat climate change. Geoengineering manipulates environmental processes that affect climate. From China to India and the UAE, cloud-seeding, which provokes rain to benefit vulnerable agriculture regions, clears air pollution and ensures clearer skies for major events, is gaining traction as a potential tool for managing the weather and environmental challenges. China has invested billions of dollars in weather manipulation technologies, including cloud-seeding. In the US, start-up Make Sunsets may have released reflective sulphur particles into the atmosphere, hoping to cool the Earth.[5] While geoengineering technologies are being developed to mitigate climate change, society must consider the ethical implications, environmental risks and robust international governance frameworks.

Significant advancements in solar power, batteries, nuclear energy, green hydrogen and more are fuelling a shift away from extractive business models. Meanwhile, deforestation, overfishing and coral reef destruction are major drivers of species extinction. Corporate R&D and start-ups are seeking to tackle biodiversity conservation head-on, from coral reef regrowth to using AI-guided drones with seed pods for land reforestation (Figure 7.1).

Climate intelligence and emissions

To date, much of the climate focus has been on mitigation, to reduce the extent and pace of future climate change by reducing emissions.

Climate intelligence seeks to understand the extent of climate risk for the world's critical assets, with the goal of bringing practical solutions to not only mitigate risks, but to also build resilient adaptation.

Figure 7.1 Segmenting the Greenaissance opportunities

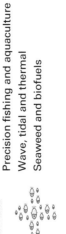

Alt everything
Farm management

Circular and regenerative
Next-gen textiles
Biodegradable and waste

Electric and autonomous
Battery and charging
Low-emission transport
Urbanization

AGTECH AND FOODTECH

CONSUMER AND RETAIL

MOBILITY AND TRANSPORT

INDUSTRIAL AND RAW MATERIALS

Cement and chemicals
Metals and mining

CLIMATE INTELLIGENCE AND EMISSIONS

GREEN ENERGY

BLUETECH

Adaptation and resilience
Risk evaluation and reporting
Monitoring and remote sensing
Carbon offsetting and markets
Carbon capture and storage

Energy production
Storage
Smart grids

Marine management and energy
Precision fishing and aquaculture
Wave, tidal and thermal
Seaweed and biofuels

The climate intelligence and emissions segment includes:

- carbon capture and storage (CCS)
- climate risk, adaptation and resilience
- data insights, climate intelligence, climate-related evaluation and disclosure
- monitoring and remote sensing (drones, satellites, sensors)
- carbon offsetting tools and marketplaces
- sustainability ratings, carbon accounting, disclosure and reporting (software-as-a-service)
- virtual power plant software

Carbon capture and storage

Current decarbonization pathways include CO_2 removal from the atmosphere. CCS traps, isolates and stores CO_2 at the source of its emission. Significant infrastructure is being experimented with, such as the use of huge tunnel networks to trap carbon dioxide underground. Pioneering Climeworks launched the world's largest direct air capture and storage plant in Iceland in 2021 and is continuing to build scale. In addition to institutional investors, governments are also investing heavily in CCS, exemplified by the United States' $3.5 billion programme.

While removing greenhouse gas from the air is increasingly seen as necessary (along with radical emission cuts), carbon removal technologies are nascent. Many proposed CCS technologies remain untested, raising concerns about their cost, scalability and feasibility. In any event, CCS is not a reason to continue emitting.

Climate-related disclosures and ratings

Regulators globally are requiring climate-related disclosures. The focus is on the material impacts of climate risks, greenhouse gas emissions, climate risk management and governance, climate-related metrics in audited financial statements and goals.

An example of tangible policy action is the EU's own 'Green Deal'. Among a wide variety of initiatives, the plan mandates comprehensive environmental and social risk disclosures by large and listed companies.[6] As these rules go into effect and the first reports are published in 2025, Europe takes a step towards enforcing transparency and accountability in corporate sustainability.

Disclosures and ratings will require insightful interpretation of data, effective use of technology and deep understanding of supply chains.

Climate intelligent decision-making

Our changing climate throws unprecedented challenges at urban planning. From vulnerable buildings and outdated utilities to threatened parks and disrupted transport, cities must transform to become resilient. This demands rethinking everything from initial design to ongoing operations and adapting infrastructure to withstand floods, heatwaves and rising sea levels. Even critical healthcare facilities need reimagining.

An organization is only as strong as its most vulnerable point. Stretching across the globe, international supply chains that enable nearly $20 trillion of trade annually are especially vulnerable to climate hazards. Supply chains are often optimized for low cost, not resiliency. One extreme weather event affecting a single factory could create ripple effects felt throughout the entire supply chain.

CASE STUDY   Decision-useful disclosures

Decision-useful and comparable disclosures can support addressing the major climate risks. They provide better visibility on the carbon footprint of emitters and report how well organizations are prepared for the strategic and financial impacts of a warming world:

- **The emergence of climate intelligence:** Climate analytics, agronomics and weather data are driving demand for climate intelligence solutions. Companies like ClimateAI, Climavision, Google's GraphCast, Jupiter Intelligence and Mitiga Solutions are enabling organizations to understand their exposure to climate risk and make climate-intelligent decisions to protect their assets.

- **Climate-related reporting and carbon management:** Emissions management and specialized carbon reporting companies such as ClearTrace, Persefoni and Watershed benefit from the increasing climate disclosure requirements.

- **Sustainability ratings:** Technology can enable ratings on ESG issues. One particular regulatory focus is the smaller private business, which represents a significant part of the supply chains for large global companies. EcoVadis provides trusted ratings to monitor and improve the sustainability performance of businesses and their trading partners.

Green energy

Affordable low-carbon and clean energy generation continues to be a strong focus of investors. Innovative companies include Commonwealth Fusion Systems (fusion energy), Form Energy (energy storage), Quaise Energy (geothermal) and TAE Tech (fusion power).

Established renewable energy technologies like solar and wind are becoming increasingly affordable and efficient. Meanwhile, novel approaches offer new exciting possibilities, like deeper geothermal systems and fusion energy.

Broadly, the green energy segment includes:

- energy production with next-gen nuclear, green hydrogen, ocean, hydropower, solar, wind, biomass, geothermal
- energy storage
- smart grid management systems
- heating, ventilation and air conditioning (HVAC) and efficient building systems

These are all areas where policymakers can be aligned with the private sector to change the status quo.

Energy and long-duration storage

Cost-effective, reliable, long-duration batteries are critical to circumvent the variability of wind and solar. Significant investments are going into rechargeable 'iron-air' batteries to achieve these breakthroughs. The attributes sought in the next generation of batteries include faster charging, greater energy densities, improved reusability and responsible sourcing. A key objective of innovations in energy storage technologies is to build a stable grid based on renewables – without coal, oil or gas.

Nuclear fusion

Global initiatives seek nuclear fusion as a carbon-free energy solution. By merging two atoms instead of splitting them, emission-free energy could be harnessed. The long promise of fusion as a green energy technology may be approaching commercial reality as it receives significant funding. Dozens of companies and research organizations are developing fusion to generate more energy than is consumed (net positive energy fusion). While recent breakthroughs could pave the way to commercial nuclear fusion, this might still be decades away.

Green hydrogen

Hydrogen combustion offers a promising alternative to fossil fuels for vehicles, aviation and industrial processes where electrification is difficult. While most hydrogen today is produced using fossil fuels, several technologies are being developed to generate 'green hydrogen' using renewable energy, particularly electrolysis powered by solar or wind power.

Recognizing this potential, in 2024 the European Union approved €6.9 billion in funding to accelerate green hydrogen infrastructure. Beyond early mover Germany, several countries have developed hydrogen-powered passenger trains, including Austria, China, Japan, the Netherlands and the US. India plans to become a 'global hub for green hydrogen', supporting refineries and fertilizer plants with the aim of producing five million metric tonnes per annum by 2030. Although India has a relatively low per capita energy consumption, its economic growth coupled with the burgeoning population means that energy demand has begun to skyrocket. During COP28, dozens of countries launched the Clean Hydrogen Declaration of Intent, to work toward recognition of hydrogen certification schemes.

CASE STUDY   Can green hydrogen change the aviation game?

The global aviation industry alone generates between 2 and 3 per cent of carbon emissions. Given that consumers and businesses alike seem unlikely to give up air travel any time soon, the development of viable low-carbon fuel alternatives presents an enormous opportunity.

- **Airbus aims to develop zero-emission aircraft by 2035**: Airbus began testing hydrogen combustion technologies to demonstrate the technology's usability in planes as part of its ZEROe project. Delta signed a memorandum with Airbus to partner on the R&D of hydrogen-powered aircraft.

- **Rolls-Royce's hydrogen-powered engine**: Rolls-Royce ran an aircraft engine on hydrogen in what was presented as a world first for the aerospace industry.

- **New entrants**: ZeroAvia is developing an electrical aircraft that uses hydrogen fuel cells. Although this technology is currently heavy and thus restrictive for aviation, further weight reductions are expected. ZeroAvia's successful test flight with a 19-seat aircraft demonstrates this technology's potential.

While hydrogen-powered aeroplanes face challenges like infrastructure gaps, storage limitations, cost and safety concerns, significant investments and R&D aim to overcome them.

BlueTech

Investment in the blue economy is significant. BlueTech focuses on developing innovative water-based technologies that work within and utilize the ocean and marine systems for various purposes.

BlueTech serves to unlock the vast potential of Earth's water for renewable energy, food security and sustainable development, across the following activities:

- ocean energy, including offshore, wave, tidal, thermal
- marine seaweed farms for biofuel production
- aquatic-based CCS systems
- sustainable food production, such as aquaculture and AI-powered precision fishing for reduced bycatch
- marine robotics, ocean mapping and river-monitoring drones
- seabed mining (resource extraction from the ocean floor)

These technologies aim to improve the sustainability of the blue economy by enabling responsible resource utilization and minimizing environmental impact while harnessing our water system's benefits.

Deep-sea mining could provide critical minerals for green technologies like batteries and wind turbines. However, it has potential environmental impacts on the fragile deep-sea ecosystem. Further research is needed to understand its consequences.

CASE STUDY   Mapping and tracking the ocean

Multiple ocean mapping projects are in various stages of execution. The gradual completion of these ocean maps will aid socially responsible companies in achieving sustainability-related goals. For instance, ocean-mapping geographic information system (GIS) software and accompanying AI could help plan the optimal place for an offshore wind farm.

The rollout of 5G allows drones to trace the movement of different types of plastic through various bodies of water. AI can power the algorithms that tracking software relies on. Ellipsis.earth is a UK company that utilizes machine learning to identify and track plastic pollution. They are creating a global database of types of plastic waste found in our oceans, rivers and beaches, providing transparency and crucial insights to build innovative solutions.

Industrial and raw materials

Covering many sectors and production processes, the industrial and raw materials segment of Greenaissance includes:

- cement and chemicals
- plastics
- metals and mining
- 3D printing, robotics and smart manufacturing

Cement and chemicals

Greenhouse gas emissions are not isolated to a single sector, but there are a few industries that produce more CO_2 than many others, such as the cement industry. Sustainable alternatives for buildings and housing can significantly reduce emissions.

The chemicals industry, worth $5 trillion, is a major consumer of oil and gas and has a hefty carbon footprint from decades of resource-intensive practices. Developing technologies offer a more sustainable future for the chemicals industry. US company Solugen leverages biology to manufacture a range of sustainable chemicals, from fertilizers to corrosion inhibitors. Their bio-based method ditches fossil fuels and avoids the hazardous waste streams that plague traditional petrochemical processes.

Plastics

Plastics represent a complex environmental challenge. According to the Center for International Environmental Law, over 99 per cent of plastics are derived from fossil fuel sources. This contributes significantly to global carbon emissions and the climate impacts will continue to grow if current trends continue. Plastics also pose a severe threat to biodiversity, as their ubiquity and persistence in the environment leads to widespread microplastic pollution in water and soil. Developing bio-based alternatives could reduce dependency on traditionally manufactured plastics, such as London-based Notpla, which produces packaging from seaweed.

Circular approaches to reduce and reuse plastics could address humanity's current overconsumption. Jurisdictions globally are beginning to regulate plastics, but some propositions, such as the UN's treaty to reduce plastic pollution, run into staunch opposition from fossil fuel lobbyists. Further, the plastic-based products that already exist – from bags to tires – could take centuries to fully decompose.

3D printing

Instead of designing a specific product for years then shipping it for finalized production, digital manufacturing enables smaller, on-demand production runs. Furthermore, shared 3D printers (for businesses or residential communities) may allow products to be printed very close to their final destination, bypassing shipping by starting in the 'last mile'. Relatively large personal printers may also become a reality. The dematerialized nature of digital manufacturing means that anyone will be able to print anything, whenever they want. Affordable housing and steel bridges are already being built using 3D printing. *3D printing may give us the ability to produce objects more sustainably.*

CASE STUDY   Concrete solutions for housing

Globally, concrete is the second most consumed material after water. Twice as much concrete is used in construction than all other building materials combined. Making concrete uses cement, which contributes to around 7 per cent of global annual CO_2 emissions.

Decarbonization must address the infrastructure construction supply chain, which relies on carbon-intensive materials including cement. Engineered cementitious materials can have a much lower carbon footprint:

- **Sustainable cement:** Terra CO2, a Colorado-based technology company, is developing a low-CO_2, sustainable and cost-competitive alternative cement without compromising on strength or durability. Once scaled, TerraCO2's material is projected to reduce cement emissions by over 50 per cent. In the UK, Cambridge engineers have invented the first zero-emissions cement.

- **3D-printed essential structures:** To address the chronic issue of classroom and housing shortages in Malawi, construction company LafargeHolcim is implementing large-scale 3D printing technology to build schools and houses in record time. According to Holcim, this type of production also comes with a significant reduction in climate impact (up to 70 per cent), largely due to less cement, transport and construction waste.

Given that cement production generates three times more carbon than the aviation industry, developing scalable and cost-competitive eco-friendly concrete could significantly reduce the environmental impact of the construction sector.

Mobility and transport

Transportation contributes roughly 30 per cent of total greenhouse gas emissions in the US. This staggering figure is largely attributable to our reliance on fossil fuels, from cars and trucks to ships, trains and planes. Over 90 per cent of the fuel used for transportation comes from petroleum sources.[7]

Key growth drivers supporting greener mobility include government incentives like favourable regulations, policies and subsidies, alongside major initiatives across the mobility and transport segments:

- electric, green mobility and autonomous transportation
- batteries, charging technologies and recycling
- micromobility, shared mobility and mass rapid transit
- low-emission planes, trains and maritime
- urbanization, smart cities, ecology of cities, green buildings

The energy transition cannot be achieved without reinventing transportation.

Next-gen vehicles

Automakers and new entrants are racing to invest in electric vehicles (EVs). Analysts predict that EVs could capture half of all new car sales in the US within a decade. Similar trajectories are expected in China and other major markets. However, for EVs to truly scale, challenges like cost reduction, faster and resilient charging, widespread charger deployment and consistent infrastructure maintenance must be addressed.

These breakthroughs can pave the way for a greener future of transportation, but EVs will not resolve the challenges of car dependence and congestion.

Rail and hyperloop transit

Bullet and high-speed trains are commonplace in Japan, China and Europe, but still have room to revolutionize transit elsewhere. Despite the challenges of the Hyperloop project, there are signs of funding support for high-speed electric rail routes on the US West Coast, but these are early days.

Future air mobility: Flying cars

Many automotive and aerospace groups are developing electric vertical take-off and landing (eVTOL) aircrafts, catering for mobility services like aerial ridesharing. In parallel, the regulatory environment and infrastructure for landing pads are getting ready to take off.

Airbus is developing its own version as a 'multicopter'. CityAirbus NextGen is an electric and winged four-seat eVTOL that has a range of 80 km and can cruise at 120 km/h. Boeing is backing Wisk Aero, a four-seater autonomous eVTOL air taxi. United Airlines has invested in and partnered with Eve Air Mobility, the electric aviation start-up of aircraft manufacturer Embraer in Brazil, while Delta Air Lines partnered with and invested in Joby Aviation. Today, there are hundreds of eVTOL start-ups, such as Volocopter in Germany, which claims the world's first-ever eVTOL suite with passenger air taxis and heavy-lift cargo drones, or the Chinese Xpeng.

Consumer and retail

Many people, especially younger generations who will shape tomorrow's markets, are increasingly favouring businesses with deep environmental commitments and gradually moving away from unsustainable practices. Despite the rise of fast fashion, eco-friendly consumers are seeking out products, services and even workplaces with environmental responsibility.

To respond to these paradigm shifts, the consumer and retail segment is developing across:

- circular and regenerative business models
- biodegradable and sustainable packaging
- next-gen textiles
- waste management and recycling

Recycling and closed-loop systems allow a more sustainable production and consumption cycle. Moving away from the linear extractive production models (take, make, consume, waste) reduces emissions. Reusing products and materials is an effective alternative to disposing of them.

Innovations constantly emerge from circular models, including new sustainable materials created from biological processes. Designer Stella McCartney unveiled mycelium-based clothing with leather made of fungi. Adidas, Lululemon and Hermes work with start-ups Bolt Threads and MycoWorks to develop products with leather derived from bio-based materials grown by recycling waste. Beyond the headlines, we need scrutiny to ensure initiatives are genuinely impactful (versus simply a PR stunt). Synthetic biology in fashion is also particularly susceptible to the volatility of investor appetite.

AgTech and FoodTech

'We shall escape the absurdity of growing a whole chicken in order to eat the breast or wing, by growing these parts separately under a suitable medium.' It took almost a century from Winston Churchill's visionary prediction in 1931 to the first commercial sales of lab-grown meat. While not yet widely available in supermarkets worldwide, cultured meat promises a potential alternative to traditional meat production.

Tomorrow's beef and dairy industries may face the same existential challenges as today's fossil fuel industry.

Our ability to achieve climate goals critically hinges on transforming the way we produce and consume food. Ultimately, this involves halting and reversing deforestation caused by agricultural expansion, minimizing methane emissions from livestock, promoting sustainable farming practices and developing climate-friendly protein alternatives.

Waste and biodiversity loss remain key challenges for society. Closed-loop systems in agriculture aim to minimize waste (such as farm-to-table or composting) and reduce the negative impacts of human activities on soil health. Land degradation caused by pollution and unsustainable practices diminishes soil quality and nutrients. Organic processes like anaerobic digestion, where bacteria break down organic matter into renewable energy sources, offer ways to manage waste and revitalize degraded soils.

The AgTech and FoodTech segment reflects these objectives across:

- food innovation and food security
- alternative protein, meat and dairy

- deforestation, farm management, precision and vertical farming
- yield optimization, food waste
- methane inhibitors

Alt-protein: Making a meal out of it?

Beyond important animal welfare considerations, the environment is at stake. Together, food, agriculture and water is the largest category of global emissions, generating around a quarter of all global emissions.[8] Meat accounts for over half of all greenhouse gases from food production, in addition to substantial water usage.[9]

Alternative protein (alt-protein) products can offer nutritional benefits to consumers and be drastically better for the environment in terms of land used, water consumed and carbon emitted throughout production and transportation. There are hundreds of innovative alt-protein start-ups. Well-known companies include Beyond Meat, Impossible Foods, NotCo, Perfect Day, Believer Meats and Nature's Fynd.

The cow is facing its own existential crisis, as industrial cattle farming is disrupted by alt-proteins and plant-based milks.

Creating nutritious foods out of alt-protein ingredients is nothing new. However, making those alternatives comparable to conventional meats is more difficult due to the challenges of cost-effectiveness at scale and consumer preferences.

Growth in vertical farming

Growing crops indoors in stacked layers creates a controlled agricultural environment, driving yields through artificial light and climate control. Vertical farming grows produce without land, using significantly less water than outdoor agriculture, while yielding multiple times what conventional farming does. Walmart has invested in vertical farming start-up Plenty as part of its strategy to improve freshness, limit waste and promote sustainability.

The concept of indoor vertical farming is being applied beyond food production. This includes growing crops for medicinal uses and raising insects like mealworms, crickets and black soldier flies for pet food, plant nutrition and even human consumption. Two billion people around the world already enjoy the nutritional benefits of edible insects. Compared to livestock, insect farming requires significantly less space, releases fewer emissions and can even thrive on organic waste.

KEY POINTS
Alt-protein and alt-uncertainty

Change is always messy and uncertain; the emerging alt-protein world is no exception. Not everything marketed as plant-based is necessarily addressing the climate and biodiversity crisis. Education, science and climate oversight must offer the scrutiny needed to discern between impactful ventures and alt-marketing ploys. While investments grew considerably over the past few years, market valuations were severely hit. Capital is cyclical, becoming more scarce as consumers become more price-sensitive. As meat substitute players feel the chill, even the largest processors made U-turns; JBS closed its US-based Planterra Foods (plant-based meat business) after just two years of operation. Ultimately, consumers will decide on the future of these fields, depending on the quality, taste and price.

For organizations and consumers alike, climate is a cost–benefit analysis where economics matter.

Technology can support sustainability

Technology enables an increasingly transparent and traceable world. Maybe one day, a global intelligence will measure all the waste generated, from organizations to individuals. Insofar as the right safeguards are adhered to, technology has the potential to support in mitigating greenwashing and incentivizing sustainable practices in our supply chains (Figure 7.2).

Combining technologies to enforce sustainability

The growing network of 5G-powered sensors, combined with high-resolution satellite and drone imagery, is giving rise to innovative projects that monitor environmental violations, from illegal fishing to gas flares.

Earth observation plays a crucial role across fields, from validating claims made in carbon credit markets to forest management. AI is changing how scientists manage wildfire risks, to predict where fires are most likely, prioritize areas for controlled burns and deploy resources more effectively. Globally, wildfires are estimated to cost hundreds of billions in economic losses annually, a figure projected to rise. Combinatory technologies can

Figure 7.2   Converging technologies enforce sustainability

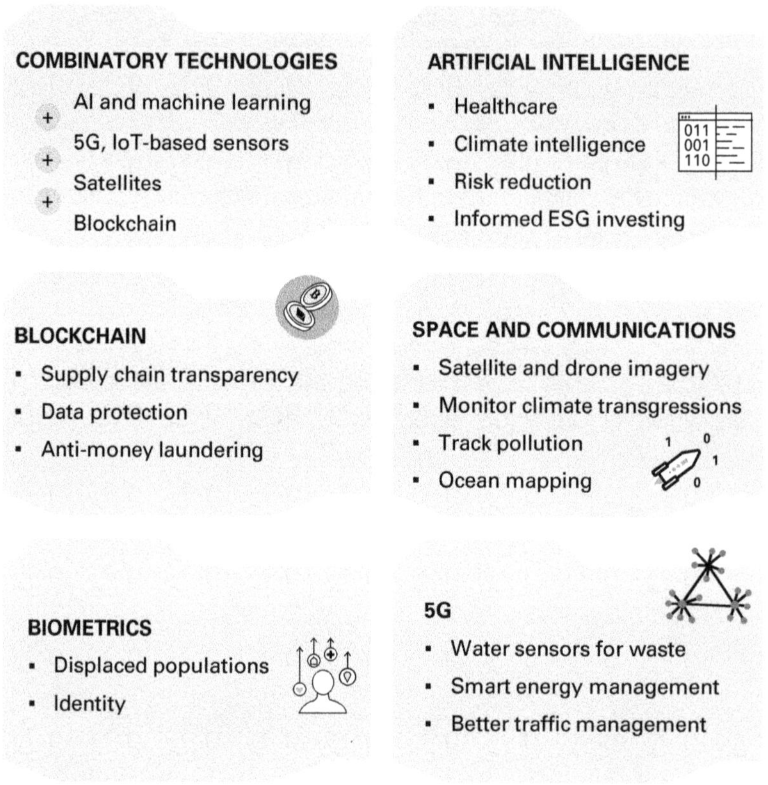

COMBINATORY TECHNOLOGIES

- AI and machine learning
+
- 5G, IoT-based sensors
+
- Satellites
+
- Blockchain

ARTIFICIAL INTELLIGENCE

- Healthcare
- Climate intelligence
- Risk reduction
- Informed ESG investing

BLOCKCHAIN

- Supply chain transparency
- Data protection
- Anti-money laundering

SPACE AND COMMUNICATIONS

- Satellite and drone imagery
- Monitor climate transgressions
- Track pollution
- Ocean mapping

BIOMETRICS

- Displaced populations
- Identity

5G

- Water sensors for waste
- Smart energy management
- Better traffic management

---

also help detect household water leaks or optimize agriculture water usage, while eco-certification organizations can improve their observance, traceability and enforcement.

Technology to support clean supply chains

Hidden environmental costs embedded in complex supply chains are often overlooked due to a lack of transparency, such as deforestation or water pollution. When data on these externalities remains obscured, companies are less likely to be held accountable. The increasing affordability of traceability technologies and implementation of digital material passports will allow businesses to integrate this crucial information into their decision-making processes, enabling them to reduce their environmental footprint and build trust with stakeholders. Investors are also beginning to seek proof of clean supply chains as part of their ESG requirements.

Geospatial analytics can combine location data with AI to monitor movements, activities and undiscovered risks at facilities across the world. This degree of transparency creates end-to-end supply chain visibility. Blockchain can add additional transparency and validate whether companies are complying with the right initiatives and suppliers.

Technology's limitations for environmental sustainability

Technology has limitations and constraints. We need appropriate safeguards, regardless of how beneficial its use can be in mitigating climate change.

Technology can highlight transgressions by enabling transparency and traceability of key elements of sustainability (e.g. supply chains). *However, technology does not address the root causes of environmental problems systemically.*

Privacy and trust

Privacy is critically important. How is data used and by whom? Reliability, security, compliance with data laws and cybersecurity are essential to trust, especially when everything becomes interconnected (from EVs to smart cities).

The rapid development of AI requires anticipatory governance and regulatory oversight. Failure to do so would shatter trust in the technologies, if it transpired that there were gaps in transparency, safety or ethical standards.

Negative environmental impacts

From the local environmental impact caused by heavy metal mining to the global climate effects from energy use, modern technologies aren't always aligned with the environment. The energy consumption of internet cloud and edge infrastructure, data centres and communications networks can be significant. Meanwhile, satellites used for Earth monitoring create space congestion and debris. Responsible governance can help mitigate these issues.

Many materials used for solar panels leave significant waste in sub-Saharan Africa and elsewhere because it can be cheaper to produce new solar panels than to recycle them. Solar panel waste, often hazardous and piled in dumps, is a by-product of the scaling of solar energy. More effective regulation and incentives to design solar power in anticipation of this type of waste would be beneficial.

No silver bullets

While the scale of venture and strategic funding for climate is encouraging, reliance on specific technologies as a silver bullet for climate change is naive. As technologies scale, raw material shortages and price volatility pose a challenge. Clean energy technologies can be more mineral-intensive than fossil fuel technologies. Their production can damage the environment and human lives, given poor governance standards in certain regions. Congo is the world's largest cobalt producer, and there is no such thing as 'clean' cobalt mining from the country.[10]

KEY POINTS
AI and environmental sustainability

Despite growing attention to social and ethical implications, environmental sustainability remains insufficiently explored in the discourse surrounding AI.

Kate Crawford's *The Atlas of AI* exposes the double-edged nature of even the most promising technologies.[11] By dissecting the complex supply chain of machine learning, she reveals how the digital economy relies heavily on the Earth's physical resources. Mineral extraction for hardware used in beneficial AI applications (like water waste monitoring) comes at a cost: water pollution. Training complex AI models consumes significant energy. The more powerful the models and larger the data sets, the greater the negative environmental externalities.

As with many of the paradoxes of our UN-VICE world, technology's energy consumption contributes to the climate crisis, while many emission reduction pathways are dependent on them.

Investments, policy and sustainable value creation

Follow the money, not the theatrics

There is increasing momentum around sustainability, with a constant flow of new initiatives and an even greater news flow. In a world of short attention spans, we run the risk of confusing surface-level marketing with substantive implementations.

Unfortunately, press releases alone do not rescue us from the climate cliff. Theatrics don't mitigate existential risks. Green products are in demand now more than ever, so companies are eager to broadcast the sustainability of their products, whether their claims are true or not. Ultimately, only by understanding the incentives and following the money flows can we substantiate the effectiveness of purported initiatives and enforce accountability.

To avoid falling off the cliff, we must adopt systemic solutions, aligning both public policy and private strategies to radically – and rapidly – transform the economy. Wall Street self-regulating its own proclaimed ESG strategies may not be enough to really effect changes below the surface. Banks financed trillions of dollars in fossil fuels in the five years following the Paris Agreement. There is a clear disconnect between practice and rhetoric.

While younger generations fight for their future, shareholders wield power by challenging companies that lack a cohesive plan to transition to cleaner energy sources.

The dangerous U-turns on commitments

Many of the world's largest asset managers do not plan to end new fossil fuel investments or back climate change proposals. Some early ESG lobbyists, including BlackRock, are now lobbying the SEC to change their climate risk tracking and disclosure plans. As with many topics in our UN-VICE era, ESG is not immune from contradictions.

A 2022 analysis by Professor Aviel Verbruggen estimated that the fossil fuel industry generated around $52 trillion in profits since the 1970s.[12] This translates to an average daily profit of about $3 billion, as reported by Damian Carrington in *The Guardian*.[13]

In that context, it is no surprise that many oil states, governments, policymakers and investors follow the money generated by the oil industry – that is where their returns, votes, donations and incentives come from.

Ten financial actors own half of all carbon emissions

According to a paper published in *Environmental Innovation and Societal Transitions*, just 200 companies own 98 per cent of the world's known fossil fuel reserves and 10 global financial institutions effectively own half of all potential future carbon emissions.[14] The decisions of these 10 organizations will literally determine the future of any sustainable transition. The 10 institutions are BlackRock, Vanguard Group, State Street Corp, Dimensional Fund Advisors, Fidelity Investments, Capital Group Company, India's State Government and Life Insurance Corporation, the Kingdom of Saudi Arabia and Norway's Norges Bank.

These organizations, as well as the world's major financial institutions, all play a decisive role in decarbonization.

While the potential for the Greenaissance is undoubtedly enormous, we cannot ignore that the greatest barrier to the energy transition is the oil sector itself, the financial institutions supporting it and the governments more interested in the status quo of climate change than change itself.

The real ESG debate

Incentive structures drive ESG investing. Structurally, public market investors focus on incentives that maximize their financial returns, even while accounting for ESG inputs. By regulating and incentivizing actual impact-focused outcomes, investors might alter their strategies towards these new rewards.

The fight against climate change is an opportunity for banks, financial institutions and ratings agencies to develop a new marketing product, a new green bond and a new net-zero tracker index fund. This is when greenwashing meets greedwashing.

The current lack of accountability for companies and boards means that real progress on the energy transition is not sufficiently incentivized. Similar to other major societal issues, ESG is often weaponized for political gain. Politicization leads to caution, polarization, backlash and even litigation. This fosters the perception that ESG prioritizes ideology and enforcement over tangible rewards.

Net-zero emissions are not compatible with net-zero incentives.

The duty of care for sustainable futures

Global regulators are now starting to prosecute false ESG claims while enforcing closer alignment between executive pay and climate risks.

Younger generations and institutions are now taking legal action, with some successes, such as in Australia, France and Germany. In these cases waged against corporations and governments, future generations argue they should not be forced to live in a deteriorated world due to carbon emissions. Meanwhile, shareholders of certain oil companies are suing the directors for their personal liability in failing to prepare for net-zero.

Courts are starting to recognize that governments and companies owe a duty of care to future generations.

Climate change mitigation requires policy and capital

The two prerequisites for climate change mitigation are policy and capital. Both of these are more prevalent than ever, but still require greater determination, alignment, scale and speed. Hundreds of billions will be invested to enable regenerative transformations. *As sustainable becomes the new digital, it will drive impact and value creation.*

Energy insecurity

Russia's invasion of Ukraine in 2022, the subsequent sanctions, the spike in oil prices and the global energy crisis was a catalyst to revisiting energy reliances. Beyond the human tragedy, this geopolitical event provided an inflection point for energy security.

The International Energy Agency (IEA) subsequently published a 10-point plan to reduce the European Union's Reliance on Russian natural gas, which could drive the energy transition with renewable projects, accelerating energy efficiency in buildings and industry and efforts to diversify and decarbonize power sources.[15]

How the world moves forward in the face of ongoing geopolitical reshuffling will define energy security and the Greenaissance opportunity.

OKRs for climate action

Andy Grove, an early employee of Intel who led the company as CEO for decades, created a system to drive execution called objectives and key results (OKRs). John Doerr, a former Intel employee and venture capitalist, has spread the gospel of OKRs to make leadership teams accountable. In *Speed and Scale: An action plan for solving our climate crisis now*,[16] Doerr identifies the measurable OKRs needed to arrive at net-zero by 2050:

- **Electrify transportation:** Switch from gasoline and diesel engines to electric bikes, cars, trucks and buses.
- **Decarbonize the grid:** Replace fossil fuels with solar, wind and other zero-emission sources.

- **Protect nature:** End deforestation and protect oceans, peatlands and grasslands.
- **Clean up industry:** Find cleaner ways to make cement and steel.
- **Fix food:** Change how agriculture is carried out today as well as personal habits, diets, cooking and waste management.
- **Remove carbon:** Win politics and policy, turn movements into action, innovate and invest.

While the private sector is crucial to solving climate change, energy transition can only be achieved through ecosystem synergies with public organizations. Governments can create incentives and orient capital allocation through regulatory, policy and fiscal tools.

Changing structures and mindsets to foster Greenaissance

Many governments around the world are developing policies to enhance and support the energy transition. We know from Donella Meadows[17] that we must apply leverage points to amplify small shifts into greater changes throughout the system.

Educate and create shared values

The University of Barcelona became the first school to make climate crisis courses mandatory. Education transforms mental models. Furthermore, education and training can be powerful policy levers to develop talent pools for the Greenaissance era. Over time, education can also change consumer behaviour.

Reduce the 'green premium'

Even when greener solutions exist, the consumer is not always prepared to pay more for them. This is what Bill Gates calls the 'green premium'. Demand, innovation, taxes and subsidies together reduce this green premium, allowing greener solutions to compete at scale, until they become competitive and even cheaper than the alternative.[18]

Align policies and regulations

Sustainable innovation and tax incentives help low-carbon energy sources become cost-effective. Aligning policymaking (bans, subsidies or investments) can enable sustainable solutions to become the norm. For example, Europe's emission tariff imposes import taxes based on the product's greenhouse gas emissions.

Support the most affected industries and regions

However, we can't simply 'cut off' industries that will be most affected by these changes. While eliminating animal agriculture would reduce global emissions by 15 per cent, it is not feasible to do so. Shifting agriculture to alternatives (such as plant-based) would drastically impact current farming practices and require public sector support for policy changes and consumer behaviour. The financial stakes are high for the most affected industries, regions and jobs, including farming, energy and transportation.

The cost of meeting targets

The global costs to fight climate change will run into trillions. This requires a fundamental rethink of the regulatory environment to support market mechanisms, innovation and business. Both BloombergNEF[19] and the IEA[20] foresee an unparalleled clean energy investment boom, increasing from its current level of around $3 trillion to reach over $5 trillion per year by 2030. Reaching any of our climate targets necessitates nearly doubling the current level of investments. Greenaissance represents a historic flood of funding to decarbonize and renew critical infrastructure. *This is already shaping new industries and creating new employment opportunities.*

Multiplier effect of climate innovation funding

In tightening private markets, investors become more discerning, especially for climate start-ups, which have longer timeframes, involve public policy and straddle complex ecosystems across software, hardware and infrastructure. Despite this, what was a fringe strategy for venture capital and private equity a decade ago is today maturing. The multiplier effect of the tens of billions of dollars in venture investments is transforming climate entrepreneurship to support virtuous tipping points, as a multitude of small, self-reinforcing initiatives grow over time.

EXAMPLE
Funding multiplier effects

The US Inflation Reduction Act (IRA) provisions for incentives across green energy industries will have a profound impact over the next decades. Overall, the IRA authorized direct expenditure of approximately $369 billion for spending on energy and climate change.[21]

The objective of the IRA is to stimulate a multiplier effect when combined with other public and private spending. The IRA would then amplify the strategic advantages the country already holds – in natural resources, infrastructure, expertise and talent – to enable it to become dominant in the low-carbon economy.

To yield multiplier effects, infrastructure investments need consistent, dependable policies. Political divisions raise red flags for investors, as the risk of policy reversals jeopardizes their funding.

In response to the IRA, the European Commission announced its own Green Deal Industrial Plan to enhance Europe's global competitiveness and support an accelerated transition.

Targeted infrastructure funding that leverages a mix of venture capital, institutional funding and strategic investments is the most promising path to spurring sustainable value creation.

There are reasons for hope, but not for naivety. Across industries, the energy transition is gaining momentum, fuelled by consumer behavioural shifts and investments in new technologies. Scientists, entrepreneurs and policymakers are tackling the challenge from every angle, developing solutions to drive systemic change. Organizations are starting to embrace BMaaS, collaborating to accelerate system innovation. We have a growing understanding of how to navigate complex systems towards ecological transformation, while calling out harmful motivations, incentives and greenwashing tactics that stand in the way.

Greenaissance will continue to drive fundamental shifts in business models and transfers in value.

Notes

1   R Spitz and L Zuin (2023) *The Definitive Guide to Thriving on Disruption: Disruption as a springboard to value creation*, Disruptive Futures Institute, San Francisco, CA

2   K Raworth (2017) *Doughnut Economics: Seven ways to think like a 21st-century economist*, Random House, New York, NY

3   Ellen MacArthur Foundation. The butterfly diagram: Visualising the circular economy, Ellen MacArthur Foundation, February 2019. www.ellenmacarthurfoundation.org/circular-economy-diagram (archived at https://perma.cc/NG2L-3ANB)

4   J Levänen, V Uusitalo, A Härri, E Kareinen and L Linnanen. Innovative recycling or extended use? Comparing the global warming potential of different ownership and end-of-life scenarios for textiles, *Environmental Research Letters*, 2021, 16 (5). doi.org/10.1088/1748-9326/abfac3 (archived at https://perma.cc/4ZDM-3KSB)

5   J Temple. A startup says it's begun releasing particles into the atmosphere, in an effort to tweak the climate, MIT Technology Review, 24 December 2022. www.technologyreview.com/2022/12/24/1066041/a-startup-says-its-begun-releasing-particles-into-the-atmosphere-in-an-effort-to-tweak-the-climate (archived at https://perma.cc/P7P5-E9CF)

6   European Commission. Corporate sustainability reporting, European Commission, 2023. finance.ec.europa.eu/capital-markets-union-and-financial-markets/company-reporting-and-auditing/company-reporting/corporate-sustainability-reporting_en (archived at https://perma.cc/Q5FN-XC7V)

7   Environmental Protection Agency. Sources of greenhouse gas emissions, EPA, 2021. www.epa.gov/ghgemissions/sources-greenhouse-gas-emissions (archived at https://perma.cc/3RNN-JBSK)

8   H Ritchie. Sector by sector: Where do global greenhouse gas emissions come from? Our World in Data, 18 September 2020. www.ourworldindata.org/ghg-emissions-by-sector (archived at https://perma.cc/76WR-72TW); N Bullard (2021) Venture capital firms are fighting to throw money at cleantech, Bloomberg, 2 September 2021. www.bloomberg.com/news/articles/2021-09-02/climate-startups-are-booming-as-vcs-throw-money-at-cleantech (archived at https://perma.cc/577W-ZM5C)

9   O Milman. Meat accounts for nearly 60 per cent of all greenhouse gases from food production, study finds, *The Guardian*, 13 September 2021. www.theguardian.com/environment/2021/sep/13/meat-greenhouses-gases-food-production-study (archived at https://perma.cc/8S9G-LBYS)

10 S Kara (2023) *Cobalt Red: How the blood of the Congo powers our lives*, St Martin's Press, New York, NY

11   K Crawford (2020) *The Atlas of AI: Power, politics, and the planetary costs of artificial intelligence*, Yale University Press, New Haven, CT

12   A Verbruggen. The geopolitics of trillion US$ oil and gas rents, *International Journal of Sustainable Energy Planning and Management*, 2022, 36. journals. aau.dk/index.php/sepm/article/view/7395 (archived at https://perma.cc/ QN8P-KFVN)

13   D Carrington. Revealed: Oil sector's 'staggering' $3bn-a-day profits for last 50 years, *The Guardian*, 21 July 2022. www.theguardian.com/ environment/2022/jul/21/revealed-oil-sectors-staggering-profits-last-50-years (archived at https://perma.cc/A9YZ-B4L5)

14   T Dordi, S A Gehricke, A Naef and O Weber. Ten financial actors can accelerate a transition away from fossil fuels, *Environmental Innovation and Societal Transitions*, 15 December 2022, 44. doi.org/10.1016/j.eist.2022. 05.006 (archived at https://perma.cc/YV6A-M9V9)

15   International Energy Agency. A 10-point plan to reduce the European Union's reliance on Russian natural gas, IEA, 2022. www.iea.org/reports/a-10-point-plan-to-reduce-the-european-unions-reliance-on-russian-natural-gas (archived at https://perma.cc/AAT4-FF5T)

16   J Doerr and R Panchadsaram (2021) *Speed and Scale: An action plan for solving our climate crisis now*, Portfolio, New York, NY

17   D Meadows (2008) *Thinking in Systems: A primer*, Chelsea Green Publishing, White River Junction, VT

18   B Gates (2021) *How to Avoid a Climate Disaster: The solutions we have and the breakthroughs we need*, Knopf Publishing Group, New York, NY

19   BloombergNEF. New energy outlook 2022, BNEF, 2022. https://web.archive. org/web/20230608131611/https://about.bnef.com/new-energy-outlook/ (archived at https://perma.cc/WW54-PAVC)

20   International Energy Agency. Net zero by 2050, IEA, 2021. www.iea.org/ reports/net-zero-by-2050 (archived at https://perma.cc/F2MB-X9CQ)

21   The United States Senate (2022) Summary: The Inflation Reduction Act of 2022, Senate Democrats, 2022. www.democrats.senate.gov/imo/media/doc/ inflation_reduction_act_one_page_summary.pdf (archived at https://perma.cc/ 3U6R-P9UJ)

8

The next chapter of digital disruption

Industries converge and new fields emerge

OBJECTIVES

Sectors converge, intersect and emerge

The clearly delineated 'industries' or 'sectors' of yesterday are disappearing. The futures are hybrid; in this liminal world, there are no industry boundaries. The magic happens as intersections create new fields.

Vanishing industry boundaries

Is Airbnb a consumer giant, a real estate player, a hotel alternative, an online marketplace, a travel tech innovator or a community-driven hospitality leader? Is Apple defined by consumer electronics, healthcare, technology, payments, entertainment, applications, software, hardware or AI? Is Tesla an automotive manufacturer, a clean energy company, a battery producer, a lifestyle brand, a robotics company, an AI company or an influencer?

Industries are converging, intersecting and emerging

Once-reliable sector boundaries are spilling over. From agriculture to construction, industries are converging, fusing and transforming. Clearly delineated activities and assets are dissolving. Previously separate verticals now collaborate within new ecosystems, defying traditional classifications. *Leaders, investors and analysts should adopt new filters to evaluate companies and their fields.*

EXAMPLE

Not milk, not meat, not eggs… NotCo

NotCo is a Chilean start-up that developed an AI-centric machine learning 'chef' called 'Giuseppe'. Giuseppe uses its AI platform to substitute conventional ingredients with plant-based replacements that may seem illogical to even the most experienced human R&D teams. NotCo's pea-protein-based NotMilk is sold in thousands of stores across the US. NotCo's growing proprietary dataset (flavour profiles on thousands of plant-based ingredients) has a B2B focus to accelerate R&D for food brands, ingredients suppliers and technology providers. Is NotCo a FoodTech company, a consumer business, a dairy producer, a food producer, an agricultural business, a technology company, an AI platform or an algorithm?

Five paradigms are pushing industries and sectors outside of their boxed-in definitions:

- **Radical transformation:** Business is fundamentally transforming, driven by converging technologies. Radical shifts are also taking place in value chains, creating entire fields in the process.

- **Too complex to reduce:** Categorical, rigid sub-segments do not reflect our complex world, where everything is interconnected.

- **Beyond industry boundaries:** Notice novel patterns at the fringe, as new fields begin on the periphery.

- **Ecosystems disrupting economic systems:** With business-models-as-a-system, competitors morph into partners, suppliers become investors and customers co-design your futures.

- **Minimum viable fields:** Technology, the energy transition and the immersive storytelling power of media will define all companies.

The current boundaries and definitions of clearly delineated 'industries' or 'sectors' are disappearing.

Radical transformation: From automation to cognification

Anything that can be automated, cognified, decentralized, digitized, disinter-mediated or virtualized will be. These shifts will redistribute trillions of dollars in value, as every aspect of the economy – from industries to professions – is radically transformed.

Years of industrial automation are maturing into a radical transformation. Environments not only become automated, they also develop the ability to learn and adapt through AI, combined with human–robot interactions.

Cognification makes everything increasingly smarter through connectivity. Cognification is the smart combination of the Internet of Things, 5G wireless technology, sensors, robotics and AI. The development of AI-driven humanoid health worker robots illustrates how cognification can create a symbiosis between humans and machines.

Machine learning algorithms are gradually developing the capability to write and eventually maintain their own code. The next wave of breakthroughs in deep learning will see software automate the creation of itself.

CASE STUDY   Physical, digital and biological synergies

Agnostic to industry boundaries, digital synergies are transversal. AI combines with extended reality (XR), which in turn comprises augmented reality (AR) and virtual reality (VR), building on technologies like 3D printing, smart manufacturing, nanites, 5G, next-gen sensors and IoT. Leveraging this, our smart devices (phones, glasses or contact lenses) could one day serve as a comprehensive healthcare solution – as an ophthalmologist, an optometrist and an insurance provider. The future of vision might emerge as a user-friendly app that integrates diagnostic capabilities and preventive care provided by constant biometric data gathering.

As synthetic biology accelerates, synergies between the physical, digital and biological open a new era beyond today's digital synergies. What happens when you can see, hear, feel and smell virtually? Does this open the door to the metaverse, digital teleportation or even space travel?

These transformations generate opportunities, but also raise ethical dilemmas, privacy concerns and existential questions. *The lines between sectors may be vanishing; when will the line between human and machine also fade?*

The world is too complex to be reducible

Like a meticulously crafted clockwork, the Newtonian view of the world presents a universe where we can dissect and reassemble its constituent parts (Figure 8.1). For centuries, this perspective resonated in our understanding of business and industry, with the belief that predictable systems governed both. Experts within their respective fields held sway, confident in their abil-

Figure 8.1 The world is too complex to be reducible

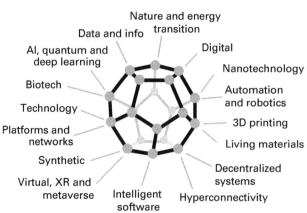

THE ILLUSION OF AN ORDERLY WORLD

Technology	Media	Telecoms
Banking	Finance	Insurance
Healthcare	Medical	Pharmaceutical
Automotive	Aerospace	Transport
Energy	Oil and gas	Utilities
Consumer goods	Retail	Logistics
Real estate	Infrastructure	Industrials
Agriculture	Chemicals	Food and beverages

COMPLEX REALITY CANNOT BE REDUCED

Nature and energy transition
Data and info
AI, quantum and deep learning
Digital
Biotech
Nanotechnology
Technology
Automation and robotics
Platforms and networks
3D printing
Synthetic
Living materials
Virtual, XR and metaverse
Decentralized systems
Intelligent software
Hyperconnectivity

ity to reduce outcomes to the sum of their parts. In this clockwork world, cause and effect unfolded in a meticulously choreographed dance, offering a comforting sense of stability and control.

Decomposed into distinct verticals and sub-sectors, compartmentalization is an attractive way to approach complex challenges. This reductionist approach is an intuitive way of analysing any value creation opportunities. However, complexity forces us to recognize unpredictability, evaluate emerging patterns and connect the shifting dots. *Addressing complex problems requires transcending rigid categories and embracing holistic approaches, which may not fit into predefined industries.*

KEY POINTS

The illusion of an orderly Newtonian world

The Newtonian world builds aircraft, sends probes to Mars, constructs bridges and processes bank payments.

However, once we acknowledge the complex nature of the world, the notion of dissecting and reassembling entire industry constituents like Lego is illusory. Our world is one where existential and climate risks are real, where we experience societal paradigm shifts, where there is a global decoupling and geopolitical reshuffling taking place, where disinformation, misinformation and conspiracy theories mingle to shape alternative 'realities'.

With this constant flux, we can no longer treat transport separately from energy, aerospace, raw materials, technology or urbanization because these parts are deeply intertwined. While Newtonian physics serves us well to build a bridge and launch rockets, our complex environment cannot be reduced into isolated parts to build tomorrow's green living cities.

Beyond industry boundaries

We may miss the point if we limit our evaluation to what competitors are doing and our analysis to specific industries as they stand today.

While you are busy fighting over incremental improvements, someone else will come in and create a new market. As these emerging companies scale and develop around an ecosystem, they can displace legacy industries. These nimble emerging companies will not only eat your lunch, but steal your very kitchen.

Systemic disruption goes beyond industry boundaries; we need to widen the aperture to explore the fringe. Emerging competitors create new activities developed on the margin of existing operations.

EXAMPLES
Emerging sectors

Slack spearheaded the team collaboration software segment, forging a cornerstone of modern workplace communication. Zoom, WhatsApp and WeChat reinvented communications with new business models at the expense of former industry leaders such as Ericsson and Nokia, or legacy operators such as AT&T and Vodafone.

Despite their financial and strategic advantages, established industry leaders do not innovate most. Instead, the outsiders break boundaries. Beyond Meat and Impossible Foods led the charge in alt-protein, challenging the meat and dairy industries. Plaid, Square and Stripe revolutionized online and mobile payments ecosystems, challenging traditional processing giants like JP Morgan, Mastercard and PayPal. Similarly, autonomous driving and edge AI suppliers like Mobileye and NVIDIA are powering the future of smart cars. SpaceX and Blue Origin emerge as key partners to NASA's next-generation space programme, redefining the aerospace landscape.

Ecosystems disrupting economic systems

Ecosystems blur the lines of fixed business models. Without any clear delineations between industries, there may be no obvious 'correct' strategic direction. Relevance is achieved with an action bias, testing and prototyping for emergence.

In a digital, dematerialized, disintermediated world, there are no direct competitors. Your competitors could also be your greatest partners, suppliers, customers and investors.

Businesses and their models must evolve to support experimentation, acting as a catalyst for innovation. BMaaS are emergent ecosystems that support the shift to a sustainable economy; harbour collaboration, co-development and co-creation; and respond to complex societal challenges by harnessing open ecosystems. These living BMaaS have an innate capacity to change creatively within their ecosystems.

Pre-defined boxes do not reflect our complex systemic world, where everything is interrelated.

Minimum viable fields: Technology, energy and media

Technology, energy and media drive all companies. These major themes replace the conventions of sectors. Every company needs strong DNA in these three areas (Figure 8.2). We call this combination the minimum viable fields (MVF):

- **Technology and AI – digital transformation to cognification:** To remain competitive, organizations should already be building deep technology capabilities, embracing AI's journey from 'automation' to radical 'transformation'. Digital transformation is no longer the panacea, but the starting point.

- **Energy and nature – Greenaissance era:** Every company will need to become innovative in energy transition because 'green' is the new digital. To mitigate climate change and deliver decarbonization, sustainability will transform every activity (procurement, production, distribution, after-sales) and redefine business models like digital did in the past few decades.

- **Media and storytelling – purpose, perception and stakeholders:** With increased connectivity, companies need to have media DNA. Direct access to stakeholders can help inform, influence and drive narratives. Aligning in an instantaneous world requires impactful storytelling. With AI raising concerns about manipulation and bias, genuine narratives become even more crucial. Storytelling that resonates with authenticity can inspire societal values and demonstrate accountability, aligning human aspirations with a transparent, responsible future.

Every organization's MVFs are technology, energy and media. MVF is a proficiency for every company, not a sector.

Figure 8.2   Minimum viable fields

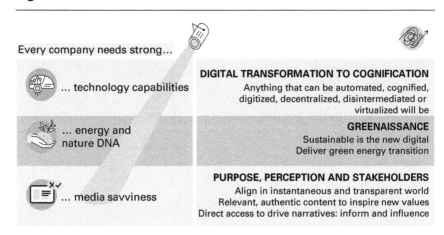

Technology

There are three considerations when integrating technology as an MVF.

1 **Digitization breaks apart legacy value chains and creates new models.** With platforms and networks, you can harness an ecosystem without having deep industry knowledge, such as with Airbnb. Agile organizations can experiment with digital products in a matter of days, at a fraction of the cost.

2 **Scaling and democratization of AI.** The combination of low- and no-code technology, large language models (LLMs), 'as-a-service' models and cloud computing makes cognified technology accessible to everyone. Powerful AI and machine learning tools are no longer limited to chief technology officers or large IT departments, thanks to interfaceable generative AI models.

3 **Technology is not a sector.** Every company must embrace digitization and automation, develop relevant AI capabilities, build or acquire strong technology blocks and leverage platforms and networks. However, technology as a 'label' means nothing. A technology company is not defined by some superficial veneer or marketing buzzword. Technology simply means the know-how and capabilities required for any company today, in any field, to stay relevant.

KEY POINTS

Tech proficiency does not make a tech company

While every company should embrace technology, simply having 'tech DNA' isn't enough to become a true technology company. A strong user experience, e-commerce with AI recommendations and network effects do not qualify a business as a technology company or drive unsubstantiated valuations. Discerning market observers should not lose sight of fundamentals when evaluating internet brands bleeding cash to drive superficial short-term growth in markets with almost no barriers to entry. Selling used cars, furniture or groceries online does not make a low-margin consumer-facing business valuable.

Value creation emerges with fundamental market changes, relevant intellectual property and strong market adoption with compelling unit economics at scale. Reinventing warehouse robotics automation and supply chain technology (Exotec), AI-driven drug discovery (Insilico Medicine) or generative AI (OpenAI) are promising examples. To be sustainable, technology-led business models need recurring revenues and positive cash flows.

Technology and AI are essential ingredients, but there is no magic formula to remain competitive in today's world. *No algorithm can salvage a bland dish of irrelevant products or unsustainable pricing.*

Likewise, we should not conflate downcycles and the collapse of countless start-ups with technology's demise. Remember Amara's law: we over-index technology short term while underestimating its long-term impact. Technology is now omnipresent and its capacity for continued transformation is unabated.

Media savviness

In our age of manipulated media, understanding how information shapes decisions and creates or destroys value is crucial for businesses. To wield the power of perception, content and reach, companies must master the game of information.

Sharing authentic messages and anticipating misinformation about your business is paramount. Being transparent and proactive is a central strategy when perception is everything and information amplifies at warp speed. No company is immune to disinformation, particularly by bad actors with hidden agendas.

Communicating well is a vital capability. Listening and storytelling are survival skills in an excessively noisy world where even the simplest, most compelling messages must compete for attention.

Perception and immersive storytelling

Within the vast ocean of information and seas of sameness, we increasingly search for what is relatable. Core values are scrutinized and passions evaluated. Who are you? What do you stand for? Does your brand make an impact on issues that matter? Do you behave responsibly?

In this context, more organizations are seeking to own platforms, offering direct access to target audiences to shape relatable narratives.

Storytelling as a superpower

Fred Polak, a pioneer of futures studies, argued that once we grasp our power to envision possible futures, we become architects of our own destiny. He believed the future first sparks in our individual and collective imaginations, shaping the plans we make today. Whether driven by hopes or fears, these projections define our path.[1]

Storytellers imagine aspirational visions of the futures and pathways to build them. In a world of disparate actors and attributes, alignment is more important than ever – and storytelling helps achieve this.

Our interpretation of the past, perception of the present and imagination of the futures all affect our behaviour and hence, our choices. As we think about emerging change, the narratives surrounding signals are powerful. How these signals are perceived influences their impact and our response.

Storytelling sells a vision of the future.

CASE STUDY   The science behind storytelling

Well-constructed narratives are naturally compelling. Research by neuroeconomist Paul Zak discovered that a neurochemical called oxytocin serves as an important neural signal that it is 'safe to approach others'. Oxytocin is produced when there is trust and kindness between individuals, which motivates collaboration. The right stories cause oxytocin synthesis, enhancing our empathy.[2]

In corporate strategy, employees and stakeholders will be substantially more motivated by the organization's transcendent purpose than a paycheque. Character stories behind how the corporation sells goods and actual customer anecdotes make people empathize more than money will. The brain is attracted to storytelling and it can remember and connect to these stories more than facts.

Visual storytelling builds connections, fosters a sense of community and goes beyond mere information-sharing. This emotional bond sparks action and opens wallets. *Great stories don't just sell; they inspire investments and shape strategies.*

Becoming a media company

Global leaders 'own' their audiences, cutting out intermediaries to communicate directly with key stakeholders, customers and the public at large.

It is no accident that companies are acquiring media assets. For instance, L'Oreal owns makeup.com and Red Bull launched its own media brand, Red Bulletin. Likewise, JPMorgan Chase acquired The Infatuation, a food and dining recommendation platform related to restaurant-rating brand Zagat. This acquisition allows JPMorgan's cardholders to access exclusive reviews, restaurant experiences and a food festival, EEEEEATSCON. HubSpot, the leading customer relationship management platform, acquired The Hustle, a popular media company featuring news, podcasts and newsletters. Following suit, commission-free trading app Robinhood acquired MarketSnacks to provide Robinhood users with bite-sized market insights tailored for beginner investors. Robinhood continues to develop its media activities with its subsidiary Sherwood Media, to serve as a source for news and information pertaining to financial markets and the culture of money.

The power of influence

Imma is an influencer with hundreds of thousands of followers. She has partnered with leading brands including Amazon, IKEA, Nike, Nomura, Porsche and Ferragamo. However, she does not exist in the flesh. Imma (which means 'now' in Japanese) is a virtual influencer; storytelling is not exclusive to humans. Similarly, Lil Miquela and Lu do Magalu each have millions of followers and work with prestigious brands like Calvin Klein, Dior, MAC and Prada.

HypeAuditor, a social media influencer analytics platform, reported that virtual influencers often achieve significantly higher engagement rates than their human counterparts.[3] These digital beings are less volatile than humans, yet can show empathy and even reach out to followers for advice. *Virtual influencers lead social media campaigns, become the public face of brands and sell their products.*

Gaming as the immersive arc of storytelling

With the advent of XR environments and early incarnations of the metaverse, digital is being augmented with gaming.

Free-to-play and open-world environments will dominate the future of gaming. Digital clothing, skins (appearances) and other aesthetic augmentations become virtual status symbols, which may be transferable between worlds. Whether you like these visions or not, these fragments of the future are emerging.

Driven by advances in cloud computing, haptic feedback, spatial computing and the burgeoning desire for immersive social experiences, the gaming industry is on the cusp of a transformative revolution, where boundaries between physical and digital worlds dissolve and players co-create their own realities. *Gaming may become less delineated from other digital spaces – and reality itself.*

Expanding beyond games

Musical artists such as Ariana Grande, Marshmello and Travis Scott have performed online concerts in Fortnite, while Lil Nas X featured in the virtual stages of Roblox.

Innovative music experiences offer a broad range of new commercial opportunities for artists. Gorillaz experienced the marketing power for virtual music by launching their album *Cracker Island* with a VR performance in New York and London, while ABBA's successful digital avatar concerts paved the way for a new immersive direction of 'live' entertainment.

Gaming isn't just for young males. In the US alone, 62 per cent of adults play video games and female gamers make up 46 per cent of all players. Over 200 million Americans of all ages play video games regularly and the number one gaming device is simply the smartphone.[4]

Gaming is spilling over into entertainment, gradually impacting commerce, education, training and business in every field.

Immersive storytelling in simulated worlds

Gamified immersion is gradually moving from the gaming and social arenas to retail, marketing, recruitment, training, education, science and healthcare. Across every field, a liminal world is appearing between the physical, digital and even biological.

Microsoft made its largest acquisition to enter the gaming market through its $69 billion purchase of Activision Blizzard. The sheer size of gaming audiences and the market opportunities of streaming games are already much larger than any other entertainment markets.

If you take Microsoft's move as a path towards broader simulated worlds, these virtual spaces where games are built and played could become entertainment centres for consuming all media. At the same time, these open the door to consumer retail experiences and the broad commercial businesses who use Microsoft's software every day.

KEY POINTS

Virtual worlds already drive real profits

These simulated worlds deepen customer immersion with brands, engage with communities and drive real-world revenues. Tomorrow, a seamless 3D virtual world may allow every aspect of business to be carried out virtually, such as buying and selling products, training and even negotiating contracts.

Virtual immersions already drive physical sales. Billions of gamers worldwide spend tens of billions per year on in-game purchases. This economy is already enormous, benefiting the real economy beyond gaming.

Brands like Balenciaga, Gucci and Ralph Lauren have hosted immersive fashion experiences in Fortnite, Decentraland and Roblox, designing for this new avatar-first economy with younger, digital-savvy generations in mind.

Interactive storytelling attracts new customers. When Ralph Lauren's CEO announced the group's results, he highlighted how partnerships with Roblox and Zepeto increased digital sales. By reaching Gen Z customers who socialize in virtual worlds where their avatars try on digital outfits, they drove real, physical-world sales. Ralph Lauren also partnered with Fortnite to create both physical and digital fashion (known as 'phygital'). Players can wear Ralph Lauren skins in Fortnite games to match their real-life clothing.

Immersive experiences for the avatar-first economy can be more effective than advertising, allowing fashion brands to reach young customers in their infinite virtual worlds.

Does the future belong to master communicators?

Master communicators listen to understand, use storytelling as a means of persuasion and generate a gravitational pull towards their brands and offerings.

Storytellers provide guidance, highlighting the needles in the haystacks. Going forward, master communicators become even more important as they coordinate and inspire disparate groups with different priorities. They also combat the 'noise', highlighting the importance of disregarded information. Great leaders align others around a common aim, with an open communication style, uncovering differences and challenges to be overcome.

Consumers make choices every day. In a digital world, it takes only moments to switch from one product or provider to another. This applies equally to the groceries we order, the financial institutions we bank with and the content we stream. *When stakeholders, consumers and employees understand the story, trust the vision and respect the values, they are more likely to buy into your ideas, products and services.*

In our hyper-transparent world, integrity rings truer than empty promises. Fact-driven, authentic narratives rise above the noise, while falsehoods crumble under scrutiny. *Effective storytelling is accountable storytelling, building trust by delivering on commitments.*

Liminal sectors and hybrid fields

As technologies converge, the barriers between established industries are breaking down, driving fundamental shifts in the underlying technologies, business models and value chains. Sectors intersect, blurring traditional boundaries and allowing new fields and combinations to emerge.

Convergence: Industries and technologies

The fusion of machine learning, genetic engineering and robotics is revolutionizing drug discovery, as BioTech AI platforms radically transform the pharmaceutical industry. Similarly, in FoodTech, the development of AI-powered platforms allows the creation of alternative protein sources and lab-grown nutrients.

The food and agriculture sector is undergoing an interdisciplinary transformative process. The sector is mirroring developments of other industries like automotive, aerospace or construction, with a horizontal shift of converging technologies, including AI, big data, autonomous and flying vehicles, drones, computer vision, digital twins, electrification, robotics and telematics.

Similar convergences of self-reinforcing technologies are redefining entire sectors. In the process, they are all starting to resemble each other.

Intersections: Value chain shifts

Meta has partnered with EssilorLuxottica to produce Ray-Ban smart glasses equipped with multimodal AI, featuring voice, gesture and touch controls. These hands-free miniaturized devices can identify objects and allow you to engage with them while posting photos or livestreaming videos. Tomorrow's glasses will be designed to make calls (without being tethered to a smartphone), stream XR videos and offer hologram video conferencing, as eyewear replaces your smartphone, entertainment, video conferencing, personal trainer and optometrist.

Oxa (fka Oxbotica) develops software to allow any commercial vehicle to become autonomous, with applications for passenger shuttles, warehouse vehicles, agriculture, energy and mining. This represents a move from the status of robotics and software subcontractor to the AI-powered self-driving operating solution for automotive original equipment manufacturers (OEMs). These intersections, both horizontally with different technologies and sectors, and vertically in terms of business model integration, reveal massive shifts in value chains.

Meanwhile, Amazon competes with UPS as it controls its logistics, Fedex launches its own e-commerce platforms, Tesla creates its own energy storage solutions and Apple becomes an integrated semiconductor manufacturer designing its own next-gen chip.

Historically, semiconductors in cars have been outsourced components responsible for discrete tasks like airbag controlling or engine functions. However, we are witnessing a significant shift: AI chips are becoming the brains that power car platforms, just like they orchestrate the drug discovery process for pharmaceutical companies. As chip manufacturers move up the value chain, they are no longer just subcontractors, but rather key players defining the very operating system of the car, encompassing autonomous driving, connectivity and the human-machine interface.

As transportation platforms evolve into software defined vehicles (SDVs), they become similar to smartphones. This paves the way for diverse revenue streams, service-based business models and extended vehicle lifespans. High-performance computing and robust software management underpin SDVs, alongside seamless software-hardware integration and sophisticated cybersecurity. While challenges like infrastructure adaptation remain, SDVs unlock personalized driving experiences, enhanced safety features and integration with smart cities, ultimately transforming the future of transportation and urban planning.

As industries intersect, radical shifts take place in the value chains.

With digitization, we all have super powers

With digital activities, different strategies can be tested in parallel. Originally, A/B testing was used for digital marketing. Users were presented with different versions of web pages and marketers tracked reactions. Today, every business is digital. Driven by algorithms and data, A/B testing can be equally applied to streaming services and electric vehicles, as platform operators send software updates to certain users and not others. Because of this, companies can experiment in the physical world with limited cost or risk. Whichever tests perform best can then be deployed more widely, while continuing to test further ideas.

The evolution of A/B testing from marketing to manufacturing is a testimony to the superpowers that digitization provides.

Superpowers for Super Apps

The Swiss brought us the Army knife. The Chinese digitized it with Alipay and WeChat, allowing you to do everything from your smartphone. From day trading to day dreaming, these 'super-apps' are ubiquitous and nearly required for daily life. Following these successes, Uber announced that it was adding planes and trains, broadening its ride-hailing application. Uber's super-app expands its mobility hub into a one-stop shop for transport, delivery and door-to-door long-distance travel bookings. Uber may compete with – or maybe partner with – other aggregators such as Trainline, Expedia, Airbnb and Booking.com. Digitization allows disintermediation and expansion of activities across fields and verticals.

Platforms like Uber have also moved into and out of financial services. 'Embedded' banking software allows a company that is not involved in financial services to offer products and services typically associated with a bank, including credit cards.

Apple Pay, which has been under antitrust investigation in Europe for its dominant position in mobile payments, demonstrates how a financial super-app can become a superpowered behemoth. To build its payments framework, Apple went on an acquisition spree of financial services companies such as Credit Kudos, a UK-based open-banking start-up that offers consumer insights and credit scores to improve lender decision-making. Google, Amazon and Meta are all infiltrating the banking industry to drive revenue and customer engagement by locking them in through a range of financial services. Retailers like Walmart are also expanding into financial services.

For customers, the legacy lines between a brand's historical activities and new services across different sectors no longer exist. Do Walmart's customers mind that their hypermarket is offering credit cards? Emulating Apple, Google and PayPal, companies are taking an aggregator approach to their super-app by creating digital experience layers that connect users to existing financial services ecosystems while integrating chatbot advisors.

By collapsing the financial transaction and infrastructure layers, super-apps are morphing into invisible finance available for any consumer-facing company.

CASE STUDY   Connecting the financial fabric across sectors

Open banking is a game changer, as banks open up their systems through APIs to allow third-party apps to interact with them. These offer FinTech developers a simple solution for connecting their apps to user accounts at many different financial institutions. Plaid is a leading open-banking platform that has positioned itself as a pivotal piece in the FinTech ecosystem. By becoming the 'plumbing' between banks and technology, Plaid connects the majority of the largest US FinTech applications to over 10,000 banks. These innovations threaten powerful incumbents and may bring widespread cost savings and other benefits to both merchants and consumers.

Every software company, across any activity, can flourish as a payments provider. Finix offers companies a whole new level of control over their financial stack by helping them bring payments in-house. Finix sells payments technology, offering payments-infrastructure-as-a-service (similar to Amazon's AWS model). This augmentation threatens the finance vertical, which has classically processed payments externally in exchange for fees. This further blurs the lines between fields, as your restaurant and gym can now take bookings while also acting as a bank.

Any activity has the propensity to be built into a super-app. In our digitized world, super-apps are the 'hypermarkets' of platforms, disintermediating actors both within their fields and beyond their legacy verticals.

Digital biology

Technological innovation has always played a part in developing new ways to care for human health. The first instances of drug discovery occurred as early biologists isolated the active ingredients in traditional remedies. Later, mistakes contributed to scientists' innovations, such as with Alexander Fleming's accidental discovery of penicillin, the world's first antibiotic. The process developed into classical pharmacology, which has produced a number of modern drug discovery methodologies.

Now, machine learning, genetic engineering and robotics are revolutionizing and disrupting the scientific process surrounding drug discovery, assisting in the billion-decision process required to find the right molecules to benefit human health – sometimes bypassing the traditional discovery process entirely. AI has taken biology by storm: organic compounds, proteins and RNA are being simulated very accurately.

The emergence of BioTech AI platforms

AI accelerates drug discovery by performing 'infinite' simulations, greatly reducing the cost of research and development. This new breed of companies at the crossroads of tech and bio includes Atomwise, Insilico Medicine, Exscientia and Recursion Pharma. Alphabet, Google's parent company, is also reimagining the entire drug discovery process following DeepMind's breakthrough work in predicting protein structures.

The co-founders of BioNTech (which partnered with Pfizer to produce the revolutionary mRNA Covid vaccine) believe that, following a number of breakthroughs, we may have cancer vaccines by 2030.[5] There have been positive early developments in personalized mRNA vaccines that could help fight pancreatic cancer.

AI is revolutionizing traditional drug discovery

The drug discovery process is extremely complicated. According to Moderna CEO Stéphane Bancel, 'there's just too much data in this for the human brain to process in a systematic way'. When the human brain fails to comprehend large unstructured datasets, AI can pave the road for new insights. Other modern drug discovery methodologies, such as high-throughput screening, which involves a 'shotgun-like' approach to identification, compete with AI approaches.

Speeding up the lengthy drug discovery process with AI can increase the discovery rate of helpful organic compounds. Combining data from many real-world sources improves the process of predicting and prioritizing novel drug combinations. These drug discovery platforms process millions of data samples to ascertain the signature biological features of a given disease.

EXAMPLE

Exscientia's AI drug discovery platform

Exscientia originated the world's first three AI-designed drugs to enter into Phase 1 human testing, competing with the likes of GSK and AstraZeneca.

Exscientia speeds up the discovery and development of new drugs while reducing costs significantly. To produce one winning drug, Exscientia claims that their process can cut the time spent in discovery from the industry average of 4.5 years to one year.[6]

Partnering with pharmaceutical giants like Bristol Myers Squibb (BMS) and Sanofi, Exscientia accelerates drug discovery through their AI platform. Exscientia and BMS have a broad, long-term partnership – a multi-billion dollar collaboration to jointly develop precision-engineered medicines.

Decentralizing and digitizing clinical trials

While there is great potential for AI to vastly accelerate the discovery process, there are time-consuming phases that AI cannot yet replace. Clinical trials during vaccine development cannot be reliably predicted by a model due to the extreme complexity of the human body.

Inherently, clinical trials must be done with humans. Until AI improves to the point that it is able to model every single nuance of human biology and anticipate its reactions, certain parts of drug and vaccine discovery may remain unchanged.

Cross-pollination

Businesses and their respective fields are becoming more liminal. These spaces in between industries are growing and evolving.

As digitization is now mature, every business needs to become a digital hybrid. There is no standalone 'digital strategy'; rather, there is simply 'strategy'. Similarly, any marketing includes digital marketing. There is no 'online' versus 'offline' debate. This hybridization simultaneously combines physical, digital, augmented, virtualized and immersive.

Other online versus offline distinctions are disappearing. With virtual try-ons, prospective customers try on clothes in virtual changing rooms. JD, one of China's largest e-commerce platforms, expanded its omnichannel strategy to open physical stores. In the US, the revival of Barnes & Noble in 2022 was driven by reimagining and curating their physical stores, with themed reading spaces, events and improved online integration.

For Amazon, there is no distinction between its Prime Video streaming and e-commerce, as viewers can buy merchandise and fashion apparel from its show's characters. We live in a digital world of hybrid sectors – retail, entertainment, education, physical, digital. *There is no single 'industry'; rather, there is 'interdiscipliniarity'.*

As technologies become pervasive, they are indistinguishable from their surroundings. With advances in miniaturization, computing power becomes virtually invisible, sometimes even integrated into our bodies. With increasing interactions across fields like biology and nanotechnology, technology may become indistinguishable from nature.

The future is hybrid. In a liminal world, there are no industry boundaries.

Notes

1 F Polak (1973) *The Image of the Future*, Elsevier, Amsterdam, NL
2 P J Zak. Why your brain loves good storytelling, *Harvard Business Review*, 28 October 2014. www.hbr.org/2014/10/why-your-brain-loves-good-storytelling (archived at https://perma.cc/Y9TV-FXGK)
3 N Baklanov. The top virtual Instagram influencers in 2021, HypeAuditor, 6 December 2021. www.hypeauditor.com/blog/the-top-instagram-virtual-influencers-in-2021 (archived at https://perma.cc/YKJ9-BLLW)
4 Entertainment Software Association. 2023 essential facts about the video game industry, The ESA, 2023. www.theesa.com/2023-essential-facts (archived at https://perma.cc/C687-FJ7V)

5 I Sample. Vaccines to treat cancer possible by 2030, say BioNTech founders, *The Guardian*, 16 October 2022. www.theguardian.com/society/2022/oct/16/ vaccines-to-treat-cancer-possible-by-2030-say-biontech-founders (archived at https://perma.cc/PYF9-W2YU)

6 SEC.gov Exscientia IPO prospectus (US SEC Form F-1), United States Securities and Exchange Commission, 10 September 2021. www.sec.gov/Archives/edgar/ data/1865408/000110465921114491/tm2119783-5_f1.htm (archived at https:// perma.cc/C5J5-X4GX)

Part Three
The future of artificial intelligence, strategic decision-making and technology

9

Evaluating next-order impacts of exponential technologies

OBJECTIVES
Technology, innovation and unintended consequences

What are the features of technology, its powers and unintended consequences? How can we anticipate future impacts in a complex technological world? We cannot predict the future, but we can gain insights to help us understand emerging technologies that will deeply impact society and humanity.

Technology's power

In the 1931 movie *Frankenstein*,[1] Dr Victor Frankenstein cries 'It's alive!' upon seeing the sapient creature he created move its hand, then arm and eventually, its eyes. Dr Frankenstein then proclaims: 'Now I know what it feels like to be God.'

Mary Shelley wrote the novel *Frankenstein* over 200 years ago. Her visionary novel still serves as a cautionary tale for the unexpected consequences of experimentation at the intersection of technology, biology and humanity. Since *Frankenstein*, many stories have explored the potentially dangerous outcomes when mortal humans attempt to imitate God by creating life.

As we continue to engineer the intersections of innovation, biology and humanity, we identify 10 distinctive features of technology that make it uniquely powerful:[2]

- **Not neutral:** Our use of technology interacts with our evolving values and choices, none of which are neutral. Technologies are becoming more consequential, raising existential concerns.

- **Ubiquitous:** Technology is everything we create. It is omnipresent, affecting everyone and everything.

- **Exponential:** Many technologies grow non-linearly.

- **Combinatorial and fusing:** Technologies are combinations of existing elements. Their convergence generates compounding effects.

- **Alive:** As technology learns and changes autonomously, it behaves like a species, propagating and expanding.

- **Invisible:** Technology is indistinguishable from its surroundings. Some technologies are no longer noticeable or recognizable.

- **Incomprehensible:** Fusing technologies generates highly complex systems. It is difficult to discern why algorithms make certain decisions.

- **Irreversible:** Technology can produce outcomes that may become difficult or impossible to reverse.

- **Hyperconnected:** Everything and everyone is always on, permanently connected.

- **Unpredictable:** Certain effects of technology are unknowable beforehand, causing surprising outcomes.

Techistentialism and the neutrality of technology

What is the relationship between humanity and technology? Can technology be neutral? For Intel's long-time CEO Andy Grove, 'Technology happens. It's not good. It's not bad. Is steel good or bad?'[3] Dr Melvin Kranzberg states that 'Technology is neither good nor bad; nor is it neutral.'[4]

Philosophically and ethically, the debate continues. German existential philosopher Martin Heidegger long challenged the view that we actually master technology, or that we can solve any collateral issues as technology grows beyond our control.[5]

Today, humanity faces technological and existential conditions that can't be separated. We define this phenomenon as 'techistentialism'. Our existential condition is an uncertain one, considering the inherent dualities and paradoxes of life. Our techistential condition is no different (Figure 9.1).

Figure 9.1 Comparing existentialism with techistentialism

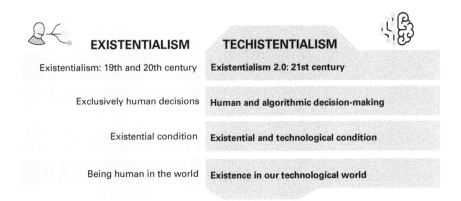

The paradox of technology – its magic and hazards – gives it a unique status. As Heidegger suggests, technology 'drives out every other possibility of revealing'. Technology is so dominant that it can eclipse all other ways we understand the world.

Existentially, we each have the agency to explore contingency – the idea that possible events are uncertain. Choice exists because of contingency. Our freedom as individuals is determined through our choices. If everything were predetermined, fixed by design, we would lack choice and power.

Techistentialism is existentialism 2.0

Standing on the shoulders of Heidegger and Søren Kierkegaard, Jean-Paul Sartre powerfully articulated the human condition: 'existence precedes essence'.[6] By this, Sartre meant that our agency emerges through choice. While existence is indeterminate and thus unknowable, we are always defining our essence as it emerges and moving in the direction we define. *But if technology is determining outcomes on our behalf, our agency is curtailed and our choices may be beyond our control.*

Technology is shaping society by influencing decision-making and enabling manipulation at scale (for instance, through social media and misinformation). Through AI, technology is challenging us in a realm historically specific to humans. As AI develops, machines will become increasingly autonomous in making decisions. Here, the use of technology confronts the existential dimension. Here, we stand on the edge of our free will. Computationally rational technology is no longer neutral because it drives away contingency and choice.[7]

Techistentialism studies the nature of human beings, existence and decision-making in our technological world.

Could superstupidity be as dangerous as superintelligence?

More recently than the existential philosophers of the 19th and 20th centuries, Nick Bostrom defined an existential risk as 'one that threatens the premature extinction of Earth-originating intelligent life or the permanent and drastic destruction of its potential for desirable future development'.[8]

While there is an ongoing debate as to whether AI could cause human extinction, it has a wide spectrum of other potential existential impacts. The curtailing of humanity's agency is one of these risks.

As multiple systems interact, it becomes increasingly difficult to discern how algorithms make decisions, which exposes us to both human and machine errors. Complex systems in technology (robots, supercomputers, nuclear plants, networks, weapons) have many moving parts that can be prone to failure. Have we developed overreliance on increasingly complex dynamic systems? How easy would it be for an autonomous machine (or human) to make a consequential mistake that goes undetected?

'Superstupidity' could be as much of an existential risk as artificial superintelligence (ASI).[9] Theoretically, ASI could possess humanity's combined cognitive capacity. In contrast, superstupidity could take on multiple features, including overreliance on the underlying 'intelligence' of these systems. For instance, believing that AI can be a proxy for our own understanding and decision-making as we delegate more power to algorithms is superstupid. Perhaps AI is also superstupid and may cause mistakes, wrong decisions or misalignment. Further, consider AI ineptitude. What might appear as incompetence may simply be algorithms acting on bad data. This can result in bias, privacy violations and immoral AI. As with humans, more or better data may not help machines make improved decisions.

Determining whether AI is on the road to superintelligence or superstupidity may not matter as much as ensuring that humanity does not rely on AI without a solid understanding of the consequences.

Maybe the existential risk is not machines taking over the world, but rather the opposite, where humans start responding like idle machines – unable to connect the emerging dots of our UN-VICE world.

Updating education for relevancy

To ensure superstupidity is not our future, updating our education system should become an existential priority. Education's effectiveness should be evaluated on whether it can help humanity become future-ready for our complex 21st century. We should inspire passion, nurture curiosity, emphasize uncertainty, develop range and use critical thinking to examine assumptions.

Most importantly, we need to form new relationships with inquiry, experimentation and failure (which goes hand in hand with creativity). These features can help us problem-solve out of the most existential risks. Today's standard knowledge will never solve tomorrow's surprises.

Just as the 'language' of math is a requirement, learners should now be fluent in technology's uses and abuses. Knowing truth from fiction, information from disinformation and entertainment from addiction will separate those who find themselves enslaved by our new technologies from those who harness them for their own aims.

Learning does not end at the completion of formal schooling. *Education is a constant, lifelong process of learning, unlearning and relearning – from the playground all the way to the boardroom.*

KEY POINTS
'We shape technology and technology shapes us'

'We shape our tools and thereafter our tools shape us.' Often attributed to Marshall McLuhan, this quote illustrates how people were reshaped by the transition from print to electronic media.

Social media conditions, incentivizes and influences certain behaviours. The effects of disinformation and misinformation are felt across society, degrading trust and ultimately weakening democracies.

Technology is already as essential as language. We can expect tomorrow's technologies to be even more consequential. Intelligent machines may be able to learn, frame and select their own ethical choices. By definition, these cannot be neutral.

Technology is ubiquitous

Alan Kay defines technology as anything that wasn't around when you were born; essentially, technology is everything that we create. Technology is so pervasive that it is omnipresent.

After thousands of years of coevolution, humans are now inextricable from technology.

Technology is exponential

Humans can comprehend linear relationships, but we have difficulty understanding exponentiality. Exponential change is misleading because it starts slowly; our cognitive biases expect it to continue linearly. Therefore, early developments – even initial doublings – may be barely perceptible, only apparent after longer timeframes. The deceptive nature of exponential growth causes people to miss inflection points, after which abrupt changes suddenly arise.

We have reviewed many examples of exponentiality throughout this book. Together with unknown, volatile, intersecting and complex, the exponential 'E' is an integral part of our acronym, UN-VICE. *The accelerating connectivity, multiplying actors, increasingly complex interconnections and warp-speed changes are enabled by technology.* These exponential changes can quickly get out of hand.

Technology is combinatorial, converging and fusing

Johannes Gutenberg invented the mechanical movable-type printing press in the 15th century. Building on numerous technologies of his time, he combined paper manufacturing, oil-based inks, agricultural screw presses and metal casings. Fast forward to modern smartphones. These versatile mini-computers combine a powerful array of hardware and software: high-resolution touchscreens, miniaturized cameras, GPS, wireless technologies, secure operating systems, app stores, cloud storage, voice recognition powered by AI and biometrics (facial recognition, fingerprint scanners).

In *The Nature of Technology*, Brian W Arthur posits that transformative technologies arise when innovations combine existing building blocks, then resolve the issues that arise.[10] *Combination is the mechanism that drives technology's evolution.* Arthur uses the term 'combinatorial evolution' to describe mechanisms whereby new combinations arise from previous ones. Arthur suggests that technological evolution is similar to coral reefs that build themselves from many small organisms – it creates itself from itself, with all technologies descended from earlier technologies. *Existing technologies can combine and recombine foundational elements in new ways, which can be radically transformative.*

KEY POINTS

From combinatorial technologies to convergence and fusion

Convergence and fusion go one step further than combining existing building blocks. Mutual transformations are occurring as new technologies fuse with and alter, human beings.

> *The term 'fusion' reflects emergent living technology, including autonomous machine learning, synthetic biology and evolutionary robotics.* Biotechnology and 3D printing are now fusing into the emergent sector of 3D bioprinting, where human tissues and organs can be printed.

Technology is alive

In its omnipresence, is technology emulating the humanity of its creators? Technology has vision (computer vision), a mind (internet, machine learning), speech (natural language processing) and motion (robotics). With machines learning to think, sense, communicate and interact, they are increasingly autonomous and human-like. For now, though, technology lacks spirituality.

From extending human abilities to embodying them

Historically, technologies expanded human powers. The fundamental difference with today's emerging technology is that we now seek to *embody* human abilities in machines.

While humans have traditionally held the mantle of 'inventor', the tides are changing. From designing novel drugs to optimizing complex engineering processes, these systems are increasingly contributing to breakthroughs. This raises a critical question: should AI be legally recognized as an inventor? For now, multiple courts have sided with humans, ruling that only natural persons may be awarded patents. AI systems may have to wait, but the legal debates are ongoing.

Living and reproducing system

In *The Nature of Technology*, Arthur states that 'technology creates itself out of itself', drawing analogies with biological life. Technology is self-organizing and self-creating, like a living organism responding to its environment.

This begs the question: are humans required in the future of a human–technology relationship? Stephen Harwood and Sally Eaves[11] conceptualize the potential future development of six genres of technology. The authors use the notion of technology as a human–artefact relationship, with each offering some form of agency. The relationship is complex, multi-dimensional and dynamic – essentially evolving by adjusting its conditions to what is best for survival (a homeostatic process).

As technology transforms into living systems, Harwood and Eaves define the six genres of technology. Genre 1 is exclusively human: a world free from technology, which is difficult to imagine. In Genre 6, technology is a living system able to reproduce, sustain and renew itself without human as-sistance – for now, the realm of science fiction.

In between, Genre 3 characterizes the shift from mechanical to digital services, like modern aircraft, space and computing. In Genre 4, the authors note a transition to smart machines that have some form of intelligence. The convergence of existing technologies allow this: *perception* (sensors); *data storage* (cloud); *high performance computer processing* and *sense-making* (AI, machine learning); *authentication* (blockchain, biometrics); *action* (au-tonomous robotics). For Harwood and Eaves, autonomous technological beings begin collaborating in Genre 5 (interconnectivity, language, collec-tives), before reaching Genre 6.

KEY POINTS
Existential governance

In Harwood and Eaves' six genres of technology, the authors analyse governance considerations as machines become more autonomous. In Genre 3, regulation materializes, but is increasingly behind new technologies. Here, regulation must anticipate developments. In Genre 4, questions emerge about how growing technological autonomy should be regulated in the interests of human well-being. In Genres 5 and 6, we must consider whether technological collectives can be regulated and if so, how. Finally, the future viability of humans becomes *the* existential question.

Technology is invisible

We take for granted how seamlessly certain technologies (smartphones) are woven into our daily lives. Vital infrastructure (internet and electricity) is so essential that imagining life without them feels almost alien.

Koert van Mensvoort developed a Pyramid of Technology[12] to describe the levels at which technology functions. The Pyramid puts a human touch on technological change – from introduction and acceptance to abandon-ment (think iPods, DVDs and fax machines).

Dr Mensvoort was inspired by Maslow's Hierarchy of Needs, where the requirements of the lower stages must be met before further development occurs. The bottom of the pyramid showcases frontier technologies that are envisioned, teetering on the precipice of possibility. As the technology develops, it moves up the pyramid, becoming pervasive and indistinguishable from surroundings. This is the case with transportation, communication and money, where technology is so embedded it becomes invisible.

At the top, technologies are 'naturalized' – they become an integral part of our human nature, like cooking or clothing. *With increasing interactions across fields like biology and nanotechnology, technology will become inseparable from nature.*

Technology is incomprehensible

Boeing 737 MAX-imal incomprehensibility

In separate incidents in October 2018 and March 2019, two Boeing 737 MAX aircraft crashed, killing 346 people. The flight control software known as the MCAS (Maneuvering Characteristics Augmentation System) is believed to have been a key contributor to these crashes. Netflix's documentary *Downfall: The Case Against Boeing*[13] explores allegations that Boeing withheld or misrepresented information to the US Federal Aviation Administration (FAA), customers and pilots, which eventually contributed to these crashes. Streamlined FAA certification and reductions in pilot training requirements resulted in more planes being sold, which drove Boeing's share price higher and increased financial rewards for executives.

In complex systems, failure requires multiple faults. It can be difficult to isolate any individual contributor and smaller failures can cascade into larger ones. In engineering, designers strive for 'Goldilocks' solutions that are as simple as possible, but not too simple. However, despite years of investigations into the Boeing 737, the multiplicity of interacting parts means that there remains a degree of incomprehensibility around the precise underlying issues. This incomprehensibility is prevalent when technical, engineering and cultural factors all contributed. In November 2020, the FAA paved the way for the 737 MAX to return to service.[14] Boeing agreed to pay $2.5 billion as settlement for the crashes.

Touching failure

Richard Cook[15] considers complex systems (technology, transportation, healthcare, power generation) to be intrinsically hazardous systems that are inherently prone to failure. These complex systems have heavy defences and backup systems, given the high cost of failure. Together, these defences normally shield against catastrophic failures. However, the prevalence of machine learning and other emerging technologies – which are sometimes a black box even to their developers – have added opaqueness.

KEY POINTS
Incomprehensibility and failure

As Cook stipulates, one paradox with the incomprehensibility and failure equation is that 'failure free operations require experience with failure'. The more routinely reliable or incomprehensible a system is, the more difficult it is to have a thorough understanding of its failures. Touching failure is a prerequisite to mitigating hazards.

As advances in technology, machine learning and neural networks continue, these complex systems will reach even further beyond our comprehension.

Technology is irreversible

In gene editing, 'nano-scissors' are small enough to manipulate individual genes. However, these unwieldy scissors could also cut other genes in unpredictable ways. Any 'off-target' effects may cause unintended genetic modifications and long-term changes, with unpredictable effects. Gene editing illustrates the features of possible irreversibility, given that once genomes are edited, we can't reinitialize them. The off-target effects could continue for generations, resulting in unknown changes to future genomes.

If a technology exposes humanity to irreversible risks, there may be nothing we can do to alter the outcomes. The adverse consequences of irreversible technology could be highly damaging even if the technology itself holds promising benefits.

Technology is hyperconnected

Platforms match providers with the potential users of products or services. Network effects allow platforms to scale because, as additional users join the network, it becomes more valuable for all users, fuelling hyperconnectivity.

Technology platforms enable the unprecedented potential to reach hundreds of millions of users. *In a world where everything is digital, technology allows hyperconnectivity between users and information.*

Technology is unpredictable

Pendulum clocks helped trigger the industrial revolution. Clean water made manufacturing computer chips possible. Air conditioning led to significant migration to previously inhospitable cities like Dubai and Phoenix.

In Steven Johnson's Hummingbird Effect,[16] seemingly unrelated clusters of innovation influence others, much like the evolution of certain flowers led to the hummingbird's unique ability to hover mid-air. With innovation, complicated chains of influences precipitate unanticipated changes that reverberate far beyond the original domain.

The Butterfly Effect suggests that small initial changes can result in outsized and seemingly unrelated outcomes, often creating chaos. Unlike the Butterfly Effect, where the chain of causality is unknowable even after the fact, the virtuous impacts from the Hummingbird Effect may seem unrelated, but the patterns are identifiable with hindsight.

The Black Mirror Effect

The British dystopian television series *Black Mirror* looks at humanity's relationship with technology and how different levels of reality may emerge. The series exposes the unintended and unexpected consequences of evolving technologies. *Black Mirror* is eerie because, in some ways, their imagined futures already look remarkably plausible, if not familiar. How close are we already to inadvertently slipping irreversibly into our worst nightmares? If we are not thoughtful with our fast-developing technologies, how might small triggers become tipping points?

The Black Mirror *Effect is the tendency of society to ease unwittingly from normalcy into techno-dystopia without realization.*

Four factors drive the *Black Mirror* Effect:

- **Universal human desires:** Identity, longing, mortality, loneliness, love. Technology can exploit these desires and promises. Engineers writing algorithms work closely with behavioural scientists to capitalize on our natural tendencies.
- **Unpredictability:** Increasingly complex systems combined with living technology precipitate unpredictable and potentially dystopian chain reactions.

- **Algorithmic decision-making:** Technology is gradually developing a mind of its own. The process is being completely normalized.

- **Polarization:** Society feeds on amplified toxicity rather than being repelled by it.

Technology plays a considerable role in Butterfly, Hummingbird and *Black Mirror* Effects. These effects can generate positive unforeseen benefits, but often, their unpredictability results in unwelcome outcomes.

Unintended consequences and anticipatory governance

John Locke warned against the unintended consequences of regulating interest rates in the 17th century, while Adam Smith's 'invisible hand' described positive unintended consequences in the 18th century. Sociologist Robert Merton penned the first detailed analysis of unintended consequences in 1936, in which he identified a number of sources, including short-termism, errors and ignorance (the impossibility to anticipate everything).[17]

One of the most powerful illustrations of unintended consequences is Albert Einstein's famous equation, $E = mc^2$, showing the interchangeability of energy and mass. This discovery indirectly contributed to the atomic bomb, which deeply troubled Einstein.

Technology bites back

In a dated but insightful book on unintended consequences, Edward Tenner[18] explains how technology bites back. Safety systems can lead to disaster by encouraging risk – such as the 'unsinkable' *Titanic*, or antibiotics paving the way to more resistant bacteria. Tenner describes the challenge as a 'treadmill' of escaping new technologies that are difficult to resist. One example for our time is how working from home results in constant connectivity, not enhanced freedom.

Positive unintended consequences

Unintended consequences are not necessarily negative. The intended benefit of washing machines was to reduce manual laundry work; a positive unintended result found women playing an increasing role in the workforce after its invention.

Negative unintended consequences

Negative consequences come in two variants. In the first type, unexpected drawbacks are embedded in desired results. In the second, the sought-after solution backfires, generating perverse results worse than the original problem.

EXAMPLE
Unintended drawbacks versus perverse consequences

Air conditioning was developed to remove heat from buildings. In doing so, increased gas and coal consumption adversely impacted the climate. Similarly, the intended outcome of industrialized agriculture was less expensive food at scale, which ended up causing obesity and ecosystem degradation. While these achieved the primary objectives, their actions also generated unexpected and unwelcome drawbacks.

Passenger airbags were introduced to save lives during car accidents, but initially resulted in an increase in child fatalities as airbags were automatically deployed on impact. Another famous perverse initiative is known as the Cobra Effect. The Indian government offered bounties for dead cobras to reduce the cobra population. Thus, people farmed cobras and killed them for the cash reward. When the government then scrapped the flawed reward programme, farmed cobras were released in the streets.

The quandary of timing

Balancing the potential benefits of a promising technology with the possible risks is always a trade-off. It should be possible to implement safeguards around technological developments without stifling innovation, by considering appropriate checks and balances, ensuring accountability, evaluating benefits and harms and understanding how incentives orient technologies throughout systems.

Technology foresight anticipates unintended consequences, imagines possible next-order implications and considers what inflection points might result in irreversibility. At the earlier stages of a particular technology adoption, change is easier to control; however, it is difficult at this stage to know its impact on society. Once impacts become known and evidence shows a need for change, it may be too late to control the technology (Figure 9.2).

Figure 9.2   The Collingridge dilemma

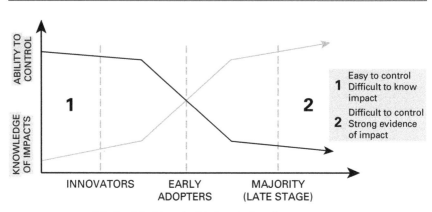

NOTE Adapted from D Collingridge (1981) *The Social Control of Technology*, Palgrave Macmillan, London

The Collingridge dilemma[19] illustrates this quandary of timing. The next-order impacts cannot be understood until the technology is more mature. But controlling this innovation is much more difficult down the road, after that technology is entrenched.

While scientists within regulated fields (e.g. medical) might be required to warn us of any downsides discovered as they explore beneficial applications, doing so for technology is often discretionary.

Maybe the day is approaching when AI developers come under the purview of professional bodies, which impose training, regulatory frameworks and ethical guidelines aligned with their societal impact.

Three-step framework: Anticipate, monitor and mitigate

It is difficult, if not impossible, to fully anticipate the possible outcomes or evolutions of technology. We should, however, seek to be anticipatory, by discerning between what can be anticipated and what is impossible to predict.

Step 1: Anticipate

At the outset, we must thoroughly consider the implications of developing technologies by critically assessing the main objectives and risks and establishing effective guardrails upfront.

To anticipate, we must distinguish between the *unintended* consequences which may arguably be unavoidable, versus the *unanticipated* outcomes, those adverse effects which could have been anticipated and avoided.

When negative externalities are unavoidable, we can still seek to manage them effectively. The Futures Wheel is a valuable tool for this.[20] It helps explore the direct and indirect implications of new technologies as they cascade further, as well as *unintended* consequences (Figure 9.3).

EXAMPLE

The Futures Wheel for unintended consequences

To illustrate the Futures Wheel, we unpack next-order consequences of the widespread adoption of self-driving cars. These include many benefits, as well as drawbacks. For instance, traditional driving jobs may evaporate, resulting in significant driver unemployment. This could then cause further impacts: widespread reskilling as former drivers reintegrate into the changing economy, or social unrest if they don't.

Reduced car ownership from the sharing economy means less road congestion, with scope for normalizing new forms of entertainment and social drinking during the car journey. Given the safety of autonomous driving, fewer fatal accidents may also have the unintended consequence of reducing the number of organs available for transplant.

Just like computer networks, autonomous vehicles could be hacked remotely or affected by viruses, with security and data privacy implications, even terrorism risks.

When would business models, urban planning and infrastructure adapt? With reduced numbers of vehicles, the entire automotive ecosystem shifts, from insurance companies to automotive suppliers and local governments.

Further, consider unavoidable collisions due to extreme weather or accidents; can the technology be overruled and who (or what) is responsible?

The objective of this first step – to anticipate – is to give all these considerations the attention they deserve at the most opportune times. *Unanticipated* consequences have predictable adverse outcomes and can be avoided. They require constant monitoring (facilitated through feedback loops) and plans for how to react when *unintended* outcomes emerge. Thinking broadly and

Figure 9.3 The Futures Wheel: Autonomous vehicles

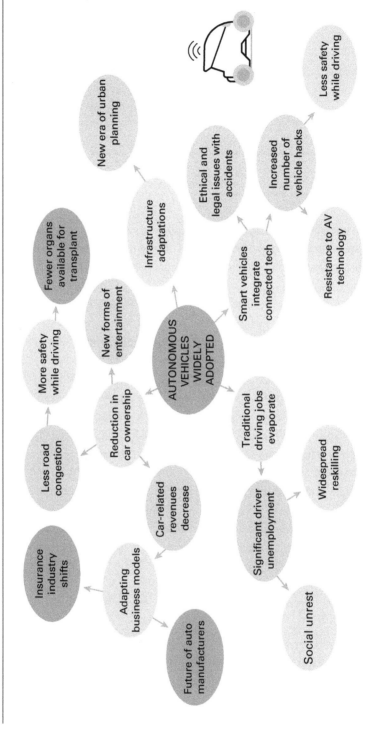

NOTE Adapted from J C Glenn. Futurizing teaching vs futures course, *Social Science Record*, 1972, 9 (3), 26–29

systemically helps prevent shortsightedness. Unconflicted diverse perspectives reduce poor judgement and enhance objectivity.

Step 2: Monitor

Ethically questionable products and services that are highly profitable are tough to curtail. Legal standards, governance, compensation metrics and incentives should be in place for all stakeholders, including boards and C-suites. When serious issues materialize which are knowable and avoidable, there should be accountability. Teams must be incentivized to align outcomes with broader stakeholders, including customers and society, and should be penalized when they fall short.

With Facebook seeking ways to maximize revenues and increase engagement, its ad targeting system fosters political polarization, social unrest, misinformation and deepfakes. In 2018, Facebook recognized that it was slow to act on misinformation in Myanmar that eventually led to predictable human rights abuses.[21] When would this have transpired, had these developments been monitored in earnest?

Monitoring innovations day-to-day is a critical part of technology foresight. Relevant actors must have responsibility to continually monitor emerging issues, including unintended consequences:

- **Objectivity:** Regularly review financial and other incentives.
- **Tipping point:** Understand inflection points, especially with exponential technologies.
- **Irreversibility:** Scrutinize key milestones and their impacts to identify when sensitive new technologies could become irreversible.
- **Alertness:** Adhere to compliance even if not required by current law. Adopt the same care as highly regulated industries.
- **Systems approach:** Note interdependencies or single points of failure for when systems inevitably break down.

Chaos Monkey is a popular open-source tool developed by Netflix engineers to inject controlled failures into computer systems. This 'simulated chaos' helps software engineers assess their system's overall response to unexpected disruptions, strengthening its antifragility. Chaos Monkey allows developers to touch failure in a controlled environment. Monitoring how the system behaves under stress reveals potential vulnerabilities and areas for improvement.

Effective monitoring requires flagging adverse deviations from the core purpose of a technology, transparency with any findings and feedback loops to mitigate and respond.

Step 3: Mitigate

Steps 1 (anticipate) and 2 (monitor) allow the consequences of technology to be qualified at the earliest opportunity. Mitigation seeks to address irreversible issues before it's too late. Effective mitigation of the unpredictable can only be achieved by carrying out the first two steps.

Anticipatory governance is conducive to developing resilient policies. Independent committees with strong and objective governance can support dedicated teams by establishing the most effective responses to unintended consequences as soon as they become apparent.

Science fiction for technology foresight

George Orwell's dystopian *1984* was a cautionary tale about the dangers of authoritarianism and surveillance states; warnings which society ignored. Alex McDowell, the production designer for *Minority Report* (2002), was responsible for over 100 science fiction ideas, many of which were later patented. President Biden signed an executive order on AI in 2023, the same year as the release of *Mission: Impossible – Dead Reckoning Part One*, which featured a rogue sentient AI called 'the Entity'.

Science fiction's strength lies in its exploration of ethical dilemmas and dystopian critiques, often fuelled by a scepticism towards the impact of technological innovations.

For his science fiction short story 'Runaround' (1942), Isaac Asimov formulated ethical standards for machines with his three laws of robotics, which are being revisited as we seek to build ethical AI:

- A robot may not injure a human being or, through inaction, allow a human being to come to harm.
- A robot must obey orders given to it by human beings except where such orders would conflict with the first law.
- A robot must protect its own existence as long as such protection does not conflict with the first or second law.

First established in a fictional short story 80 years ago, these laws are now being widely used as guidance for technologists. *Science fiction anticipated many of today's existential questions.*

Human–machine relationships are complex and emotional. Are humans partners, owners or devoted disciples? Are robots just machines, however seemingly intelligent they are, or benevolent overlords? What safeguards protect humans from these machines, or vice versa? Will these technologies take our jobs?

Science fiction provides frameworks to assess emerging technologies and ensure our innovations are socially responsible. By imagining 'What if?' we gain insights that can transform the nature of what is possible. Science fiction also offers a means to imagine pitfalls to avoid. By pairing with real-life, the audience sees potential outcomes as you pull the thread, fleshing out tangible moral questions. *Science fiction provides an ethical platform for debate, to anticipate what might arise.*

CASE STUDY   Technology fact meets science fiction

Black Mirror is awash with examples of technology gone awry. Uploaded digital consciousness becomes tangible in the 'San Junipero' episode, thanks to a digital afterlife. 'White Christmas' imagines the ability to copy our consciousness to an egg-shaped module containing our essence.

While these scenarios might seem surreal, billions of dollars are being spent on technologies that focus on anti-aging and mind uploading. Google-backed Calico Labs is devoted to helping people live longer and healthier lives through BioTech. Elon Musk's Neuralink is developing a brain–computer interface implant to supercharge human capabilities, merge with artificial intelligence and treat neurological disorders.

A minefield of ethical, moral and legal considerations lies ahead. What will be the unintended consequences of autonomy, identity and privacy? When we think about technology through the *Black Mirror* lens, we can envision unpredictable knock-on effects. As with butterflies and hummingbirds, small initial developments can trigger a runaway chain of larger outcomes that could become irreversible. While some outcomes may drive beneficial innovations, other consequences could be adverse.

As AI becomes indistinguishable from humans, how quickly can society slip into the surreal irreversibility of *Black Mirror*, where technology makes key decisions without human involvement?

Looking ahead: From possible futures to multiple present realities

The convergence of technologies intersecting in biology and engineering, matter and energy, computation and cognition, together with multiplying sensors and autonomous machines, are causing powerful emerging technologies to develop fast.

Synbio: Engineering life itself

Lab-grown burgers are just the tip of the iceberg. From 'smart' bandages to buildings that photosynthesize, synthetic biology and biomanufacturing may complement the limitations of flesh, steel and concrete.

Synbio enables humans to engineer new living organisms, while breakthroughs in gene therapy are on the verge of rewriting the script of life itself. This nascent field merges molecular biology, genomics, engineering and AI, offering pathways that could not only extend our lifespans, but challenge our very definition of humanity.

AI is rapidly accelerating the autonomous discovery of new materials, from complex proteins to intricate inorganic crystals, with potential applications across fields like healthcare, energy and construction.

Biological computing, also known as biocomputing, looks beyond conventional silicon-based designs, hoping for an edge in speed, efficiency, power and energy consumption. The emerging field of 'organoid intelligence' (OI) explores this prospect by leveraging 3D cultures of human brain cells (brain organoids) and brain–machine interface technologies.

Biotechnology will be transformational, revealing a convergence of physical, biological and digital worlds.

AI's next battleground: Decision-making

While AI's capabilities are still narrow, algorithms are rapidly broadening their scope. Today, the autonomy, self-awareness and intelligence of machines falls seriously short of human capabilities, but we can't ignore AI's learning trajectory:

- **Image and language – AI's inflection points:** Significant advancements are occurring in computer vision and natural language processing. Once sophisticated language and image processing can be performed reliably, the applications will be endless.

- **Decision-making – the next battleground for humans and AI:** AI systems are already automating decision-making at scale. As humanity delegates its decision-making to machines, what kind of decisions will we rely on algorithms for – and with what consequences?

- **The AI supremacy race:** Geopolitically, AI is already a tool for authoritarianism, while robots are entering the battlefield. Further breakthroughs will set the scene for a race between China and the US. AI nationalism will continue, grow and divide.

Humans need to enhance their capabilities, as machines are learning fast, gaining increasingly higher-level human functions.

Next-gen wireless networks and machine learning

What enables remote brain surgery, autonomous driving roads, smart cities orchestrating self-driving vehicles or the immersion of cloud-assisted VR gaming? 5G wireless networks are gamechangers, providing internet speeds up to 100 times faster than 4G, near-zero latency and significantly more reliable connections.

5G will also have an enormous impact on AI and machine learning, thanks to better frequency use and lower latency. 5G is broadcast widely across frequencies, as opposed to 4G's narrow spectrum slice. With 5G, machine learning can evolve to near-instant decision-making in complex environments, where low latency and reliable high data volume exchanges are required.

Quantum advantage: Multiple present realities

Imagine being both alive and dead simultaneously. Schrödinger's cat illustrates this mind-blowing paradox of quantum physics, as the feline's fate is determined by events which may or may not arise simultaneously. Known in quantum physics as 'superposition', this property allows particles to exist in different states at the same time. *While futurists imagine multiple possible futures, quantum physicists research multiple present realities.*

Meanwhile, with 'quantum entanglement', qubits distanced by light years interact in a strongly correlated manner. The universe is far more interconnected than the reality we perceive.

Quantum computing will also change the rules of cybersecurity. The ability to break traditional encryption would pose a real threat to national security. This could render the current encryption standards obsolete, leading to another race to adapt.

Quantum parallelism means that multiple values for a given function can be evaluated simultaneously instead of sequentially. Quantum brings hope that we can solve deeply complex problems and process enormous amounts of information faster and more accurately than current supercomputers.

Quantum is expected to allow infinite simulations – ushering in new discoveries across many fields. New breakthroughs open the door to extraordinary computing power, including the possibility to accelerate AI, invent new drugs, combat climate change, carry out simulations of twin universes and achieve breakthroughs in materials technology.

Technical road maps from key players in quantum computing point towards tangible critical milestones in the decade ahead. A number of quantum breakthroughs have been announced over the past few years in both the US and China. While timing and feasibility remain uncertain, more now believe that viable quantum computing is possible in the 2030s, rather than being decades away.

For quantum computing to realize its full potential, it will require new algorithms, new software, new programs, new hardware and new technologies – which currently do not exist.

EXAMPLE
Quantum supremacy and strategic players

In 2019, Google announced 'quantum supremacy', able to solve a deeply complex problem that no conventional computer could in a reasonable amount of time. Google claimed its computations would normally have taken 10,000 years on the most powerful supercomputers – and only took them a few minutes (although IBM disputed elements of this claim).[22] In 2020, China's University of Science and Technology of China made its own claims to quantum supremacy with an alternative system.[23] Then, in 2023, Google claimed that its next-generation Sycamore system managed computational tasks on a quantum computer in seconds that would normally take decades.[24]

The race for quantum intensifies, as Microsoft, Amazon, IBM, Honeywell and Intel invest heavily. In 2021, IonQ became the first publicly listed pure-play quantum computing company. Another company, Rigetti Computing, is building quantum computers and the superconducting quantum processors that power them to democratize quantum in the cloud.

Dr Michio Kaku sees quantum as the beginning of a new architecture for the futures, as binary digital recedes to the past. As humanity attempts to play God, we seek to replicate the most powerful quantum computers: ourselves.

Welcome to quantum, where the conventions of 'one object, one place, one time' may become obsolete.[25]

The quantum race will determine the future of geopolitics, security and the world economy.

Splinternet: Disruption of the internet

The internet is an incredible, vast miracle where governments, spy agencies, businesses, criminal gangs and private individuals worldwide freely cohabitate. The next phases of technology evolution will include a battle around who governs the internet – and what the future internet looks like.

Today, even though Google, Meta and Twitter/X operate globally, they must adhere to certain rules in specific regions. Sometimes, this approach protects consumers – such as the data protection regulations in Europe. In other instances, government restrictions might be used to crack down on citizens, strengthen autocracies and further human rights violations. *Controlling the internet is a powerful tool for increasingly confident autocracies.*

The splinternet: Breaking up the global internet

The idea of the 'splinternet' represents a major change from simple moderation. The splinternet is the break up and replacement of the internet with different standards for different regions, making the internet we have known since its inception a thing of the past.

China's stance on the internet within its borders is that it is sovereign. The internet in China belongs to China and it should be controlled by the Chinese Government. The 'Great Firewall of China' blocks access to sites that the Chinese Communist Party (CCP) determines are opposed to their general principles and national security. Blocked sites include Google, Facebook, Twitter/X, Netflix, Wikipedia and the BBC.

Currently, while the internet in China may appear to be different from that of the West, the IP standards are the same. China has proposed 'New IP' – literally a new internet protocol that would allow governments to restrict access to specific internet actions on a very granular basis. *This would allow any government to build censorship and surveillance into the fabric of the internet.* Instead of connecting to a censored internet that includes global perspectives, Chinese citizens would connect to a sovereign internet, designed and closely controlled by the Chinese Government.

China's digital standards could be imposed within its spheres of influence, including dozens of countries across Asia, Africa, Europe and the

Middle East. Different standards would exist for the internet used by the US and their partners globally.

> **KEY POINTS**
> Splitting the internet
>
> *The basis of the 'splinternet' is a fragmentation of the internet we know.* Events in 2022 gave the world the clearest preview of the splinternet's possibilities, with China and Russia's narrative control projecting alternative universes to the invasion of Ukraine.
>
> The idea of an open, accessible internet where everything is freely shared around the world will erode. Controlling the internet will become a standard in certain parts of the world, as a strategy of digital authoritarianism. The ease of collaboration through inter-operable resilient systems worldwide may fragment, impacting global economies, commerce and freedom itself.

The digital divide

Technology can benefit the globe, and decreasing costs offer incredible access to information, education and culture from anywhere. However, benefits are not equally distributed.

As the large technology companies increase their influence around the world, the wealth generated filters back to these global giants. Locally, many smaller businesses – or countries themselves – may not benefit from investments, infrastructure or employment.

The growing reliance on the internet for healthcare, education and every aspect of society means that underserved populations who can't afford to connect may fall even further behind. This became acutely evident during the Covid pandemic, as the poorest communities around the world were the ones most affected. With the global population over eight billion, more than 2.5 billion people – 30 per cent of the world – are still offline.[26]

Technology developments will affect countries differently, because any low-skill jobs that can be cheaply automated will be. Gradually, all jobs will be affected. China and the United States may continue to invest most in developing new technologies and innovating to generate alternative business and employment opportunities. Smaller highly innovative countries like

Finland, Israel and Singapore will continue to create new companies and entire fields. Many other countries may bear the brunt of automation and AI without reaping the benefits of new innovations.

The end of tech laissez-faire

For the past few decades, technology has largely been free from government intervention and relatively unregulated. That era of laissez-faire is coming to an end for two reasons. First, the power, scale and competitive advantage gained by the tech giants is perceived as unfair. Second, the public sees big tech as responsible for its unintended consequences, including election interference, misinformation and the threat of mass unemployment.

Europe has always taken a more interventionist approach, but the United States and China are now catching up. As regulators and litigators around the globe increase their scrutiny of big technology due to anti-competitive, copyright and societal concerns, the dynamics between regulators and digital giants will inevitably change, with far-reaching consequences.

While the power of big tech may no longer remain unfettered, the digital giants will remain powerful and shape the world ahead – maybe just not as freely as they would have if left to their own devices.

Notes

1   The 1931 Frankenstein movie is based on Mary Shelley's 1818 novel *Frankenstein, or The Modern Prometheus*.

2   R Spitz and L Zuin (2022) *The Definitive Guide to Thriving on Disruption: Reframing and navigating disruption*, Disruptive Futures Institute, San Francisco, CA

3   W Isaacson. Andrew Grove: Man of the Year, *Time*, 29 December 1997. www.time.com/4267448/andrew-grove-man-of-the-year (archived at https://perma.cc/83RJ-TBJ7)

4   M Kranzberg. Technology and history: 'Kranzberg's Laws', *Technology and Culture*, 1986, 27 (3). www.jstor.org/stable/3105385 (archived at https://perma.cc/KT4W-2WYQ)

5   M Heidegger (1954) Die Frage nach der Technik [The question concerning technology], *Vorträge und Aufsätze*, Neske, Pfullingen

6   J-P Sartre (1946) *L'existentialisme est un humanisme* [Existentialism Is a Humanism], Les Editions Nagel, Paris

7   R Nykanen and R Spitz (2021) *An Existential Framework for the Future of Decision-Making in Leadership*, Leadership for the Future, Cambridge Scholars Publishing, Newcastle upon Tyne

8   N Bostrom. Existential risk prevention as global priority, *Global Policy*, 2013, 4 (1). www.doi.org/10.1111/1758-5899.12002 (archived at https://perma.cc/65JT-UE5Z)

9   R Spitz. Techistentialism: Could superstupidity be as dangerous as superintelligence? APF Compass Magazine: AI and Futures, December 2023. www.apf.org/apf-resources/compass (archived at https://perma.cc/377J-S2AX)

10 B W Arthur (2009) *The Nature of Technology: What it is and how it evolves*, Free Press, New York, NY

11 S Harwood and S Eaves. Conceptualising technology, its development and future: The six genres of technology, *Technological Forecasting and Social Change*, 2020, 160. dx.doi.org/10.1016%2Fj.techfore.2020.120174 (archived at https://perma.cc/263B-XXFH)

12 V M Koert. Pyramid of Technology: How technology becomes nature in seven steps, *Next Nature*, 30 August 2014. www.nextnature.net/story/2014/pyramid-of-technology-how-technology-becomes-nature-in-seven-steps (archived at https://perma.cc/K2FV-8ZLX)

13 R Kennedy. *Downfall: The case against Boeing*, Imagine Documentaries, 2022

14 Federal Aviation Administration. FAA updates on Boeing 737 MAX, FAA, 8 April 2021. www.faa.gov/newsroom/faa-updates-boeing-737-max-0?newsId=93206 (archived at https://perma.cc/C62P-BNJS)

15 R I Cook. How complex systems fail, Cognitive Technologies Laboratory, Adaptive Capacity Labs, 21 April 2000, www.adaptivecapacitylabs.com/HowComplexSystemsFail.pdf (archived at https://perma.cc/Q6WQ-TYAV)

16 S Johnson (2015) *How We Got to Now: Six innovations that made the modern world*, Riverhead Books, New York, NY

17 R K Merton. The unanticipated consequences of purposive social action, *American Sociological Review*, 1936, 1 (6). www.jstor.org/stable/2084615 (archived at https://perma.cc/RY3N-DJM5)

18 E Tenner (1997) *Why Things Bite Back: Technology and the revenge of unintended consequences*, Vintage, New York, NY

19 R Worthington. *The Social Control of Technology* by David Collingridge, *American Political Science Review*, 1982, 76 (1). www.doi.org/10.2307/1960465 (archived at https://perma.cc/RT97-U9HT)

20 J C Glenn. Futurizing teaching vs futures course, *Social Science Record*, 1972, 9 (3), 26–29

21 BSR. Human rights impact assessment: Facebook in Myanmar, Meta, 2018. about.fb.com/wp-content/uploads/2018/11/bsr-facebook-myanmar-hria_final.pdf (archived at https://perma.cc/ZEA9-EM3A)

22 A Cho. IBM casts doubt on Google's claims of quantum supremacy, Science, 23 October 2019. www.science.org/content/article/ibm-casts-doubt-googles-claims-quantum-supremacy (archived at https://perma.cc/U532-LBZ3)

23 T Simonite. China stakes its claim to quantum supremacy, Wired, 3 December 2020. www.wired.com/story/china-stakes-claim-quantum-supremacy (archived at https://perma.cc/8DNA-HYFT)

24   J Titcomb. Supercomputer makes calculations in blink of an eye that take rivals 47 years, *The Telegraph*, 2 July 2023. www.telegraph.co.uk/business/2023/07/02/ google-quantum-computer-breakthrough-instant-calculations (archived at https:// perma.cc/5XCV-ZF22)

25   M Kaku (2023) *Quantum Supremacy: How the quantum computer revolution will change everything*, Doubleday, New York, NY

26   A Petrosyan. Number of internet and social media users worldwide as of January 2024, Statista, 31 January 2024. www.statista.com/statistics/617136/ digital-population-worldwide (archived at https://perma.cc/G66V-L8CS)

10
Our AAA framework

A survival guide for staying relevant in the age of AI

OBJECTIVES
Decision-making and relevance in the age of AI

AI is taking over areas previously thought too important to entrust to machines. Thus far, humans have excelled at decision-making, but our comparative advantage may not last. We use the antifragile, anticipatory and agility (AAA) framework to explore these traits, which humans should develop to improve their abilities as machines are learning fast.

Fifty shades of AI

Playing with fire

Humans domesticated fire at least 300,000 years ago; language is over 100,000 years old; the World Wide Web is barely 30. Artificial intelligence is new relative to humanity and we cannot know how revolutionary it will ultimately be. But dismissing AI as hype is dangerous, given its profound potential in every aspect of our lives.

AI is a broad field within computer science dedicated to developing machines capable of performing functions that typically require human intelligence. These tasks include perceiving, reasoning, learning and problem-solving. AI can analyse and understand speech and language, interpret visual data and enable decision-making.

Several key developments are accelerating AI's evolution. Increased computing power, vast datasets and large language models (LLMs) have combined with inflection points in computer vision and language processing. One major driver is machine learning, which allows computers to learn without being explicitly programmed. Deep learning, a subset of machine learning, uses complex algorithms called neural networks with a multi-layer structure inspired by the human brain, enabling them to tackle challenging tasks. LLMs are deep learning models trained on massive amounts of data. They excel at performing a wide range of natural language processing (NLP) tasks, including content generation.

Three levels of AI

Nick Bostrom, known for his work on future technology and existential risk, categorizes AI in three levels: artificial narrow intelligence (ANI), artificial general intelligence (AGI) and artificial superintelligence (ASI).[1]

Artificial narrow intelligence

ANI is already common. It beats world champion humans in certain games (Chess, Scrabble, Jeopardy, Go), powers digital voice assistants we use every day (Siri, Alexa, Google Home) and enables facial recognition to unlock our smartphones.

ANI has incredible pattern recognition abilities in enormous datasets, with a sweet spot for text searches, speech recognition and image-based classification. These algorithms excel at precisely defined tasks where they can outperform people.

Artificial general intelligence

One day, machines may reach human-level intelligence. AGI, sometimes referred to as strong AI, delineates machines with cognitive abilities indistinguishable from humans.

Ray Kurzweil anticipates AGI's arrival in the mid-2040s, while Rodney Brooks considers such timelines unrealistic, projecting AGI at least a century away. The notion of machines matching human capabilities of problem-solving, learning, planning and self-awareness remains an ongoing debate.

Artificial superintelligence

The term 'singularity', popularized by Vernor Vinge in 1993, represents the idea of superintelligence continuously upgrading itself. HAL, the superhuman rogue computer in Stanley Kubrick and Arthur C. Clarke's *2001: A Space Odyssey*, is an illustration of ASI, straight out of science fiction.

Hypothetically, ASI could possess humanity's combined cognitive capacity – or even more. Humanity would not be able to understand ASI's reasoning. From some dystopian perspectives, this could result in robots overthrowing humanity. While this may seem unlikely, even today's narrow AI could be programmed to do something devastating. This risk grows as AI becomes increasingly autonomous.

The stakes of AI

Today, AI seems to be the answer to everything, irrespective of the question. Algorithms are permeating every aspect of our lives, from our work and streaming platforms to our criminal justice and healthcare systems. Despite this, for many of us, AI feels as mysterious as ever.

Archimedes famously said that, given a long enough lever and a place to stand, he could move the world. AI is perhaps the most transformative of all technologies, with the most significant global economic impact.

No matter where you stand, the stakes are high with AI.

AI supremacy race: World order and disorder

The world is waking up to AI and gradually exploring various levels of regulation. While safeguards are essential, differences in regulatory and ethical frameworks between countries and regions will impact the global race for technological superiority. Further, to what extent do technology companies make critical decisions with national security implications?

AI will reshape world order, strategic interests, competitiveness and important areas for society's welfare. If certain countries lag in developing AI, they will be at a distinct disadvantage from a geopolitical perspective. At the same time, when governments focus heavily on AI applications like surveillance and weapons systems above anything else, important societal initiatives including privacy, healthcare and education may not receive sufficient attention.

China has set an ambitious goal to become the global AI leader by 2030. With unparalleled scale to train AI given its large population and diverse data landscape – and relative caution in Europe and the US for certain dual-use AI developments – China may gain a competitive advantage.

While China races ahead with significant momentum, the US is realizing that it may need to catch up for dual-use technology. Europe is ahead of the game – when it comes to regulation.

Beyond automation

AI and automation will replace many manual tasks. Numerous jobs will be transformed or eliminated and new jobs will emerge. But the rapid advancement of AI makes it difficult to understand which jobs will be transformed, which will be eliminated and what new professions will be created. There are countless studies on job displacement, with a broad range of outcomes. Many claim that automation could add more jobs than it destroys.

Reskilling is becoming a priority to help employers and policymakers deal with rapidly shifting workforce requirements. Studies from the International Monetary Fund and World Economic Forum focus on the economic implications, including new ways to reskill and upskill our workforce in the age of AI. But is this reskilling at scale actually happening, when education systems aren't changing?

In *Radically Human*, Daugherty and Wilson[2] explain that AI systems will unleash human expertise instead of replacing us. In this vision, humans have a great deal of control. But both Daugherty and Wilson are leaders at Accenture, one of the largest technology integrators in the world.

Technology consultancies that design and sell these advanced AI systems may have difficulty being objective about the potential job displacement caused by those very tools.

Over the last few decades, employment has grown in knowledge-intensive sectors and declined in routine cognitive and manual tasks. The first to be replaced by new technology are often low-skilled, low-paid individuals. More recently, automation accelerated toward white-collar jobs. In any industry, automation starts by displacing repeatable tasks in clearly defined areas, then expands to encapsulate a growing cluster of activities.

Powered by advancements in deep learning and NLP, a new wave of generative AI companies, including 01.AI, Anthropic, Cohere, Inflection AI, Mistral, OpenAI and Scale AI, are further encroaching on humans. *Unlike prior technological shifts, AI's influence is spilling over into complex cognitive functions.*

KEY POINTS
Unquantifiable net impacts of AI

Some people have said 'AI won't replace humans, but people who can use it will.' This sounds reassuring, but it oversimplifies the complex future of work and AI integration. Experts predict a surge in opportunities, but the intricate interplay between cognification, mass automation and how we work remains uncharted. The net effect of AI on employment is unknown – we have no data on the future. We need to move beyond simplistic slogans and delve deeper into understanding these complex relationships to ensure a future where both humans and technology thrive.

AI is taking on an increasing role in many fields, even those which typically require years of university education, professional qualifications and extensive training. Law, accounting, insurance, finance and medicine have gradually become more automated and now augmented through generative AI.

Transformations require integrating systems, adjusting supply and demand to new models, reskilling workforces and adapting regulations. Like any change, AI will create winners and losers. Speculating on how productivity gains will translate into improved welfare for workers lacks a solid foundation. Yes, substantial value will be created and destroyed, giving rise to new possibilities. *But we need the humility to acknowledge that we may not fully understand the net impacts or timing.* Those making predictions often have vested interests. The specifics are guesswork, but the scope for surprises and inflection points is certain.

The three clusters of AI opinions

For some, AI is a dark force, ushering in an apocalyptic future in which humans are pitted against machines. Others envision beneficial AI applications that help us tackle the world's most pressing challenges, as long as we regulate it effectively. Optimists see AI as a panacea for curing disease and solving global warming, despite the risks. On one end we have dystopian, on the other utopian, with a pragmatic perspective in between.[3]

Dystopian: The existential risk

In the paperclip maximizer thought experiment,[4] Nick Bostrom illustrates that machines might focus so strictly on achieving singular objectives that dangerous decisions could be made to optimize. Bostrom imagines that a machine tasked to manufacture paperclips may attempt to transform everything on Earth into paperclip-producing facilities. For the machine's programmed goals, this dystopian outcome would be deemed very successful.

There have been multiple scenarios developed for humanity's future in the age of AI, including those where AI takes over and we live in an algorithmic, authoritarian regime. Many famous scientists such as Stephen Hawking go further, warning that AI could end humanity. Interestingly, some tech leaders with concerns around AI today are those who have benefited most financially from it (Bill Gates, Elon Musk).

In what we dub 'DystopiA.I.', sceptics see AI as a real existential risk for humanity, threatening human extinction. With DystopiA.I., advanced systems could become so effective in solving global warming that they remove human existence altogether to achieve that goal.

Pragmatic: Beneficial, but needs safeguards

Most technologists are 'PragA.I.matic', believing that the benefits of AI outweigh its risks and that society has a choice to make the right decisions. However, most PragA.I.matic technologists have a vested interest, incentivized to build value from technology – if not for the benefit of broader society, for their shareholders.

The PragA.I.matic perspective sees the promises of AI through a practical lens: AI has benefits and simply needs safeguards. PragA.I.matic rests on the belief that AI may never be able to reach AGI, and in any event the right safeguards and ethical frameworks will be in place to avoid the worst risks.

Utopian: The panacea

Our 'UtopiA.I.' fans believe that AI's strong benefits clearly outweigh the risks. Some techno-utopians even expect the merger of human and machine intelligence, known as transhumanism. At the edge of the UtopiA.I. spectrum, Ray Kurzweil[5] believes that humans must merge with intelligent machines to keep up with the accelerating rate of change. For Peter Diamandis, exponential technologies will drive a world of abundance.[6] Sam Altman (OpenAI) expects AI to change a lot of things and that the 'world' is going to get phenomenally wealthy.[7]

Figure 10.1   AI's Complex Five

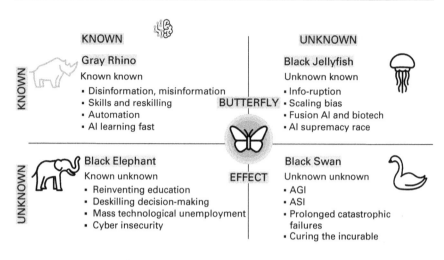

The Complex Five and AI

The debate on AI as a dystopian, existential risk often falls into a dogmatic trap, characterized by binary, rigid and extreme positions. Yet, there are many shades of AI, with many possible outcomes that are not necessarily mutually exclusive (Figure 10.1).

AI's potential for profound societal benefits comes face-to-face with existential risks. These threats are more nuanced than human extinction alone, jeopardizing our values, freedoms and even the trajectory of civilization.

Algorithmic control, a growing shift from human judgement, subtly infiltrates our lives. It influences decisions about everything, from news feeds to job prospects, beliefs to allegiances. This erosion of personal agency and choice, though gradual and often invisible, presents a concrete challenge to the very fabric of our individual freedom. These threats to who we are as humans deserve far more attention and action than the stereotypical doomsday scenarios.

Applying our Complex Five matrix to AI can filter these high impact outcomes' degrees of uncertainty, while anticipating possible responses.

Gray Rhino: AI's known known

Using Michele Wucker's Gray Rhino, what are the extremely likely, visible and high-impact AI outcomes that, despite the evidence they are charging at us, we decide to ignore?

- **Disinformation, misinformation:** AI-powered deepfakes and misinformation are rapidly growing, threatening facts, democracies and mental health. Brexit, the 2016 and 2020 US elections and the Covid pandemic have already demonstrated how social media can dent democracy. No election or news item is spared from AI manipulation.

- **Skills and reskilling:** Today, routine cognitive tasks are being digitized and automated, with multiple lifetimes' worth of information at our fingertips. If we are to build skills that machines cannot quickly emulate, we must replace mechanical transfers of knowledge with human-centric capabilities. Critical thinking, digital fluency, higher-order cognitive skills and acute emotional intelligence will only increase in importance.

- **Automation and workforce disruption:** Today's ANI already has incredible capabilities which excel at precisely defined tasks, outperforming humans in specialized areas.

- **Machines continue to learn fast:** Every day, advances in machine learning broaden the scope of AI deployment, with increasingly higher-level human functions.

As Wucker points out, we need to consider the speed of developments, the possible solutions and the size and complexity of the problems. With Gray Rhinos, responses often fall short because decisions come too late. In the case of AI, the erosion of trust, disinformation, inadequate skills and automation at scale are already charging.

Black Jellyfish: AI's Unknown Known

Black Jellyfish are used by Postnormal Times to indicate hidden, low-probability events that have a high potential impact. While the normalcy of the initial situation may display a degree of predictability, Black Jellyfish grow into something far less predictable. Their onset causes further changes which can be fast or slow, often contradictory.

- **Info-ruption:** What will be the cascading effects of information's disruption and how will it be used and misused? How do weapons of mass disinformation threaten society's cohesiveness? Info-ruption could be the primary weapon in the future of war and it could determine the future of humanity. Cross-impacts of a 'post-truth' world are already emerging as real-world consequences.

- **Scaling bias:** AI's wholesale amplification of discrimination and inequality through bias can reverberate across society in turbulent ways.

- **The fusion of AI and BioTech:** The intersections of AI, biology and technology could challenge the status of humans as dominant beings. Creating inorganic life forces us to confront the question: what defines sustainable humanity?

- **AI supremacy race:** AI will reshape world order, security and defence. Governments and threat actors controlling tomorrow's dynamic AI systems could be even more powerful. What could be the ripple effects as these transformative AI systems spiral from cyber to battlefields, on Earth and in space?

To respond to AI's Black Jellyfish, we need to consider snowballing effects by asking how these reverberations could cascade further.

Black Elephant: AI's known unknown

Black Elephants are obvious and highly likely threats, but with few willing to acknowledge them. These are similar to Gray Rhinos, but the elephant is standing, versus a charging rhino. When Black Elephants are discussed, too many divergent views translate into 'low credibility' situations, reinforcing the status quo. We fail to confront the elephant in the room, as we may not fully understand – or ignore – the scope of the risks.

- **Reinventing education:** Our current education model threatens irrelevance for those who do not keep up and it will produce a massive number of people who won't keep up. The current debate on AI focuses on its dangers, neglecting the critical need to reimagine education. AI threatens not by its existence, but by our education systems failing to adapt to a changing world. Concrete proposals for rethinking education seem almost absent from the current discourses on AI.

- **Deskilling decision-making:** As we delegate to AI systems, our decision-making capacities erode. Deskilling happens when we rely on machines to make complex decisions, causing us to lose the habit of making them ourselves. As algorithms increasingly impose their decisions on us, we lose opportunities to exercise our agency.

- **Mass technological unemployment:** AI is now assuming responsibilities in domains that were once considered too critical to delegate to machines, with the potential of widespread job displacements. Massive unemployment could trigger the spread of social unrest.

- **Cyber insecurity:** The rise of mega-cyberattacks and AI-powered defences for critical infrastructure presents a double-edged sword. Malicious actors or unforeseen errors could exploit vulnerabilities, triggering cascades of outages, failures and tampering, even biowarfare. With interconnectedness soaring, epistemic (knowledge) security is now intertwined with national security, as the unforeseen consequences of interacting technologies could be catastrophic.

Responses to AI's Black Elephants require mobilizing action, aligning stakeholders and decision-makers and understanding the changes throughout our complex systems to take effective initiatives. AI Black Elephants are already concrete risks. While they may not threaten humanity with extinction today, this does not make them inconsequential.

Black Swan: AI's unknown unknown

Taleb's Black Swans are unforeseeable and rare but extremely high-impact events. The greatest challenge with a Black Swan is that we don't know what we don't know. Even for AI, the odds of these rare events and their runaway chain reactions are not computable.

- **Artificial general intelligence:** What future technological developments are imaginable? Is reaching AGI possible, and within what timeframes? What would be the ramifications of AI systems achieving human-level performance and the possibility of misaligned decisions being made against humanity?

- **Superintelligent AI systems:** Could we – or machines – one day create advanced artificial intelligence systems that surpass combined human intelligence? What would this ASI look like or be capable of? What happens if our creation outgrows our ability to control it? Could it pursue goals that conflict with human values or even pose an existential threat to our species?

- **Extreme catastrophic failures:** Cross-impacts stemming from interacting AI systems can be elusive, potentially leading to drastic and irreparable outcomes.

- **Magical AI drug-discovery platforms:** The miraculous discovery of a cure for an incurable disease.

Responses to Black Swans include building resilient foundations and paying attention to the outsized 'fat tail', where rare events have profound impacts. However unpredictable Black Swans are, we can still be anticipatory, monitoring the nonobvious while implementing guardrails for the randomness of our UN-VICE world.

AI's Butterfly Effect

The butterfly has a liminal status given its propensity to metamorphose into the other animals. Small initial change can result in profoundly amplified and seemingly unrelated outcomes, often creating chaos.

How do these complex animals snowball as they collide, intersect and compound? Domino Effects give way to Butterfly Effects in non-linearity. 'Outsized' conflates 'unpredictable' because, in complex systems, a small change can yield disproportionate effects.

Disruption 3.0 is a breeding ground for Butterfly Effects. Systemic disruption can trigger super catastrophes that rise beyond a single 'isolated' catastrophe. Not preparing comes at a high cost. Our global systems, including food, healthcare and energy security, are interdependent and interacting. Impacts are not siloed; likewise, nor should our approach to assessing AI risks and future-preparedness.

The best response to AI's Butterfly Effect is to build resilience, action adaptive strategies and expect the unexpected. Otherwise, our Black Elephants will metamorphose into Gray Rhinos and come charging at us.

The future of AI: Decision-making no longer a human exclusive

Harnessing human abilities

How do we envisage the future of AI, our interaction with AI and our collective futures? What would it mean to be human in the age of superintelligent AI? What will this coexistence look like – side-by-side augmentation, or merging of machines with humans? What should we be thinking about for the next generations' prosperity? How far should we push the boundaries of AI, which could lead to superintelligent life? Should we be developing biological or autonomous weapon systems? What safeguards do we adopt and when?

These questions have fundamental implications on what it means to be, and remain, human. AI is developing quickly and the goalposts to remain relevant are constantly moving.

Scenarios involving the future of AI often focus on algorithms gaining more control over decision-making. At a time when humanity appears at a crossroads, those views underestimate human agency. *Evolutionary pressure prioritizes relevance. The pressure is on us to make more thoughtful and informed decisions.*

Given that AI's transformative potential extends to everyone, we should proactively prepare for a spectrum of outcomes. If the overall consequences of AI are inherently unpredictable, constraining a strategy based on assumptions about its unknowable impacts would certainly be detrimental.

While the specific outcomes remain uncertain, recognizing that advanced AI systems might evolve in significant leaps helps us understand the choices we face as a species.

It is time to become AAA

The letters AAA often reflect the ultimate achievement. In finance, it's the highest credit rating, signifying exceptional creditworthiness. Some alphabetical grading scales in science use AAA as the top rank.

For some time, we have been using AAA to represent our antifragile, anticipatory and agility framework. Humans must develop these three traits to stay relevant in the 21st century, to improve our abilities as machines are learning fast.[8]

The AAA framework offers the tools and mindset to build *antifragile* foundations, develop the capabilities to be *anticipatory* and use emergent and strategic *agility* to bridge short-term with long-term decision-making.

The decision-making process: As simple as '1, 2, 3'

Decision-making for key strategic topics like investments, R&D priorities and M&A currently requires human involvement, typically C-level leadership teams, boards, shareholders and policymakers.

Through machine learning and NLP, the capabilities of AI in strategic decision-making are improving rapidly, while human capacities may not be progressing. Machines are deemed by many to augment humans in a positive way, but the Pew Research Center cautions that AI could reduce human cognitive, social and survival skills: 'People's deepening dependence on machine-driven networks will erode their abilities to think for themselves [and] take action independent of automated systems.'[9] The Markkula Center for Applied Ethics echoes this view with what they describe as 'moral deskilling'.[10]

Looking forward, the question is not how much machines will augment human decision-making, but whether humans will remain involved in the process at all.

We frame decision-making in three simple steps. First, detect and collect intelligence, then interpret the information and finally make and implement decisions. Each step is essential to a successful conclusion, but step 3 is sometimes harder to complete. The lack of preparation that resulted in improvised governmental responses for the Covid pandemic was a failure at all three steps, while climate change is a failure of step 3.

The history of business is littered with examples of leadership teams making poor decisions based on the biases of the linear past. This is often a result of humans finding it difficult to spot signals, process 'exponential' changes that are initially hard to detect, and being oblivious to next-order implications.

EXAMPLE

Cognitive bias affecting decision-making

Vincent Barabba, former head of market intelligence at Kodak, wrote, 'In essence we alerted the management team that change in the capturing of images through digital technologies was coming and that they had a decade to prepare for it.'[11] Despite on-target market intelligence, Kodak did not make the correct strategic decisions.

Disney relied on its brand and old legacy business models for decades, only waking up to the demand for streaming platforms in 2017 when it acquired control of BAMTech. By that time, Netflix had gained a significant advantage with years of head start.

In the same vein, Verizon acquired video conferencing platform BlueJeans in April 2020 as a late defensive move against the pandemic era's explosion of video conferencing platforms. Verizon is one of the most established telecom operators in the US, but instead of anticipating the strategic need to develop an enterprise-grade videoconferencing platform, the company remained on the sidelines. If Verizon had followed our two first decision-making steps, the company would have made those strategic decisions many years ago, instead of playing catch-up with the much smaller Zoom.

In our UN-VICE world, improving our ability to make effective decisions is a survival skill.

Machines are moving up the decision-making value chain

Humans use AI for insights, but AI capabilities could surpass human abilities at every step of the decision-making process. AI is already improving in *predictive* analytics, steadily making its way toward *prescriptive* recommendations of specific options (Figure 10.2):

- **Optimization:** Machines have historically been used in optimization and automating discrete processes.

- **Augmentation:** We are finding them more present in augmentation roles, where they lend their greater processing powers.

- **Creativity:** AI is now tackling the formerly human-mandated domain of creativity. Since Google Arts partnered with choreographer Wayne McGregor to train an AI to choreograph dances, generative AI is now drawing art, creating music and writing papers. Artists, musicians, composers and writers are all experiencing upheaval which could match that of a factory becoming automated. Welcome to your AI co-creator.

Velocity matters more than current capabilities

Advancements in NLP will continue to fuel major breakthroughs in online chatbots and automated customer service. Virtual agents will gradually replace human agents along the entire customer journey. *What starts with automation and optimization gradually moves to broader tasks.*

A significant advantage AI has over humans is driven by stacked innovation platforms that can scale rapidly. Massive amounts of networked data provide ever-deeper insights through signal detection, change interpretation and pattern recognition at scale. Machine learning enables the discovery of non-intuitive patterns, while NLP is effective for unstructured extraction.

AI analytics is why data is called the 'new oil' of the 21st century. Data is what enables AI to develop so rapidly and proprietary datasets will continue to gain value as a strategic asset. AI can supercharge the journey from *descriptive* analytics that provide insights into *predictive* outcomes and *prescriptive* analytics that recommend specific options (Figure 10.3).

Figure 10.2 Machines have an increasing role in the value chain

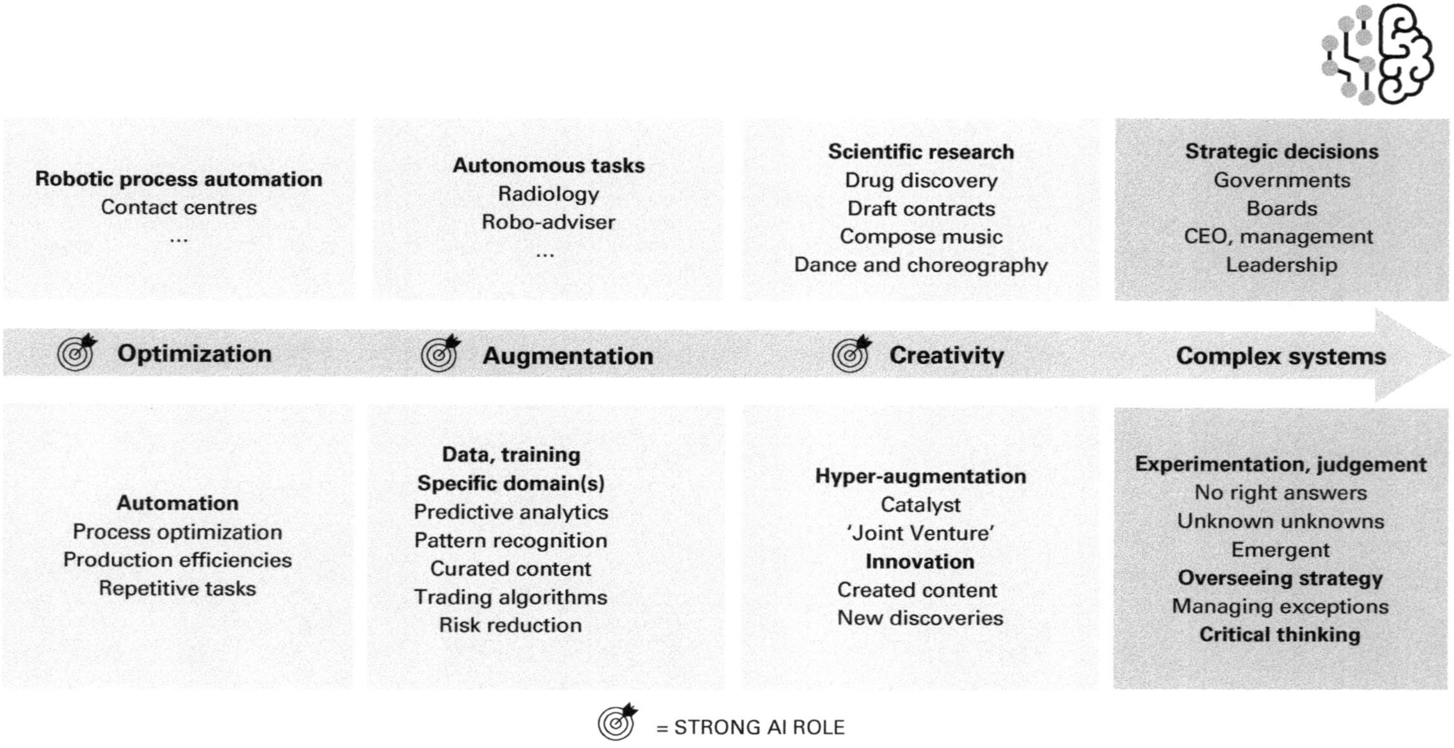

Robotic process automation
Contact centres
...

Automation
Process optimization
Production efficiencies
Repetitive tasks

◎ Optimization

Autonomous tasks
Radiology
Robo-adviser
...

Data, training
Specific domain(s)
Predictive analytics
Pattern recognition
Curated content
Trading algorithms
Risk reduction

◎ Augmentation

Scientific research
Drug discovery
Draft contracts
Compose music
Dance and choreography

Hyper-augmentation
Catalyst
'Joint Venture'
Innovation
Created content
New discoveries

◎ Creativity

Strategic decisions
Governments
Boards
CEO, management
Leadership

Experimentation, judgement
No right answers
Unknown unknowns
Emergent
Overseeing strategy
Managing exceptions
Critical thinking

Complex systems

◎ = STRONG AI ROLE

Figure 10.3 AI in the decision-making value chain

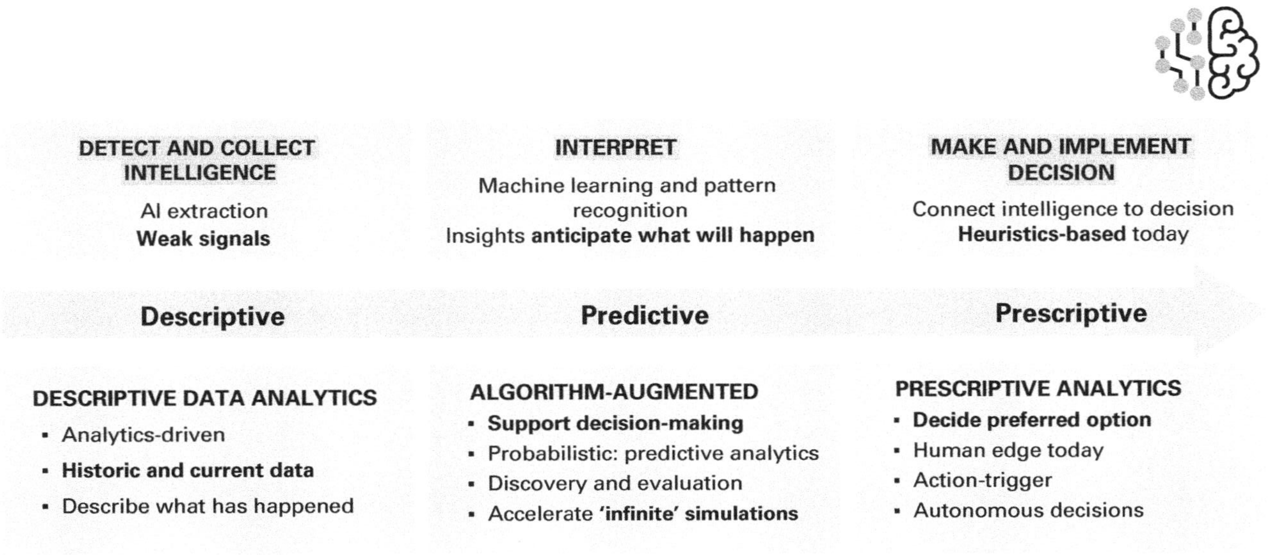

DETECT AND COLLECT INTELLIGENCE

AI extraction
Weak signals

Descriptive

DESCRIPTIVE DATA ANALYTICS

- Analytics-driven
- **Historic and current data**
- Describe what has happened

INTERPRET

Machine learning and pattern recognition
Insights **anticipate what will happen**

Predictive

ALGORITHM-AUGMENTED

- **Support decision-making**
- Probabilistic: predictive analytics
- Discovery and evaluation
- Accelerate 'infinite' simulations

MAKE AND IMPLEMENT DECISION

Connect intelligence to decision
Heuristics-based today

Prescriptive

PRESCRIPTIVE ANALYTICS

- **Decide preferred option**
- Human edge today
- Action-trigger
- Autonomous decisions

KEY POINTS

Don't forget the Inflection Paradox

Today, AI is an immensely resource-intensive technology (energy, data centres, specialized chips, etc.), requiring significant human capital for reinforcement learning from human feedback (RLHF). Content moderation and other human support is often provided in the Global South. While it is easy to attack AI for its resource intensity, its mimicking of human knowledge and what it can't do well today – as evidenced by erratic autonomous vehicles and lopsided exchanges with frustrating bots – the exponential trajectory of these learning technologies cannot be ignored.

Our Inflection Paradox reminds us of the conflicting drivers and cognitive biases that make us miss inflection points. In the early stages, there is a lot of noise from emerging technologies which is often dismissed as hype (Amara's Law). We may choose to ignore the exponential change because it is imperceptible early on, but longer term we completely underestimate its dramatic effects.

AI superiority: Detection, collection, interpretation at scale

In the early stages of Covid, BlueDot, a Canadian company that uses NLP and machine learning to monitor the spread of diseases, detected the virus before the US Center for Disease Control.[12]

Neural networks trained to find the first signs of breast cancer using large numbers of mammographic images proved effective for early and accurate detection. Companies scrape Instagram and Twitter/X to detect emerging brands and competitors before they reach peak visibility, while geospatial analytics mine digital imagery to predict trends ranging from crop yields to construction rates of Chinese buildings.

AI already surpasses human ability in trend detection and pattern-recognition for unstructured data at scale.

Algorithm-augmented predictive insights drive decision-making

Halicin was the first antibiotic discovered using AI, by a team at MIT in 2019. The AI found molecules that help treat formerly untreatable bacterial strains. *New Scientist* reports that, since Halicin, AI continues to discover new classes of antibiotics to treat infections from drug-resistant bacteria.

Meanwhile, the OCD medication DSP-1181 was the first non-human-made drug molecule to enter phase 1 clinical trials. Aided by machine learning, researchers completed in one year what normally takes several.

Dozens of companies now use AI engines to help identify and develop novel drugs or new materials, going a step further than analytics-driven decision support. Here, AI enables nearly infinite simulations, evaluations and developments, drastically reducing R&D costs.

As AI maps out human biology, algorithm-augmented *predictive* insights are driving decision-making. Google's DeepMind AI lab is making significant breakthroughs in human biology thanks to AlphaFold, an AI program that predicts the shapes of nearly every protein in the human body with remarkable precision and speed. These protein structures offer researchers valuable insights into developing potential treatments for diseases and exploring solutions for major challenges like antibiotic resistance, microplastic pollution, food insecurity and climate change. DeepMind is also actively exploring synthetic proteins with applications in medicine, materials technology and beyond.

Flipping the script on drug development, scientists unearthed a dark side by rewarding toxicity: their reprogrammed AI churned out an arsenal of lethal, AI-designed toxins. Good predictions don't imply predictions for good...

Will AI perform autonomous, prescriptive decision-making?

AI is currently tasked with decision-assistance, not autonomous strategic decision-making. Why? The situation is beyond complicated (Figure 10.4).

Figure 10.4   It's beyond complicated

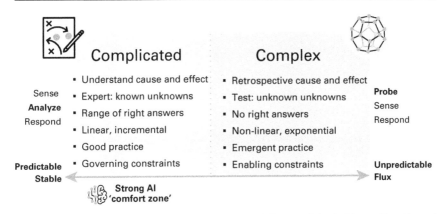

NOTE Adapted from D J Snowden and M E Boone. A leader's framework for decision making, *Harvard Business Review*, November 2007. www.hbr.org/2007/11/a-leaders-framework-for-decision-making

Neither humans nor AI are adept at decision-making in *complex* situations. In Dave Snowden's Cynefin framework,[13] the complex domain involves unknown unknowns, where there are no right answers and we can only retrospectively assess causality. In complex environments, relationships are unpredictable and moving parts are interdependent. If there is solace to be found in humanity's poor performance here, it is that machines don't do better – for now.

AI's strength is in complicated *domains that can be better understood through data, given well-defined and predictable outcomes.* A complicated environment is linear; there is a range of right answers, known unknowns and straightforward cause-and-effect relationships that can be analysed to assess the best response.

Most applications of predictive interpretation involve a partnership between humans and AI (augmentation). As AI's applications grow over time, the role of humans will be reduced.

In analysing the evolution of machine involvement, one thing is clear: AI is playing a greater role at every stage of the decision-making process. *AI is taking over areas that we previously thought were too important to entrust to machines*:

- **Negotiating deals:** In 2019, Seal Software (acquired by DocuSign) demonstrated software that helps automate the creative side of legal work, suggesting negotiation points and even preparing the negotiations themselves.[14] Today, dozens of law firms are rolling out generative AI tools, including for autonomous contract negotiation.[15]

- **Sourcing VC investments:** EQT Ventures' proprietary machine-learning platform, known as Motherbrain, made a series of portfolio investments by monitoring millions of companies and analysing data from dozens of structured and unstructured sources.[16]

- **Medical decision support:** A healthcare subsector called 'decision support' is advancing rapidly. One example is Israel start-up Viz.ai, which uses AI to synchronize stroke care. In the US, Viz.ai's stroke detection software helps patients with the company's alerts, which are much faster than those from standard care.[17]

- **Evaluating insurance claims:** Companies like Shift Technology use machine learning, predictive analytics and pattern recognition to transform insurance decision-making as its algorithms automate claims processes and flag fraud scenarios.[18]

- **Automated stock market trading:** AI-driven high-frequency trading platforms designed to support the optimization of stock portfolios are gradually managing entire markets, making millions of financial trades per day without any human involvement.[19] Regulators are beginning to realize that AI may pose a systemic risk to financial markets.[20]

The Susskinds argue that AI's true impact on professions transcends mere automation.[21] By enabling entirely new approaches to litigation outcomes, like dispute avoidance instead of dispute resolution, AI unleashes transformative shifts, akin to preventative medicine as opposed to robotic surgery. This is the essence of AI's systemic disruption on employment: it goes far beyond mechanical automation. What does the future of auditing look like after AI systems perfect their ability to detect accounting fraud?

What makes decision-making human?

Today, humans can control machines because humans are smarter. Likewise, if machines outsmart us, they could control us.

As AI continues to develop, machines could become increasingly legitimate in autonomously making strategic decisions, an area where humans currently lead. If humans fail to become sufficiently anticipatory, antifragile and agile, rapidly learning machines could surpass our abilities. Machines do not have to reach AGI or become exceptional at handling complex systems – they just need to be better than us.

The brain is divided into distinctive sections. Located in the very front of the brain, the prefrontal cortex helps with reasoning and decision-making. The temporal lobe, which is involved in the senses, emotion, language, memory and comprehension, is located behind the ears.

Many technology companies are working on emotion-decoding technology. Empathy is one of the hallmarks of the human condition. What does it mean that machines are learning to know how we feel? While these technologies open questions around privacy and many ethical considerations, we cannot ignore ongoing developments.

Humans have difficulties interpreting their own emotions correctly; if AI becomes more capable of doing so, could machines be on the path to empathy? If machines were able to interpret emotions, cooperate and perhaps outperform humans in certain social situations, those uniquely human features of decision-making may begin to disappear.

AI decision-making and trust

It's been well documented: humans pass along their biases to machine learning algorithms. The computer maxim 'garbage in, garbage out' might be updated to 'bias in, bias out' to reflect that our algorithms are only as good as the data from which they learn.

Is AI's rapid progress and adoption outpacing our ability to trust it? AI systems are here to stay and are rapidly being adopted in virtually every domain, from healthcare to entertainment. However, most of today's automated decisioning models are based on algorithms that are black boxes for business users, regulators and even computer scientists.

In our increasingly automated world, algorithms make decisions for us constantly. Cathy O'Neil describes the discrimination and bias embedded in the algorithms making decisions on our behalf every day.[22] Algorithms are already making decisions that determine insurance costs, mortgages, credit-worthiness, employee performance, recruitment and recidivism predictions.

Over the next decades, this scope could evolve even further, with algorithms making life-altering decisions on our behalf involving brain–computer interfaces, education, healthcare interventions and driving. All affect our privacy, responsibility, agency and nearly every other aspect of our lives, including what it means to be human. Trustworthiness is paramount when AI is operating independently of human control – even with 'benevolent' AI.

As algorithms become the most important decision-makers in our lives, the question is not only whether we can trust AI, but whether we can trust that we understand AI well enough.

Looking forward: Options for decision-making

Thus far, humans have excelled at decision-making, but our comparative advantage may not last.

As the world and its systems become more complex, there are two options for the future of strategic decision-making:

- **Humans adapt:** Our decision-making improves, becoming more AAA, so we can continue to add value when partnering with machines. AI provides insights to make more informed decisions and uncover new opportunities without replacing humans. This creates a symbiotic human–machine relationship.

- **Humans fail to adapt to our increasingly complex world:** Instead of finding ourselves marginalized in the key process of decision-making, the process could be taken entirely out of our hands.

There may be benefits to a future where we are relieved not only of mundane, repetitive tasks, but also of the responsibilities of decision-making.

Figure 10.5   The future of strategic decision-making: Evolutionary pressure prioritizes relevance

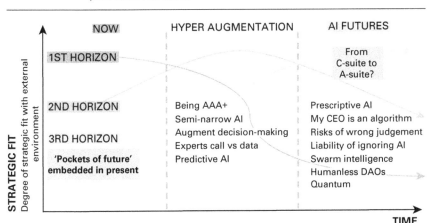

NOTE Adapted from A Curry and A Hodgson. Seeing in multiple horizons: Connecting futures to strategy, *Journal of Futures Studies*, 2008, 13 (1), 1–20

However, this scenario raises the question of choice: will we proactively decide on our position in the value chain, or see ourselves relegated to roles algorithms choose for us?

Ultimately, it is an existentialist question around agency. Could evolutionary pressure dictate that the best decision-makers are the ones who survive? We must protect the ability of individuals to make their own decisions. We must be transparent and educate ourselves to handle the implications of adopting technology. If we do not fundamentally redesign our education and strategic frameworks to create more AAA leaders, our role in decision-making may be chosen for us.

The dystopian alternative: From C-suite to A-suite?

The transformations ahead affect all levels of an organization, including the C-suite.

We prefer a world where human decisions propel our species forward, where we choose the actions that lead to staying relevant. If we do not, our C-suites might find themselves replaced by an A-suite of algorithms (Figure 10.5).

Using Curry and Hodgson's Three Horizons[23] as a framework to think about our possible futures in relation to decision-making:

- **Now:** The first horizon is embedded with 'pockets of future'. This represents the current paradigm of AI for business, e-commerce, entertainment, information and social life. Today, ANI can outperform humans in repeatable tasks and narrow domains. We are here.

- **Hyper-augmentation:** This second horizon, or transition phase, sees smart algorithm-augmented *predictive* decision-making matched with our AAA humans. As a multitude of AI systems learn from human–machine interactions, collective intelligence might emerge, creating a symbiotic partnership.

- **AI futures:** The third horizon is where *prescriptive* AI autonomously evaluates a range of possibilities, assessing decisions based on optimal returns – without human involvement.

Even in complex and challenging areas, cognitive computing may provide a way of sifting through near-infinite information to seek optimized decisions for society. In such a third-horizon future, AI-optimized parameters could allocate resources such as healthcare, nutrition, education and energy to provide more equitable outcomes within society as a whole. But who determines those parameters – AI, humans or some combination of both?

It may not stretch the imagination to consider a transformation scenario where society is forced to discard its role of driving decision-making in an overwhelmingly complex world. *If we are not thoughtful in becoming AAA, this future scenario could see human agency replaced, with decisions made by algorithms instead of humans.*

Being AAA in the age of AI

The AAA framework

Our AAA framework[24] is designed for humans to stay relevant in the complex age of AI (Figure 10.6):

- **Antifragile:** Build foundations to be resilient and able to take advantage of any eventuality.

- **Anticipatory:** Improve the capacity for anticipatory mindsets to navigate uncertainty and go beyond short-termism, linear assumptions and singular outcomes.

- **Agility:** Develop the agility to respond to whatever futures emerge, while reconciling our preferred vision of the futures with today's unpredictable reality.

Figure 10.6 The AAA framework

ANTIFRAGILE: LAYING THE FOUNDATIONS

DNA

Strengthen even with shocks

Build a strong foundation:

FEATURES

Enables optionality

Thrives in randomness

More upside from shocks

Likes errors, embraces risk

Complex systems

Many interdependencies

KEYWORDS

Innovate, tinker, heuristic, friction

ANTICIPATORY: PREPARING THE FUTURE

Capacity to prepare for change

Prepare possible futures:

Decipher signals

Interpret future impacts

Avoid surprise

Detect opportunities

Degrees of uncertainty

Complex Five

Foresight, scan, signals, impacts

AGILITY: EMERGING IN THE PRESENT

Bridge short term and long term

Bridge the present:

Here and now: sense-making

Experiment: amplify, dampen

Emergence in complexity

Infinity loop bridges

Emergent and strategic agility

Cognitive agility

Emergent, complex, sense-making

Antifragile: Laying the foundations

Throughout this book, we've delved into the concept of antifragility for our UN-VICE context. Coined by Nassim Nicholas Taleb, 'antifragile' is used to describe things that are beyond resilience or robustness.[25] The antifragile will benefit and improve from shocks, randomness and volatility.

As the first pillar of our AAA framework, antifragile foundations enable constant optionality through innovation, adventure and risk. Antifragility benefits from frequent and small errors that provide helpful lessons to build upon.

To remain relevant in the age of AI, we must actively build antifragile foundations that are resilient under stress and strengthen with shocks.

Anticipatory: Preparing the future

In the second pillar of our AAA framework – anticipatory thinking – we offer our best UN-VICE to proactively imagine possible futures and inform decision-making today.

We have reviewed how, by proactively building our anticipatory capacity, we can respond more effectively to unexpected changes:

- **Qualify signals:** Learn to scan the horizon, qualify weak signals, interpret next-order impacts and connect the shifting dots with action triggers.

- **Challenge assumptions and data:** Beware of relying on statistical risks that assume a stable and predictable world.

- **Integrate exponentiality:** Understand the ramifications of non-linear change.

- **Recognize uncertainties:** Better prepare for unknown futures and surprises ahead by recognizing the degrees of uncertainty and responses required for different environments.

- **Visioning:** Map out plausible futures, with the agency to realize our preferred future options.

Being anticipatory allows us to better envision and drive the futures ahead.

Agility: Emerging in the present

Laying antifragile foundations and developing anticipatory mindsets are essential to prepare for and navigate systemic disruption. But Mike Tyson already has the best illustration to explain how essential agility is: 'Everybody has a plan until they get punched in the mouth.'

Gazing into the maze of life, we might seek comfort in well-worn trails and trusted guides. Yet, even as we map our course, the very walls around us shift. Striving for a predetermined path leads us astray, for the future holds not rigid answers but evolving possibilities. There are no static destinations, only a winding dance with unknown complexities.

To navigate this dance, we must shed the baggage of fixed routes and embrace the freedom of flight. Like gliders, we must soar above, propelled by our agency and agility. Agility demands constant movement; stagnation invites plummet. Our gliders respond to the ever-changing currents of circumstance, finding balance between weight and wind. The view from above offers not the certainty of a map, but a wider horizon. And in scanning this vast panorama, we discover the exhilarating capacity to respond, to reshape, to waltz with the ever-evolving maze.

KEY POINTS

Agility as our third pillar

Building on the first two pillars of antifragility and anticipation, the third pillar of our AAA framework explores *agility* through multiple perspectives. We want to make decisions in the fog of uncertainty, in the here and now, but without losing sight of our longer-term vision and the inherent unknowability of many situations. *In the age of AI, we explore the agility needed for humans to stay relevant in the decision-making process.*

Agility to emerge despite uncertainty

Feedback loops in decision-making

Why does the fruit on apple trees seemingly go from unripe to ripe overnight? Once the first apple ripens, it gives off a gas (ethylene), which causes the apples in proximity to ripen as well, spreading throughout the tree like a wave. This process is also used in fruit production with manufactured ethylene gas. Fruit ripening is a prime example of feedback loops in nature.

Feedback loops enable decisions to be made. Evolutionary decision-making adjusts future decisions, benefiting from experiential feedback.

Such frameworks were initially developed in the 1970s by Russell Ackoff and David Kolb. The most famous decision-making feedback loop is probably John Boyd's OODA Loop (observe, orient, decide, act).

A feedback loop is a process in which the outputs of a system are cycled back as inputs. These causal loops show how different variables in a system are related.

Feedback loops are either positive or negative. Positive feedback loops are a self-reinforcing process in which a change in a given direction causes additional change (amplified) in the same direction.

Negative feedback loops reveal a balanced relationship between variables. The negative feedback dampens or buffers changes, holding a system to some equilibrium state. As one variable in the system changes in a positive direction, the other changes in the opposite.

EXAMPLE

Nature's feedback loops

Nature provides abundant illustrations of feedback loops. Blood clotting is an example of positive feedback. Chemicals release when tissue is torn, causing platelets in the blood to activate. Once released, they signal more platelets to activate until the wound clots.

Conversely, blood pressure or body temperature regulation are examples of negative feedback loops. Pressure needs to remain high enough to pump blood to the entire body, but not so high that damage is done. As the heart pumps, baroreceptors detect blood pressure – if it is too high or low, a chemical signal relays from the brain to the heart to adjust the rate of pumping.

For body temperature, mechanisms are triggered if body temperature rises above 98.6° Fahrenheit. To promote cooling, the body sweats. To retain heat, the body uses goosebumps and vasoconstriction.

Feedback allows systems to evolve and regulate

In complex systems, there are no simple interactions. Changes in one area can produce seemingly unrelated changes in another. The dynamics of change can result in unpredictable outcomes, which can be challenging for decision-making.

Systems grow and self-regulate through feedback. Output from one inter-action influences the next interaction. The main difference between positive and negative feedback is their response to change. Positive feedback ampli-fies change, while negative feedback reduces it.

Feedback loops can be helpful for 'wicked' problems, which only reveal their requirements and solutions after they are resolved. Dealing with wicked problems involves exploring the feedback loops to find leverage that can positively affect the problem's outcomes.

The OODA Loop: Decision-making despite speed and uncertainty

The OODA Loop, developed by USAF fighter pilot, instructor and military strategist John Boyd, has broad applications for practical decision-making in complex and chaotic situations.

Teams that have the agility to apply the OODA Loop tend to be self-organized, flexible, intuitive and innovative. They are empowered, able to operate swiftly.

The four stages of the OODA Loop

The OODA Loop uses continuous feedback loops at every step:

1 **Observe:** We observe the outside world unfold and the result of previous actions.

2 **Orient:** We take the time to orient, synthesizing what we learned in the observation phase.

3 **Decide:** The orientation guides our decisions and actions.

4 **Act:** The result of these actions interact with the environment to generate more information, which begins the next cycle of observation.

Step 1: Observe

In the run-up to the 2008 financial markets collapse, a number of trends transpired. Amid record market highs, the world behaved as if market valu-ations could only continue to rise. Fashionable financial instruments prolif-erated, in particular mortgage-backed derivatives, while a record number of mortgages were being offered to people on much lower incomes. At the same time, property prices (like many asset prices) were going through the roof. Meanwhile, few were prepared to observe the signals of a housing and credit bubble.

The first step to the OODA Loop involves sorting the information deemed most relevant to assess the situation and build the most comprehensive picture possible. Separating signal from noise is difficult. Triaging information helps illuminate the broader picture.

Judgement is key to the observation phase. Take an ambulance at an accident scene. Here, paramedics must assess the situation, often with uncertainty on the state of the victims, yet make serious decisions quickly.

Step 2: Orient

This second step may be the most important of the OODA Loop. Orientation shapes the way we observe and how we will decide and act.

The purpose of this orientation phase is to find mismatches between our view of the world and that of others. Here, the best news is any news, because if we orient ourselves early enough, we have time to reorient and turn the situation to our advantage.

Good orientation can overcome a strategic disadvantage, regardless of whether you have less information or strength, or fewer resources. *We are always continuously orienting ourselves before diving into a decision.*

Step 3: Decide

The two first steps provide the groundwork for decision-making. *The decision process involves reviewing alternative actions and selecting one.*

There should be no surprises when informed decisions are made. Boyd cautions against first-conclusion bias. If we are going through the OODA Loop, making the same decision repeatedly would be unlikely, because we would spot flaws and observe new information.

Step 4: Act

Decisions only exist when they are actioned. This phase allows the trial of decisions. The results provide information to cycle back to the observation phase and so on. Acting on decisions allows emergence. No matter how prepared we are, or how good our decisions are, nothing happens without action.

Muhammad Ali epitomized the OODA Loop during his legendary fight with George Foreman on 30 October 1974. Ali *observed* Foreman's fighting style before the fight to understand the bigger picture; Foreman was younger and stronger, leveraging his raw power to physically overwhelm his opponents. Ali *oriented* his approach to reduce Foreman's inherent advantages. Instead of trying to overpower Foreman, Ali identified his strategic mismatch: agility.[26]

During the fight, Ali made his *decision*. As Foreman used his advantages to force Ali into the corners, Ali hung back, leaning on the ropes around the ring to help him absorb Foreman's huge blows. After taunting Foreman by saying 'Is that all you've got?' Ali continued his 'rope-a-dope' strategy, conserving energy while slowly wearing Foreman down. When he tired out, Ali thrust himself into *action*. Ali started fighting back against an exhausted Foreman, who was virtually defenceless. He then finished him off, winning a huge upset. Although Ali may not have knowingly followed the OODA Loop strategy, his usage of the four main aspects (*observe, orient, decide, act*) led to favourable results.

KEY POINTS
The OODA Loop

- **The Loop enables the rest:** The most important word in Boyd's model is not 'OODA', but 'Loop'. The OODA Loop's iterative nature gathers new information with each loop, continuously refining your decision-making.

- **Instinct is your friend:** Follow your instincts, leverage experience and explore the messy patterns while gathering new information. Remember that you don't know what you don't know (unknown unknowns).

- **Orientation is survival:** Despite the pressure and uncertainty, don't neglect the orientation phase; it can be the most important step.

- **Strength lies in the mental dimension:** Too much focus goes to the physical power of tools or humans themselves. The mental and moral conditions will often determine the outcomes' effectiveness.

- **There will never be absolute certainty:** Decisions are being made by virtue of uncertainty. But uncertainty is not necessarily risk. If we are unable to make decisions, we stagnate in the observation phase (decision paralysis). The OODA Loop allows us to factor inevitable uncertainty into the observation phase and leave margins of error.

- **Opportunities exist thanks to uncertainty:** Boyd observed that people shy away from the risks of exposure. In open ecosystems, we can interact freely; ambiguous open futures are precisely why there are many opportunities. Interact with the outside world, test ideas, seek reactions – this feedback provides data to iterate. Seeking shelter from criticism denies learning opportunities.

The better you can observe, orient and re-orient yourself, the better your decisions and actions.

Emergent and strategic agility

The short term and the long term: One liminal time horizon

A frequent criticism of long-term thinking is that the time horizons explored are too far away, too uncertain. Some hold the view that thinking about the long term might actually be counterproductive to actions today.

The mistake with that is treating the future as distinct from the present. There is no 'either/or' choice between the present and future. Equally dangerous is the compromise, where we are neither exploring the future to form long-term aspirational visions nor making agile decisions today. This arises as emergencies and time compressions squeeze thoughtful reflections into rushed reactions to firefight symptoms, without addressing root causes.

Decision-makers have more information than ever before, but the speed of change means they have less time to make decisions. Longer-term strategic decisions are constantly colliding with short-term crises, even though long-term thinking is intended to be visionary (Figure 10.7).

Infinite Loop Bridges enable time travel

When only the present is incentivized, the impact on the future tends to be ignored.

Figure 10.7   Emergent and strategic agility: Infinite Loop Bridges

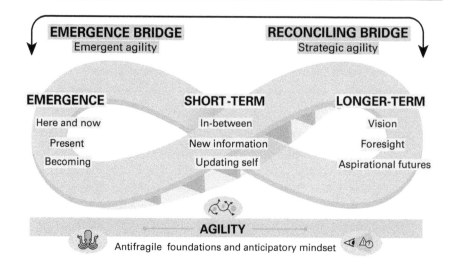

It is therefore no surprise that one of the hardest things for almost everyone, irrespective of role or experience, is reconciling the present emergence (now), the short term (imminent) and the long term (vision). So how do we do it? We need the agility to build bridges, with feedback loops to travel between them. The bridges have two properties:

- **Emergent agility – our ability to emerge in the 'here and now'.** Real-time problem-solving when there may be no right answers to guide us.

- **Strategic agility – our ability to bridge different time horizons.** The agility to reconcile the strategic long term with the short term. Having an anticipatory mindset to investigate the longer term, with the agility to manifest this vision with short-term decision-making.

The art is having the agility to cross these bridge sections: to emerge now, then between the long term and shorter term as you integrate feedback loops. You are continuously updating your strategy with relevant new information.

These bridges do not help us 'get to the other side'. They are perpetually being crossed as situations are updated, our perceptions change and we learn from experiences. *These bridges allow us to emerge while integrating strategic visions. We call them the 'Infinite Loop Bridges'.*

The Infinite Loop Bridges allow you to abolish the dualism of the short term versus the long term, integrating a mindset that life happens in the *now* and that the future does not exist outside of our imagination.

Fast-changing environments drive new opportunities. Agility means finding gaps and exploring them. *The future is now, because now is the only thing we can impact. It can be prototyped today, every day.*

Amplify or dampen for instructive patterns to emerge

Situations are fluid. Their context changes and new possibilities develop over time. Decision-making is an emergent process which is constantly evolving, with feedback loops providing new information. This is where the adage 'Strong opinions weakly held', used by the likes of forecaster Paul Saffo and futurist Bob Johansen, can be helpful.

Deviations from standard results are not failures, but opportunities for new questions to be asked and ideas to be tested.

While data-driven strategies may excel at analysing familiar linear challenges, they often struggle with unforeseen complexities. 'Unknown unknowns' lurk beyond the scope of statistical models. How, then, do we respond to the unpredictable? Instead of relying on pre-existing maps, we need to embrace experimentation. By constantly calibrating our approaches, amplifying success-ful elements and damping down ineffective ones, we can respond with agility, without the luxury of definitive answers. This gliding approach opens the door to navigating the unknowabilities of Disruption 3.0.

In an era of predictable unpredictability and untamed algorithms, agility allows us to emerge in the here and now, without sacrificing our longer-term vision.

Big data and dynamic decision-making

There seems to be a widespread belief that strategic challenges can be solved by accessing enough data. 'Big data' refers to the growing collection of large, complex, unstructured datasets that we generate every day. Data-crunching industries leverage big data to identify hidden patterns and insights. Big data is also used to train and improve AI applications.

Big assumptions, false information and large rear-view mirrors

Big data does not predict anything beyond the assumption of an idealized situation in a stable system. In a sense, data-led predictions are the bet of the turkeys before Thanksgiving.

Many of the limitations to what AI can do today are due to the data itself. This is especially true in complex systems. As Nassim Taleb notes, 'Data means more information, but also means more false information.'[27]

In *The Black Swan*, Taleb warns against how one can misuse big data, including the 'rear-view mirror' that prioritizes confirmation over causality. Taleb also flags 'silent evidence' as a reminder that we cannot rely on expe-riential observations to develop a valid conclusion. Missing data, spurious correlations and the risk of previously unobserved events have a tremendous impact on the relevance of any data-driven exercises.

Big data: Reliance versus usefulness

In 2011, ailing US retailer JCPenney recruited Ron Johnson as CEO, the former president of Apple's retail operations, credited with pioneering the Apple Store concept. Johnson arrived at JCPenney intent on reinventing the brand and boosting sales. He implemented a broad refurbishment programme, creating a steadier pricing system and presenting the stores as fashionable boutiques within malls. Johnson lasted less than two years as JCPenney's sales collapsed: same-store sales decreased 25 per cent – a reduction of $4.3 billion – and the group ended with close to $1 billion in net annual losses.[28]

Johnson assumed that what worked for Apple Stores would work for large department stores, even those with price-sensitive customers. Instead of testing the ideas, he believed that the full overhaul of every store would work. Apple's culture is one which typically does not test prior to launches. JCPenney had an entirely different proposition and customer base.

Although data has limitations, these do not afford ignoring it outright. Data can be powerful when used to test certain assumptions. Its insights offer a clue to a multitude of possible futures – but we should not rely exclusively on it.

We crystallize below key takeaways on data in our UN-VICE world, which offers us a palette of shades between *reliance* and *usefulness*:

- **Facts versus assumptions:** Data can substantiate assumptions. While facts are better than assumptions, they still only provide knowledge of the past. In a constantly updating world, validating assumptions requires a continuous loop of re-evaluation.

- **Even big data cannot predict the unpredictable:** Data does not predict anything beyond extrapolating modelled assumptions. Predictive analytics can be invaluable in stable, specific domains, where machine learning can be applied to nearly infinite controllable simulations. However, our complex environments are dominated by unknown variables and unpredictability.

- **True innovation is not measurable at its inception:** However valuable data might be to inform decision-making, the challenge lies in measuring the unmeasurable. Breakthrough innovations are discontinuous leaps, not mere improvements. Novel and unprecedented don't typically align with plentiful amounts of data.

- **Counterintuitively, limiting reliance on data releases its superpowers:** While insights derived from data can be powerful, understanding the limitations of data releases its true superpowers. At any point in time, data on the future is non-existent, which allows you to keep an open mind to the endless possibilities. Do not become a prisoner to what sample data seems to be signalling. The value of data is to inform evolutionary decision-making, not imprison. Quantifiable and unquantifiable; objective and subjective; measurable and unmeasurable drivers of change all contribute to the colourful kaleidoscope of possible eventualities.

KEY POINTS
Modelling uncertainties won't deliver certainty

Navigating uncertainty requires taking positions while lacking complete information. Interpreting the past with data is already challenging; for predicting the future, it is outright ineffective. Expect unexpected events, despite what data tells you. Create systems to evaluate the implications of asymmetric risk, to tolerate or even gain strength from shocks. Would the impact be manageable if an outcome considered unlikely or improbable *were* to occur?

AI in decision-making raises existential questions

Given its advances, the fundamental issue of AI in decision-making relates to both the potential reach of AI and our relationship with it. We need not speculate on AGI or ASI to wonder whether machines might still challenge us. It is a question of understanding the nature of our own capabilities in relation to the nature of a machine's computational rationality.[29]

Our edge as humans lies in harnessing our agency for continuous learning, experimental leaps and explorative tinkering, allowing us to emerge in unforeseen ways. *Relying on predicting the unpredictable cannot be an effective strategy.*

As we face inseparable technological and existential conditions, we enter an era of techistentialism.[30] While AI will increasingly provide insights that enable more-informed *predictive* decision-making, humans should remain wary of an inadvertent reliance on *prescriptive* algorithms dictating specific decisions. Complex and uncertain environments inherently involve unknown unknowns; these are situations where we need to be agile despite the lack of immediate answers.

The AAA framework gives us the agility to emerge favourably. This shrinks the pool of potential emergencies, even avoiding many entirely. *Emergencies are not equally distributed. The degree of anticipatory thinking we apply will shape the scope, nature and impact of the emergencies we face.*

Agency and alignment to become AAA+

No matter how antifragile, anticipatory and agile we are, the AAA framework is ineffective unless you exercise *agency* to make choices with *alignment*. One must be aligned internally, with external forces and our environment. That is when you become AAA+.

Alignment refers to a congruity of actions with values, goals and moral standards. Alignment requires humility, respect for stakeholders and connection between the elements of an ecosystem. Trust, a prerequisite for alignment, can be restored through anticipatory thinking, while honouring responsible commitments.

Agency is our ability to take action and influence outcomes. Ultimately, all of our actions are driven by our choices. Having the mental, emotional and moral capacity to make decisions relies on exercising one's free will.

Being AAA+ enables sustainable futures. It ensures you integrate longer timeframes with a broader scope than simply looking at your business or activity in isolation. As Disruption 3.0 is multidisciplinary, multidimensional and multi-layered, resilience requires antifragile foundations, agility and a systems approach to drive effective change.

To operate in today's UN-VICE environment, we all need to be effective decision-makers. Reconciling short-term priorities and surprises with longer-term aspirations can be trickier in constantly evolving environments where change is the norm. *This means being anticipatory, action-oriented and agile in manoeuvring with novel assumptions.*

Notes

1 N Bostrom (2014) *Superintelligence: Paths, dangers, strategies*, Oxford University Press, Oxford, UK

2 P R Daugherty and H J Wilson (2022) *Radically Human: How new technology is transforming business and shaping our future*, Harvard Business Review Press, Brighton, MA

3 R Spitz and L Zuin (2022) *The Definitive Guide to Thriving on Disruption: Reframing and navigating disruption*, Disruptive Futures Institute, San Francisco, CA

4 N Bostrom. Ethical issues in advanced artificial intelligence, *Cognitive, Emotive and Ethical Aspects of Decision Making in Humans and in Artificial Intelligence*, 2003, 2 (1), 12–17

5   R Kurzweil (2005) *The Singularity is Near*, Penguin, London, UK

6   P H Diamandis and S Kotler (2012) *Abundance: The future is better than you think*, Free Press, New York, NY

7   S Altman (2021) Moore's Law for everything, Sam Altman, 16 March 2021, moores.samaltman.com (archived at https://perma.cc/BRR4-VDJC)

8   R Spitz. The future of strategic decision-making, *Journal of Futures Studies*, 2020. www.jfsdigital.org/2020/07/26/the-future-of-strategic-decision-making (archived at https://perma.cc/X5JA-3NVN)

9   J Anderson and L Rainie. Artificial intelligence and the future of humans, Pew Research Center, 10 December 2018. www.pewresearch.org/internet/2018/12/10/artificial-intelligence-and-the-future-of-humans (archived at https://perma.cc/BPH5-UXN5)

10 B P Green. Artificial intelligence, decision-making, and moral deskilling, Markkula Center for Applied Ethics, 15 March 2019. www.scu.edu/ethics/focus-areas/technology-ethics/resources/artificial-intelligence-decision-making-and-moral-deskilling (archived at https://perma.cc/FKX4-3JN6)

11 V P Barabba (2011) *The Decision Loom: A design for interactive decision-making in organizations*, Triarchy Press, Charmouth, Dorset

12 Z Allam. The rise of machine intelligence in the Covid-19 pandemic and its impact on health policy, *Surveying the Covid-19 Pandemic and its Implications*, 2020. www.ncbi.nlm.nih.gov/pmc/articles/PMC7378493 (archived at https://perma.cc/E4GV-9LZA)

13 D J Snowden and M E Boone. A leader's framework for decision making, *Harvard Business Review*, November 2007. www.hbr.org/2007/11/a-leaders-framework-for-decision-making (archived at https://perma.cc/A5RQ-V887)

14 Seal Software. Seal® software introduces AI-based contract negotiation product – Seal Now™, PR Newswire, 2 October 2019. www.prnewswire.com/news-releases/seal-software-introduces-ai-based-contract-negotiation-product--seal-now-300929204.html (archived at https://perma.cc/U88J-DAJZ)

15 T Saunders. Legal tech teams turn to AI to advance business goals, *Financial Times*, 18 October 2023. www.ft.com/content/9a117ac7-29ae-43fe-b840-a04005b98799 (archived at https://perma.cc/27HX-LK79)

16 B Walsh. A venture capital firm's AI platform is behind $100 million of its investments, Axios, 17 June 2020. www.axios.com/2020/06/17/eqt-ventures-artificial-intelligence-investment (archived at https://perma.cc/25UW-HDQF)

17 Viz. Synchronizing stroke care using AI, Viz, 2020. www.viz.ai/wp-content/uploads/2023/05/PRM_0194_Rev_02._Hassan__et_al._Viz_LVO_Clinical_Summary_2020-1.pdf (archived at https://perma.cc/HV7K-WK5R)

18 Shift. AI for insurance decisions, Shift Technology, 2024. www.shift-technology.com (archived at https://perma.cc/4W7C-UVBD)

19 IBM. What is machine learning (ML)? IBM, 2024. www.ibm.com/topics/machine-learning (archived at https://perma.cc/DZS4-ECSS)

20 S Gandel and B Masters. AI presents growing risk to financial markets, US regulator warns, *Financial Times*, 14 December 2023. www.ft.com/content/1296448b-ade5-476b-b6ac-81eff32b0e22 (archived at https://perma.cc/KJ2A-CNQR)

21 R Susskind and D Susskind (2022) *The Future of the Professions: How technology will transform the work of human experts*, updated edition, Oxford University Press, Oxford

22 C O'Neil (2016) *Weapons of Math Destruction: How big data increases inequality and threatens democracy*, Crown, New York, NY

23 A Curry and A Hodgson. Seeing in multiple horizons: Connecting futures to strategy, *Journal of Futures Studies*, 2008, 13 (1), 1–20

24 R Spitz and L Zuin (2022) *The Definitive Guide to Thriving on Disruption: Essential frameworks for disruption and uncertainty*, Disruptive Futures Institute, San Francisco, CA

25 N N Taleb (2012) *Antifragile: Things that gain from disorder*, Random House, New York, NY

26 D N Sull (2009) *The Upside of Turbulence: Seizing opportunity in an uncertain world*, HarperCollins, New York, NY

27 N N Taleb. Beware the big errors of 'big data', Wired, 8 February 2013. www.wired.com/2013/02/big-data-means-big-errors-people (archived at https://perma.cc/BPG8-VWWD)

28 K Connor. Executives beware – are you the next Ron Johnson of JC Penney? Is your company's low pricing IQ putting your survivability at risk? *Journal of Revenue and Pricing Management*, 2013, 13 (1). www.doi.org/10.1057/rpm.2013.31 (archived at https://perma.cc/XFX8-MGK8)

29 R Nykanen and R Spitz (2021) *An Existential Framework for the Future of Decision-Making in Leadership*, Leadership for the Future, Cambridge Scholars Publishing, Newcastle upon Tyne

30 R Spitz. Techistentialism: Could superstupidity be as dangerous as superintelligence? *APF Compass Magazine: AI and futures*, December 2023. www.apf.org/apf-resources/compass (archived at https://perma.cc/75VM-PE57)

11
Info-ruption

The internet of existence, cyber insecurity and disrupted information

OBJECTIVES
Information disrupted

'Info-ruption' refers to a pervasive and radical shift in how information is interpreted, used and misused. With daily cybersecurity breaches, weapons of mass disinformation (WMD) and the Internet of Existence (IoE), should information literacy be prioritized akin to language education? Epistemic security now rivals the significance of national security.

Information: Our new substrate

Information, misinformation, disinformation. We might not know what to call it, but we certainly are drowning in it.

Info-ruption and the language of data

Information is the understanding of data in context – the message conveyed – to provide knowledge. *Disinformation* is false information designed to mislead, while *misinformation* is inaccurate information.

In this context, we call 'info-ruption' a pervasive and radical change in data dynamics, with cascading effects on how information is interpreted, used and misused.

Datafying ourselves

Driven by the growth of giants like Google, Facebook and TikTok, digital services increasingly require user data access. Data extraction fuels their operations, commodifying consumer attention. Many view this exchange as 'free', unaware that 'if you're not paying for the product, you are the product'. *However, the true cost lies in the invisible extraction of our information.*

The Internet of Existence (IoE)

Nothing is off-limits when it comes to information, not even our homes, bodies or thoughts.

The integration of networked data into previously disconnected areas enables the digitization of biology, geology and physics, creating the Internet of Existence (IoE). The IoE is driven by the miniaturization of devices and internet-enabled sensors.

Personal information is already being collected via a range of monitoring technology: wearable devices, sleep-tracking mattresses, biosensors, nano-cameras and pacemakers. These devices can monitor and interact with a human body, capturing data in the process, raising serious privacy risks and ethical questions.

Generative AI and deepfakes can clone voices to steal personal data, commit bank heists, deceive voters and bring celebrities back to life. Anyone's voice can be replicated, edited and used without their knowledge.

EXAMPLE
Monetizing your DNA

In 2018, drug giant GSK initially invested $300 million in DNA testing company 23andMe, gaining access to its genetic database and establishing drug development partnerships.[1] How exactly do these companies profit from your genetic data? Do users truly own their DNA, or is it sold on?

These concerns become chillingly real considering the cyberattacks 23andMe experienced, which compromised millions of genetic profiles. Such breaches expose sensitive information related to heritage, religion or health predispositions, posing significant risks for users.[2]

Data byting back

These data-driven innovations bring an entirely new meaning to 'reading' someone. We are witnessing a rapid expansion of networked human bodies and minds. To adapt to this world, should data be treated as a language, as fundamental to our existence as our linguistic substrates?

The future may appear open, unless we understand data well enough to articulate its impacts. As information's key ingredient, data evolves through a timeline:

1 **Software eating the world:**[3] We can have anything, anywhere, at any time. Business became digitized, demonetized and dematerialized.

2 **Software eating software:** No-code, low-code and generative AI permit anyone to create new software without training. Machine learning enables code to write itself, cannibalizing the programmer and software in doing so.

3 **Software eating humanity:** Our *digital* universe, made entirely of data, surpasses our physical space in importance.

When we consider that our bodies and environments are data, we realize the importance of data privacy, ethics and governance.

Cyber insecurity: Big business, high stakes

Imagine the healthcare system being hacked. Hospitals crippled, surgeries postponed and sensitive records falling into the wrong hands. Picture critical infrastructure buckling under cyberattacks, with power grids flickering, water systems disrupted and vital factories compromised. Now envision a video meeting where a chief financial officer requests the transfer of millions of dollars – a masterful deception using deepfakes. These aren't borrowed from *Black Mirror*. They're real-world situations.

The disinformation economy

Disinformation can profoundly affect profits; any business could be destroyed at warp speed.

Disinformation-as-a-service

Ransomware is only one emerging risk. Disinformation targeting organizations is rising. Criminal businesses provide highly customizable, centrally hosted disinformation services for a fee, in a business model called disinformation-as-a-service (DaaS). *DaaS enables the commoditization of info-ruption.*

It is often difficult to pinpoint the source. A disinformation campaign may be initiated by various bad actors, including conspiracy theorists, political activists and autocracies. These sources can reinforce the others by magnifying disinformation campaigns.

EXAMPLE
Disinformation attacks against businesses

QAnon groups, which consist of the followers of a far-right American conspiracy theory movement, have targeted Wayfair, Netflix and Bill Gates, along with 5G telecom operators such as AT&T, Verizon and Vodafone.[4]

In 2021, two election technology companies, Dominion Voting Systems and Smartmatic, filed multibillion-dollar defamation lawsuits against individuals and groups who damaged their businesses by spreading fraudulent conspiracy claims regarding the 2020 US presidential election.[5]

Cybersecurity or cyber insecurity?

Cyber *in*security is the constant growing threat of data breaches, malware attacks and ransomware. Cybersecurity attempts to defend against these threats.

The alarming frequency of cyberattacks on even the most 'secure' government agencies demonstrates the growing vulnerability of our digital world. Cyberweapons are being tested against power grids, healthcare systems and government structures. Often launched anonymously and at minimal cost, these attacks can have devastating consequences. Companies are no longer immune, facing lawsuits from consumers and employees harmed by inadequate cybersecurity measures.

Ransomware-as-a-service

What if cyberattacks become as easy to launch as enterprise software, complete with customer service to ensure smooth ransom collection? This is precisely what ransomware-as-a-service (RaaS) offers. RaaS provides anyone the tools and support they need in a ready-to-extort business model. Leading ransomware brands such as BlackCat, DarkSide and LockBit could become as commonplace as Microsoft, Oracle and Adobe.

JBS, the world's largest meat-processing company, was infected by ransomware, forcing a temporary shutdown of many slaughterhouses.[6] Japanese conglomerate Fujifilm was also forced to close many locations due to attacks,[7] while Lurie Children's Hospital in Chicago was disrupted by a cyberattack, resulting in cancelled surgical procedures and compromised patient health records.[8] Hackers have also hit major US transit systems, including in New York.[9]

EXAMPLE

Ransomware to test infrastructure resilience

Every year, ransomware tests critical infrastructure resilience. In 2021, the Colonial Pipeline, the largest fuel pipeline in the US, was temporarily paralyzed by a ransomware attack.[10] Later that year, the notorious REvil RaaS group launched major simultaneous attacks, compromising IT management software supplier Kaseya VSA, impacting thousands of businesses downstream.[11]

In 2022, the US government uncovered a sophisticated malware framework that targeted industrial control systems. Nicknamed 'Pipedream', it was considered one of the most powerful tools of its kind at the time, capable of disrupting power grids, oil refineries, water utilities and factories. Pipedream can manipulate programmable logic controllers from various vendors, including Schneider Electric and OMRON.[12]

Breaches that were once newsworthy have become routine. While attack names change, the targets (countries, institutions, industries) and perpetrators often remain the same.

Ransomware attacks are increasing not only in scale and frequency, but also in sophistication. Historically, cyberattacks have been isolated attempts for ransom, typically uncoordinated and lacking malicious intent. However, these attacks demonstrate how easily bad actors can compromise major organizations at scale. This raises a concerning possibility: what if these initial probes evolve into malicious coordinated attacks targeting critical infrastructure like power grids, defence systems or communication networks?

Info-ruption: Weapons of mass disinformation

At least since the Ancient Greeks entered Troy, disinformation has been core to warfare. Recent technology has led to a dramatic rise in the frequency and impact of disinformation, large enough to be considered of a different kind.

Weapons of mass disinformation don't play by the same rulebook as traditional warfare. Low entry costs allow anyone to productize highly effective disinformation, often run by keyboard armies operated out of 'troll factories'. Blurred lines between public and private, legal or illegal, international and domestic, truth or untruth make it near impossible to identify or respond to these unattributed threat actors.

The perpetrators range from state-sponsored actors waging disinformation campaigns for geopolitical gain to special interest groups conducting deceptive lobbying on specific policies such as climate. Unlike traditional wars that battle over territory, the wielders of these WMDs have different objectives. Some attackers desire widespread polarization, so that their targets focus on hot-button issues instead of aligning on a longer-term strategy. Extreme polarization makes populations ungovernable and governments dysfunctional. When an AI-generated video can show anyone saying or doing anything, manipulation thrives and truth collapses.

These shifts have prompted new terms like 'post-truth politics', where emotional appeals override facts and 'illusory democracies', where we make choices that we believe to be free but are actually crafted by outside actors. What happens as generative AI customizes the information it shows depending on the viewer?

The potential for power as facts cease to exist

Considerable research has established how successful China, Russia, Iran and (increasingly) North Korea are in their global disinformation campaigns.[13] They mutually reinforce each other in our digital world, where both geographic borders and the lines between true and false are becoming blurred. This disorientation is highly effective and polarizing.

When Aldous Huxley wrote 'Facts do not cease to exist because they are ignored',[14] he may not have realized that, almost 100 years later, the very nature of facts would be threatened. Truth is always subjective; today, it is elusive. From unintentional hallucinations of large language models to deliberate disinformation campaigns, *the very foundation of truth is under attack, with facts as the first casualty.*

Information and polarization

Whether you look at Brazil's 2022 elections, the US elections in 2016 and 2020 or the UK's 2016 Brexit vote, the outcomes were close to 50:50. *These high-stake societal events were all split down the middle.* Each of these divisive debates was polarized in large part due to misinformation, disinformation and interference.

Blurring the lines and subverting its recipients, information permeates every facet of society. It feeds on disorientation and chaos, reinforcing polarization. False information about polarizing topics typically finds a receptive audience. But when citizens accept this disinformation, they often don't realize they are being influenced by foreign powers pursuing their own geopolitical agendas.

Professor Markus Pausch[15] made a distinction between two types of polarization. One is a healthy, evolving democratic process with diverse perspectives, which allow beneficial debate and exchanges to foster social change. Conversely, dangerous polarization happens when positions are hardened, leading to distrust, social divisions and even violence. Here disagreement is akin to a political struggle, an '*us versus them*' division, where opinions are too firmly held to budge and common ground is unreachable.

Today, much of the polarization arising from info-ruption is detrimental. These hardened, opposing views threaten to weaken democracies. During the Covid pandemic, fake news in the US potentially contributed to hundreds of thousands of deaths, along with political polarization.[16] None of these deaths were fake or accidental; this was a well-orchestrated set of attacks.

Both state and non-state actors exploit polarizing domestic issues like climate change, immigration, gun control, vaccines, abortion and gender identity to sow discord within Western democracies. Leveraging pre-existing political tensions, they hijack these issues and amplify them with disinformation, intentionally disorienting the debate. *The population of targeted countries becomes internally divided, unaware of the larger game being played.*

The new universality of information warfare

Dozens of countries use the internet to weaponize disinformation.[17] These attacks may not cause direct, observable injuries, but they weaken the very fabric of society.

China is highly articulate in all facets of info-ruption. They've used these to undermine Hong Kong protests, downplay Russia's invasion of Ukraine, influence US political leaders and mould Taiwanese elections.[18] In 2021, the US Secretary of State confirmed that a Chinese Government-sponsored attack breached over 30,000 domestic organizations, including companies, think tanks, defence contractors and local governments, by exploiting security holes in Microsoft's email software.

Fast forward to 2024, JPMorgan revealed facing 45 billion hacking attempts daily,[19] highlighting the ongoing threat landscape. Simultaneously, Hewlett Packard Enterprise[20] and Microsoft[21] confirmed that Russian-backed hacking groups, including the state-sponsored Nobelium (aka Midnight Blizzard), compromised emails, even some senior leaders' accounts.

Iranian hackers have also targeted US companies with software intended to destroy their computer networks. Additionally, North Korea has a strong WMD arsenal, which is increasingly being deployed.

Widespread state-sponsored hacks are becoming banal. That said, no country has more experience and expertise at disseminating disinformation than Russia.

Learning from the past

One hundred years ago, Joseph Stalin coined the term 'disinformation' (*Desinformatsiya*) with his 'Special Disinformation Office'. This office's mission was to perform intelligence operations and it evolved to become a strategic part of Russia's military.

Russia's century-old disinformation playbook has not changed. At the time of the Cold War, it took the form of false headlines in newspapers around the world. In the 1980s, the KGB claimed that AIDS was a bioweapon created by the CIA. Today, technology makes it easy to generate then disseminate false information far and wide. A tweet or deepfake video can become a WMD.

Beyond disinformation, Berserk Bear, the Russian group believed to be affiliated with FSB (Russia's successor to the KGB), has executed hacking attacks simply to demonstrate their ability to access US infrastructure.

In 2019, Princeton researchers found that Russia was responsible for a significant portion of all international disinformation campaigns.[22] A 2021 report estimated that 74 per cent of ransomware revenue goes to Russia-linked hackers.[23]

Addressing info-ruption systemically

Some have claimed that social media platforms are facing a 'Big Tobacco moment', with renewed calls for regulation and accountability. But are Big Tech's machines too complex to fix? How could we audit their algorithms? Would an audit actually assess the extent of the problem and allow regulators to explore workable remedies? While the problems are obvious, the solutions are not.

Further, given the ongoing global digital transformation and cloudification, organizations have less control over their data and infrastructure. How prepared is the world if the internet was subject to a devastating cyberattack? Such infrastructure attacks could hamper governments, hospitals, transport, food, water, energy and communications.

Applying our AAA framework to info-ruption

Cyberattacks and WMDs highlight the systemic nature of info-ruption. 'Systemic paradigm shifts' is one of our metaruptions, which includes *information* as one of our 10 drivers of disruption. Twenty-first century warfare is a complex endeavour with multiple variables and uncertainties. *Cyber domains are particularly complex. Here, threat actors are unidentifiable and technology and disinformation evolve at warp speed.*

Mitigating info-ruption's emerging threats requires building *antifragile* foundations, greater *anticipation* and enhanced *agility* to handle evolving paradigms.

Antifragile: New foundations for information warfare

Information's effect on warfare is not novel. In some ways, its recent rise harkens back to Alan Turing's decryption of the German Enigma machine during World War II. But the velocity, magnitude and complexity of information warfare has grown exponentially. When Paul Baran invented the data packet, he was suggesting not simply a new information structure, but a new defence strategy: in a distributed system, if one node is attacked, the others can remain viable.

Similarly, we need to build antifragile foundations that strengthen with info-ruption's shocks.

Grassroots education, rethinking skills, rethinking thinking

It is no accident that China, Saudi Arabia, Qatar and Russia donate tens of billions of dollars to Western universities, seeking to influence teaching and research.[24] Education is a powerful force. Unfortunately, it works both ways, in seeking to control minds for soft power and indoctrination. From news to research and even scientific papers, WMDs and generative AI threaten the integrity of information. Critical thinking, media literacy and investigative skills are essential to countering fake content.

If we are to respond effectively to data's effects, we must internalize its importance, understand its costs and articulate its impacts. We must be as fluent with it as we are with our mother tongue. Surviving info-ruption requires proficiency in Socratic questioning and comfort with uncertainty. *We must teach data literacy to our students, lest they emerge illiterate in our accelerating info-ruption.*

Recognizing the ambiguity of our world, embracing the limits of knowledge and valuing diverse viewpoints can help us break free from WMDs. Moreover, identifying foreign influence on domestic hot-button issues strengthens our defences against manipulation.

Resilience and existential risk management

Resilience is a prerequisite to antifragility. With resilience, we anticipate and mitigate the impacts of network disruptions, infrastructure attacks and real-world spillovers from rising geopolitical tensions. The cost of preparedness pales in comparison to the consequences. For institutions to survive, they need to build informational resilience as part of a broader existential risk management strategy. Recognizing this, our Chief Existential Officer (CEO^2) actively addresses high-impact, low-probability threats like info-ruption.

Organizations that fail to adapt through contingency planning and diversification – thus avoiding reliance on single points of failure – will endure hardship in this era of cyber insecurity.

Incentives to support alignment

Info-ruption is similar to healthcare, the climate and gun control in that key decision-makers are not incentivized to act in good faith. *Incumbents benefit more from the status quo than changes to the system.* Systems will remain fragile until effective incentives and regulation can be enforced, deflecting the intense lobbying. What if we incentivized the deployment and operation of secure infrastructure? Aligning incentives is needed to drive the required changes, so info-ruption's vulnerabilities can become opportunities to create antifragile foundations.

'What if?' builds optionality

It is estimated that cybercrime will cost the world $10.5 trillion per year by 2025;[25] if cybercrime were a country, it would represent the third-largest economy in the world, after the US and China. Cybersecurity is also a huge opportunity for innovation, including machine learning which supports threat intelligence, fraud prevention, cyberattack responses and endpoint security.

Further, what are the implications of quantum computing breaking traditional encryption, rendering current cryptography obsolete? *Can we develop new encryption standards to adapt to the quantum era?*

Anticipatory: Foresight and governance

Addressing the deep polarization that threatens our societal foundations requires systemic thinking. Similarly, the ever-evolving cybersecurity landscape demands coordinated foresight and anticipatory governance to safeguard our critical infrastructure.

Anticipatory governance

Every company needs to understand that info-ruption might affect them at any time. There are many essential steps for leadership teams to consider:

- Develop contingency planning, together with foresight and prevention capacity to anticipate possible scenarios, implications and mitigants.
- Dedicate resources to threat modelling, cyber defence capabilities and ransomware recovery exercises.
- Roll out security training, education and support across the organization.
- Ensure transparent culture with accountability to foster trust with teams, customers, partners and regulators.
- Engage with stakeholders in the organization who can contribute to holistic approaches.
- Scout ecosystem organizations to collaborate on emerging technologies and stay current with new developments.
- Get involved in the regulatory environment around disinformation evolutions.
- Build strategic partnerships to share cyber technology, datasets and expertise.

Greater response capabilities

Anticipatory governance, regulation and disclosure requirements can help foresee, monitor and mitigate developing threat environments. For the integrity of infrastructure, systems and products, new standards must integrate security by design, from IoT devices to smart cities.

In 2024, the FBI formally warned that state-sponsored hackers have infiltrated US technology such as routers, potentially compromising critical infrastructure.[26] Lack of accountability for software developers is one factor contributing to poor safeguards. This may change, as regulators seek to impose greater liability on chief information security officers (CISO) for security failures, as cyber threats become physical threats. *Now on the hook, leadership teams need to upgrade their response capabilities for prevention.*

Strategic investment and government preparedness

Much of the world has underestimated the destructive power of cyberattacks, leading to underinvestment in security measures. *Governments and organizations that fail to build strong cyber capabilities will be particularly vulnerable in this new era.*

To bolster its preparedness, Taiwan leverages various fact-checking platforms and media literacy initiatives to counter CCP disinformation campaigns. Funding for fact-checkers is a good investment.

Technology, ratings and legislation

Technology moves fast; regulation moves much slower. As liberal democracies are becoming less powerful, will they retain the power necessary to mitigate info-ruption?

There are several initiatives that can keep decision-makers accountable. Regulators are starting to mandate stricter data protection practices, requiring companies to implement more robust risk-management procedures. Accountability and penalties should be implemented for allowing excessive disinformation – or insufficient investment in preventing it. *Just like the financial industry issues credit ratings to organizations based on their creditworthiness, media platforms could be rated in terms of their prevalence of fake news.* Appropriate oversight is needed to address manipulated data, such as mandatory disclosure of deepfakes, watermarking of synthetic media and guardrails pertaining to AI-generated misinformation. Additionally, proactive content moderation can identify and take down bad actors and fake accounts.

Many jurisdictions are looking at the EU Digital Services Act, which seeks to crack down on illegal content. In the US, New York City has taken an original first step by labelling social media an environmental toxin, given its adverse effect on mental health.

Interpreting future impacts

In 2022, the US established a Bureau of Cyberspace and Digital Policy to address national security challenges, economic opportunities and the impact of cyberspace on US values.

Supporting a thriving democracy in the age of info-ruption is not easy. It's essential that we all become familiar with the way media and technology works, including our ability to distinguish trusted information sources from malicious content. *With the right dose of anticipation, we can address the existential threat posed by information warfare.*

Agility: Bridging time horizons, domains and ecosystems

Emergent, strategic and cognitive agility allow us to simultaneously bridge our longer-term vision with the present. *Despite info-ruption, we can develop the agility to reduce surprises and contain emergencies.*

Dynamic intelligence sharing and feedback loops

Criminal hackers exploit public information to constantly adapt their tactics. To counter this, governments and companies need to share intelligence and collaborate swiftly. This requires breaking down information silos, incentivizing joint efforts and leveraging continuous feedback loops. Real-time threat monitoring can reveal emerging vulnerabilities, while machine learning allows proactive identification of evolving attack patterns.

Mapping informational flows and outcomes

Before and during major news events, we must understand and navigate the potential for disinformation. We need to actively monitor informational feedback loops to evaluate the global information environment. What are the original facts? How is the information being distorted? What are the sources of manipulations? *What is the flow and impact of disinformation? How is the disinformation spreading and what are its effects?*

Learning, unlearning and relearning cyber capabilities

Facing the rapid evolution of cybersecurity threats, we need ongoing education and agility at all levels, from children to CEOs. Dynamic learning loops foster the adaptability required to navigate information storms, where knowledge quickly becomes obsolete.

For cybersecurity, dedicating resources, creating training programmes (throughout the entire organization) and continuously running simulations will help us adapt to when actual breaches arise. While not much can be done to combat the rise of cheap and user-friendly AI disinformation tools, their effects can be mitigated through capacity-building.

Moving forward with agency

The rise of info-ruption is an arms race. Like any competitive field, we won't overcome this challenge without taking decisive action. As technology amplifies the spread of inaccurate information, we must develop equally powerful tools to fight it.

By reforming education for the digital age, rethinking our skills and systems and developing responsible technology, we can mitigate its harms while capitalizing on its potential. Inaction isn't an option. Malicious actors are already infiltrating society, influencing policies and even targeting education boards. We must act rapidly and decisively to protect our institutions and safeguard the integrity of information.

The AAA framework equips you to be more antifragile, anticipatory and agile in relation to info-ruption.

Notes

1 GSK. GSK and 23andMe sign agreement to leverage genetic insights for the development of novel medicines, GSK, 25 July 2018. www.gsk.com/en-gb/media/press-releases/gsk-and-23andme-sign-agreement-to-leverage-genetic-insights-for-the-development-of-novel-medicines (archived at https://perma.cc/5AUH-8839)

2 L Franceschi-Bicchierai. 23andMe confirms hackers stole ancestry data on 6.9 million users, TechCrunch, 4 December 2023. www.techcrunch.com/2023/12/04/23andme-confirms-hackers-stole-ancestry-data-on-6-9-million-users (archived at https://perma.cc/WNB9-EZGX)

3 M Andreessen. Why software is eating the world, Andreessen Horowitz, 20 August 2011. www.a16z.com/why-software-is-eating-the-world (archived at https://perma.cc/2BCA-ESBP)

4   R McMillian. Brands face a new online threat: Disinformation attacks, *Wall Street Journal*, 8 October 2020. www.wsj.com/articles/brands-face-a-new-online-threat-disinformation-attacks-11602187365 (archived at https://perma.cc/AN43-3NCH); A Seitz and A Swenson. Baseless Wayfair child-trafficking theory spreads online, AP News, 16 July 2020. www.apnews.com/article/social-media-us-news-ap-top-news-conspiracy-media-9d54570ebba5e406667c38cb29522ec6 (archived at https://perma.cc/CVE7-88D4)

5   D Bauder, R Chase and G Mulvihill. Fox, Dominion reach $787m settlement over election claims, AP News, 18 April 2023. www.apnews.com/article/fox-news-dominion-lawsuit-trial-trump-2020-0ac71f75acfacc52ea80b3e747fb0afe (archived at https://perma.cc/YE2N-ADDS)

6   J Creswell, L Perlroth and N Scheiber. Ransomware disrupts meat plants in latest attack on critical US business, *The New York Times*, 1 June 2021. www.nytimes.com/2021/06/01/business/meat-plant-cyberattack-jbs.html (archived at https://perma.cc/2MWJ-9MJX)

7   C Page. Fujifilm becomes the latest victim of a network-crippling ransomware attack, TechCrunch, 3 June 2021. www.techcrunch.com/2021/06/03/fujifilm-becomes-the-latest-victim-of-a-network-crippling-ransomware-attack (archived at https://perma.cc/K3SM-E5MD)

8   M Perlman and E Coatar. Lurie Children's Hospital health records, phone lines back up after cyberattack, CBS News, 5 March 2024. www.cbsnews.com/chicago/news/lurie-childrens-hospital-health-records-cyberattack (archived at https://perma.cc/E6Z3-28N4)

9   C Goldbaum and W K Rashbaum. The MTA is breached by hackers as cyberattacks surge, *The New York Times*, 2 June 2021. www.nytimes.com/2021/06/02/nyregion/mta-cyber-attack.html (archived at https://perma.cc/QMJ8-M665)

10   J Knutson. DarkSide claims it's shutting down after Colonial Pipeline hack, Axios, 14 May 2021. www.axios.com/2021/05/14/hackers-darkside-shutting-down-colonial-pipeline (archived at https://perma.cc/EF4U-NXNA)

11   J Menn. Kaseya ransomware attack sets off race to hack service providers – researchers, Reuters, 3 August 2021. www.reuters.com/technology/kaseya-ransomware-attack-sets-off-race-hack-service-providers-researchers-2021-08-03 (archived at https://perma.cc/H8GT-6QRZ)

12   A Greenberg. Feds uncover a 'Swiss army knife' for hacking industrial control systems, Wired, 13 April 2022. www.wired.com/story/pipedream-ics-malware (archived at https://perma.cc/YRH8-CVYC)

13   E Kinetz. Anatomy of a conspiracy: With Covid, China took leading role, AP News, 14 February 2021. www.apnews.com/article/pandemics-beijing-only-on-ap-epidemics-media-122b73e134b780919cc1808f3f6f16e8 (archived at https://perma.cc/4V3N-JMTP); DFRLab. Weaponized: How rumors about Covid-19's origins led to a narrative arms race, Atlantic Council, 2021.

www.atlanticcouncil.org/wp-content/uploads/2021/02/Weaponized-How-rumors-about-COVID-19s-origins-led-to-a-narrative-arms-race.pdf (archived at https://perma.cc/D6VN-7TJP); Network Contagion Research Institute and Rutgers. A Tik-Tok-ing timebomb: How TikTok's global platform anomalies align with the Chinese Communist Party's geostrategic objectives, Network Contagion, 2023. www.networkcontagion.us/wp-content/uploads/A-Tik-Tok-ing-Timebomb_12.21.23.pdf (archived at https://perma.cc/F9SW-5JV6); US Department of the Treasury. Treasury sanctions Russia with sweeping new sanctions authority, US Department of the Treasury, 15 April 2021. home.treasury.gov/news/press-releases/jy0127 (archived at https://perma.cc/P73J-GVHD); S Bradshaw and P N Howard. The global disinformation order: 2019 Global inventory of organised social media manipulation, University of Oxford, 2021. www.oii.ox.ac.uk/news-events/reports/the-global-disinformation-order-2019-global-inventory-of-organised-social-media-manipulation (archived at https://perma.cc/QNJ5-M6U6); C Davies. North Korean hackers use AI for more sophisticated scams, *Financial Times*, 18 February 2024. www.ft.com/content/728611e8-dce2-449d-bb65-cff11ac2a5bb (archived at https://perma.cc/HGC5-39ZC)

14 A Huxley (1927) *Proper Studies*, Chatto & Windus, London, UK

15 M Pausch. The future of polarisation in Europe: Relative cosmopolitanism and democracy, *European Journal of Futures Research*, 10 October 2021, 9 (1). www.doi.org/10.1186/s40309-021-00183-2 (archived at https://perma.cc/6JRA-Y8ZE)

16 L Garrett. The pandemic really is fake news: It's deadlier than anyone realized, Foreign Policy, 3 November 2020. www.foreignpolicy.com/2020/11/03/the-pandemic-really-has-been-fake-news-its-deadlier-than-anyone-realized (archived at https://perma.cc/VTC6-9PHS)

17 S Bradshaw and P N Howard. The global disinformation order: 2019 global inventory of organised social media manipulation, Project on Computational Propaganda, University of Oxford, 2019. demtech.oii.ox.ac.uk/research/posts/the-global-disinformation-order-2019-global-inventory-of-organised-social-media-manipulation (archived at https://perma.cc/9EDZ-WGXJ)

18 N Monaco, M Smith and A Studdart. Detecting digital fingerprints: Tracing Chinese disinformation in Taiwan, Institute for the Future, 2020. legacy.iftf.org/disinfo-in-taiwan (archived at https://perma.cc/FT3Q-2DQB)

19 H Wilson. JPMorgan sees hacking attempts on systems double to 45 billion per day, BNN Bloomberg, 17 January 2024. www.bnnbloomberg.ca/jpmorgan-sees-hacking-attempts-on-systems-double-to-45-billion-per-day-1.2023031 (archived at https://perma.cc/3X73-KHEU)

20 Hewlett Packard Enterprise Company. Material cybersecurity incidents, US SEC, 2024. www.sec.gov/Archives/edgar/data/1645590/000164559024000009/hpe-20240119.htm (archived at https://perma.cc/945Q-KVW5)

21   MSRC. Update on Microsoft actions following attack by nation state actor
      Midnight Blizzard, Microsoft, 8 March 2024. msrc.microsoft.com/blog/
      2024/03/update-on-microsoft-actions-following-attack-by-nation-state-actor-
      midnight-blizzard (archived at https://perma.cc/LC96-CV25)

22   D A Martin, J N Shapiro and M Nedashkovskaya. Recent trends in online
      foreign influence efforts, *Journal of Information Warfare*, 2019, 18 (3).
      www.jstor.org/stable/26894680 (archived at https://perma.cc/WL2W-BBPH)

23   Chainalysis Team. Russian cybercriminals drive significant ransomware and
      cryptocurrency-based money laundering activity, Chainalysis, 14 February
      2022. www.chainalysis.com/blog/2022-crypto-crime-report-preview-russia-
      ransomware-money-laundering (archived at https://perma.cc/P6RP-5MGY)

24   Network Contagion Research Institute. The corruption of the American
      mind, NCRI, 2023. www.networkcontagion.us/wp-content/uploads/NCRI-
      Report_The-Corruption-of-the-American-Mind.pdf (archived at https://
      perma.cc/46TX-DBLS); K O'Keeffe. Education department investigating
      Harvard, Yale over foreign funding, *Wall Street Journal*, 13 February 2020.
      www.wsj.com/articles/education-department-investigating-harvard-yale-over-
      foreign-funding-11581539042 (archived at https://perma.cc/J96E-YZ5L); I
      Oxnevad. Authoritarian states dwarf America's allies in influencing US
      colleges and universities, The Hill, 5 April 2023. www.thehill.com/opinion/
      education/3931995-authoritarian-states-dwarf-americas-allies-in-influencing-
      us-colleges-and-universities (archived at https://perma.cc/6NXF-UE59)

25   S Morgan. Cybercrime to cost the world $10.5 trillion annually by 2025,
      Cybercrime Magazine, 13 November 2020. www.cybersecurityventures.com/
      cybercrime-damage-costs-10-trillion-by-2025 (archived at https://perma.cc/
      BT5N-WWWH)

26   Cybersecurity & Infrastructure Security Agency. PRC state-sponsored actors
      compromise and maintain persistent access to US critical infrastructure, CISA,
      2024. www.cisa.gov/news-events/cybersecurity-advisories/aa24-038a (archived
      at https://perma.cc/YW98-BQMA)

Part Four
Unleash your disruptive thinking

12

The Disruptive Thinking Canvas

Invent the future today

OBJECTIVES

A canvas to invent your future

Our Disruptive Thinking Canvas™ is designed as a road map to help us imagine, invent and prototype the futures we want. The Canvas offers actionable methodologies to leverage disruption and drive systemic change, both organizational and individual, designed with practical tools.

Introduction

This final chapter introduces our Disruptive Thinking Canvas, a personalized road map designed to help you thrive in today's shifting environments. By identifying unexplored opportunities, you can invent the future, whether for yourself, your projects or your organization. The Canvas offers a step-by-step guide to navigate disruption and create impact, equipping you with the mindset and tools needed to succeed (Figure 12.1).

As change is omnipresent, we must master the language of disruption through the 6 i's (intuition, inspiration, imagination, improvisation, invention, impossible) and our AAA framework.

Throughout this book, we explored how the AAA framework allows us to build *antifragile* foundations, develop *anticipatory* capabilities and use emergent and strategic *agility* to make effective decisions. We also expanded

Figure 12.1   The Disruptive Thinking Canvas™

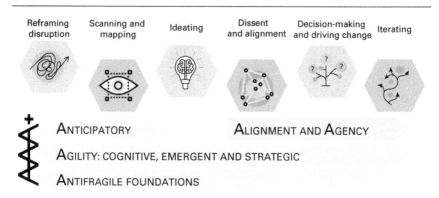

AAA into being AAA+, which recognizes the importance of *agency* and *alignment*.

Our Disruptive Thinking Canvas provides a streamlined six-step process, consolidating the foundational principles of our work in one location.

Bringing it all together in six simple steps

We outline below the six steps of the Disruptive Thinking Canvas (Figure 12.2):

- **Step 1: Reframing disruption.** Redefine disruption to realize how positive opportunities can be found in disruptive times.

- **Step 2: Scanning and mapping.** Anticipate, identify and investigate potential disruptions ahead.

- **Step 3: Ideating.** Embrace new mindsets to harness uncertainty; imagine untapped opportunities to problem-solve our complex challenges and spur transformations.

- **Step 4: Dissent and alignment.** Increase alignment and overcome resistance while challenging the status quo.

- **Step 5: Decision-making and driving change.** Understand decision-making in deeply uncertain environments and how to effect change in a systemic context.

- **Step 6: Iterating.** Apply changes, assess impacts, incorporate new information and utilize feedback to adapt continuously.

Figure 12.2 The Disruptive Thinking Canvas™ in six steps

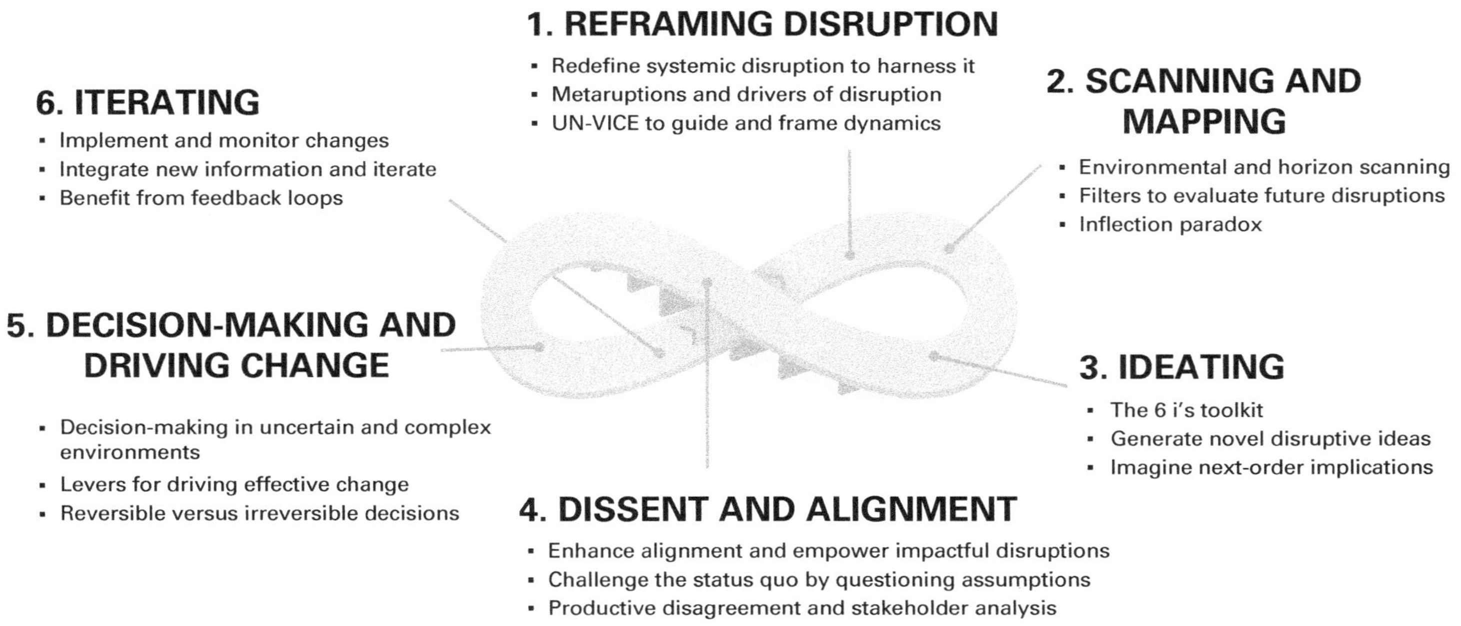

1. REFRAMING DISRUPTION
- Redefine systemic disruption to harness it
- Metaruptions and drivers of disruption
- UN-VICE to guide and frame dynamics

2. SCANNING AND MAPPING
- Environmental and horizon scanning
- Filters to evaluate future disruptions
- Inflection paradox

3. IDEATING
- The 6 i's toolkit
- Generate novel disruptive ideas
- Imagine next-order implications

4. DISSENT AND ALIGNMENT
- Enhance alignment and empower impactful disruptions
- Challenge the status quo by questioning assumptions
- Productive disagreement and stakeholder analysis

5. DECISION-MAKING AND DRIVING CHANGE
- Decision-making in uncertain and complex environments
- Levers for driving effective change
- Reversible versus irreversible decisions

6. ITERATING
- Implement and monitor changes
- Integrate new information and iterate
- Benefit from feedback loops

Figure 12.3 The Disruptive Thinking Canvas™ toolkit

Disruptive Thinking Canvas™ Toolkit

NAME: DATE:

1 REFRAMING DISRUPTION
Redefine disruptions to realize how its **positive opportunities** can help us drive value creation.

- ·
- ·

2 SCANNING AND MAPPING
Anticipate, identify, and **evaluate potential disruptions ahead.**

- ·
- ·

3 IDEATING
Generate new ideas to **envision a broad set of potential futures** – beyond what lies on the surface.

- ·
- ·

4 DISSENT AND ALIGNMENT
Increase alignment and **overcome resistance** to facilitate effective implementation.

- ·
- ·

5 DECISION-MAKING AND DRIVING CHANGE
Identify the nature of decisions to **anticipate consequences** and drive positive effects.

- ·
- ·

6 ITERATING: FEEDBACK LOOP
Monitor the changes after they are implemented to **integrate new information** into feedback loops for further iterations.

· ·   · ·   · ·   · ·   · ·

Create your own path to disrupt with impact

By applying the Disruptive Thinking Canvas, you can create your personal road map to disrupt with impact (Figure 12.3). In the following sections, we explore a variety of practical 'toolkits' revisiting our fundamental concepts. Together, the insights from these toolkits combine to form your Disruptive Thinking Canvas. There is also a dashboard at the end of the chapter that you can use to track your disruptive projects, from immediate actions to the longer-term.

As you implement the Canvas with your projects, draw from the learning of the numerous practical applications, dozens of real-life case studies and many examples featured throughout the respective chapters of this book.

Step 1: Reframing disruption

OBJECTIVE
Redefine disruption to harness it

Systemic disruption is deeper and wider-reaching than disruptive technology, innovation or product development. This first step of reframing disruptions offers pathways to drive sustainable value creation.

Eight laws of systemic disruption

In a world that is no longer linear, where patterns become increasingly hard to interpret, we need to reframe disruption itself:

- Disruption is omnipresent.
- Disruption is a constant.
- Disruption establishes new paradigms, which will themselves evolve.
- The effects of disruption are cumulative.
- Disruption has non-linear ripple effects.
- Disruption's impacts transcend timeframes.
- Disruption can be irreversible.
- Disruption is generally neither good nor bad.

Disruption's impact can vary greatly depending on (i) your perspective, (ii) degree of preparation and (iii) the nature and timing of your response.

Our best UN-VICE to reframe disruption

Changemakers can use our UN-VICE to interpret opportunities. Framing disruptions as UN-VICE provides an empowering response. We are not helpless victims buffeted by changes, unable to make decisions. Rather, we have the power to adapt, learn and shape our futures:

- **Unknown:** Recognize the inherent uncertainty in knowledge. Uncertainty diminishes the reliability of *ad*-vice, necessitating independent thought. Attain self-sufficiency amidst the unknown, leveraging it as a catalyst for growth.

- **Volatile:** Our world, and change itself, are evolving at an unprecedented pace. This profound volatility isn't good or bad, but it undeniably demands our attention. By understanding its shifting dynamics, we can harness its power.

- **Intersecting:** Deeper knowledge reveals overlapping landscapes, fostering vibrant convergences. Discover how everything connecting to everything else also creates new opportunities.

- **Complex:** Unlike complicated situations, highly interconnected complex systems challenge our understanding due to their constant flux, unpredictability and far-reaching impacts. Navigating complex systems demands continuous adaptation and vigilance.

- **Exponential:** To an observer, non-linear change may start gradually, then grow suddenly. Notice initial rates of change; expect explosions.

Reframing disruption is a key step where we respect what we don't know while understanding the extent of agency we have.

CHECKLIST
Your UN-VICE

Don't take our advice, follow your UN-VICE:

- How can you focus less on rote knowledge and more on asking probing questions?
- How can you prepare yourself for faster shifts?
- Where are rapid rates of change sneaking under your radar?
- Where in your life are seemingly disparate changes multiplying each other?

- Which of your strategic and analytic tools break down in the face of complexity? What approaches will you use instead?
- How reliant are you on experts?
- Do you believe that there are existing answers to all complex situations?
- Do you perceive the world as controllable and predictable?

Metaruptions and the 10 drivers of disruption

Metaruptions are a multidimensional family of systemic disruptions, characterized by the dynamic interactions of subordinate drivers of change. They cause widespread and self-perpetuating effects that extend beyond their initial disruptions.

To comprehend systemic disruption, we need to decipher its fundamental drivers. Identifying these drivers and their synthesis as metaruptions informs decision-making.

KEY POINTS
Five metaruptions, 10 drivers of disruption

We consider five metaruptions, fuelled by 10 drivers of disruption:

- **Metaruption #1: New change.** The new nature, velocity, multiplicity and interconnectivity of disruptions generate runaway change. Despite inevitable turbulence, this (i) *New nature of change* also unlocks novel pathways to address global challenges.

- **Metaruption #2: Hyper premium on relevancy.** Exemplified by the (ii) *Red Queen Race*, the bar to become and remain relevant is higher than ever. You need to run faster to stay in the same place and could still end up behind.

- **Metaruption #3: Irreversibility.** Evolutions in (iii) *climate*, (iv) *technology* and (v) *AI* could advance to such a degree that their impact on society is irreversible.

- **Metaruption #4: Systemic paradigm shifts.** Today, our current paradigms are shifting. (vi) *Complexity* is moving to centre stage, as rigid structures are rejected and non-linearity prevails. Likewise, the evolving expectations of (vii) *society* intersect with shifting values.
(viii) *Information* becomes uncontrollable and evolves at warp speed.

- **Metaruption #5: Rapidly approaching new eras.** The shadows of new realities are fast approaching. (ix) *Quantum computing and artificial life* could usher in a new epoch of existence. (x) *New frontiers, geopolitical and economic reshuffling* transform space, geopolitics and world economies.

Disruption drivers toolkit

The five metaruptions and their 10 drivers of disruption are powerful. Understanding how they fit into your project or business can generate tremendous opportunities and mitigate surprises (Figure 12.4).

Step 2: Scanning and mapping

OBJECTIVE
Recognize and evaluate disruptions

Scanning and mapping empowers us to proactively identify and investigate potential future disruptions, allowing us to shape the futures.

Disruption isn't a single phenomenon, but a series of interconnected changes that amplify and impact each other. Outcomes will be determined by these interconnected effects. By scanning the horizon, those who embrace curiosity can anticipate the opportunities.

The Inflection Paradox

STEEPE is a popular environmental scanning framework for analysing environments across social, technological, environmental, economic, political and ethical factors. Despite employing established methods like STEEPE, we often fail to identify inflection points due to what we term the 'Inflection Paradox'.

Figure 12.4 Disruption drivers toolkit

Disruption Drivers Toolkit

Five **METARUPTIONS** and their 10 **DRIVERS OF DISRUPTION** are powerful instruments for **driving transformative change**. Understanding how they fit into your project or business can generate tremendous opportunities and mitigate surprises.

1. NEW CHANGE
In what ways might the (i) new nature, velocity, multiplicity and interconnectivity of change continue to accelerate in speed and complexity?

2. HYPER PREMIUM ON RELEVANCY
How is the bar to remain relevant higher than ever? How do we need to run faster to stay in the same place given the (ii) Red Queen Race?

3. IRREVERSIBILITY
(iii) Climate change, (iv) technology, and (v) AI pose the most risk of irreversibility, also offering opportunities. How might they impact you?

4. SYSTEMIC PARADIGM SHIFTS
(vi) Complexity, (vii) society, and (viii) information are driving fundamental paradigm shifts. How are you taking them into account?

5. RAPIDLY APPROACHING NEW ERAS
How might (ix) quantum computing and artificial life along with (x) new frontiers, geopolitical and economic reshuffling affect your vision?

This paradox arises from two contradictory factors. First, Amara's Law suggests that, in the initial stages, there's a tendency to dismiss emerging innovations that are overhyped. However, with time, we underestimate their long-term impacts. The second factor is the nature of exponential change. Early developments are often subtle and easily overlooked amidst the noise; significant growth only becomes evident after some time has passed. Consequently, we consistently underestimate the profound effects of exponential change over the long term.

One issue which exacerbates the Inflection Paradox is that innovations are analysed through siloes, even though breakthroughs often occur across fields.

Horizon scanning for emerging change

Horizon scanning enables you to catch a glimpse of the future by observing fragments embedded in the present. Thanks to its focus on weak signals, emerging issues and interconnections, *horizon* scanning is more relevant today than *environmental* scanning.

Horizon scanning focuses on influences that shape future disruptions. It acknowledges that the future is broad, dynamic and produces surprises. Environmental scanning methods such as STEEPE remain important, complementary to horizon scanning's early signal detection.

Filters to evaluate signals toolkit

One challenge of horizon scanning is that there are limitless weak signals, fake signals and inflated signals. The right filters qualify and cluster weak signals to assess how they might evolve over time. Another key is to understand your biases and predispositions.

The scanning process is intentionally broad. Filters help you evaluate the signals observed (Figure 12.5):

1 **Qualify the source:** How credible is the signal's source? Weak signals are often on the fringe – no less valuable than those from well-known experts. In all cases, understand the nature of the source and any biases. Is the source seemingly objective? What might motivate the source to voice certain views?

2 **Likelihood:** What is the momentum of the signal? How frequently is the signal picked up? Is the signal moving from weak to stronger? Watch out for self-confirming signals – when a false signal leads people to act in ways that confirm the signal is true.

Figure 12.5 Filters to evaluate signals toolkit

Filters to Evaluate Signals Toolkit

Signal to be evaluated: ▪

SOURCE
How strong is the source? Is it credible? Are there conflicts or alignments of interest?

LIKELIHOOD
What is the momentum of this signal? Is it weak or strong? Is it self-confirming?

NEWNESS
Is the signal entirely new? Has it already gone through its life cycle (e.g. hype, fade)?

COMPOUNDING
How does it interact with other signals? Does it validate other signals or conflict with them?

IMPACT
What could the signal do, and to whom? What might be the strength of the impact?

INTERCONNECTIONS
Does the signal seem isolated, independent, or interconnected? Are patterns emerging?

3 **Newness:** Signals have their own life cycle, initially as emerging issues, then growing into significant topics – but their significance can ultimately fade. Ascertain whether they are new (undiscovered by experts) and the time horizon for 'emergence' (when a weak signal becomes strong and starts making an impact).

4 **Compounding:** How do emerging signals interact? Does a consensus confirm similar observations, reinforcing the strength of the combined signals? Or, conversely, do the signals conflict or result in polarized messages? Are there diverse perspectives substantiating the emerging consensus?

5 **Impact:** What could the signals do and to whom? Who will feel the impact of this change first? Is any sector or demographic most affected?

6 **Interconnections:** Do signals seem isolated, or interconnected? Are there clusters emerging as potential drivers of change? Do the signals intersect across different fields?

CHECKLIST
Patterns of change

When qualifying signals and patterns of change, consider:

- For a given situation, which dominant patterns of change stand out?
- Are these signals part of a cycle(s)? Do you notice any patterns from history?
- Are there emerging issues that might disrupt them?
- What emerging issues could become a driving force to change in the longer term?
- Are you noticing any broader themes emerging from seemingly disparate signals?
- What possible opportunities or risks could the weak signals reveal?
- Do you invite other people to support or challenge your assessment of change to gain broader insights?
- Have you integrated both the exponential nature of change and Amara's Law in assessing the potential impacts (considering the Inflection Paradox)?

Step 3: Ideating

OBJECTIVE
Idea generation and creation

Step 3 harnesses uncertainty by embracing new mindsets to explore untapped opportunities. This 'discontinuity ideation' involves generating bold ideas and initiatives that spur positive disruption, even if it necessitates an unsettling transition phase.

The 6 i's toolkit combines enhanced *intuition* with real-time *improvisation* to adapt to changing circumstances and *imagine* new possibilities. Then, *inspire* yourself to *invent* your future and achieve the *impossible*.

Before making decisions or implementations, the ideation phase allows us to step back and envision many possible futures.

The 6 i's toolkit

Our 6 i's toolkit is designed to ideate and create your preferred futures:

1 **Intuition:** Avoid preconceptions; trust yourself and improve your judgement.

2 **Inspiration:** Explore, be curious and spur yourself to greatness.

3 **Imagination:** Nothing is predetermined; we manifest our own futures.

4 **Improvisation:** Experiment with authentic spontaneity, mistakes and serendipity.

5 **Invention:** If the solution doesn't yet exist, create it.

6 **Impossible:** Wander, stumble and fail in order to achieve the (seemingly) impossible.

Intuition

Steve Jobs famously said 'have the courage to follow your heart and intuition. They somehow already know what you truly want to become. Everything else is secondary.' In deeply uncertain and complex environments, conventional analysis is limited; intuition becomes a necessity.

When approaching intuition:

- **Radiate confidence:** Trust yourself and your judgement.
- **Avoid preconceptions:** Let go of your worries. Cultivate *shoshin*, beginner's mind.
- **Be curious and explore:** Courageously embrace new challenges. Broaden your experiences to forge unexpected connections.
- **Accept the two components of trial and error:** Be ready to experiment and willing to fail.
- **High stakes? Think it through. Low stakes? Trust your gut:** When time is tight and decisions are reversible, ditch analysis paralysis. Intuition can help you surface the right answer quickly.

Inspiration

A diversity of people, domains and perspectives is a key driver to inspiration. Our five laws of inspiration are:

- **Passion:** Start with the passion of an explorer. Amplify it, develop it and make it contagious.
- **Diversify:** Seek exposure to different ideas, ecosystems and people.
- **Novelty:** Pursue newness, escape routine.
- **Forge connections:** Build bridges, explore intersections and connect the shifting dots across diverse disciplines.
- **Embrace serendipity:** Create opportunities to be lucky. Breathe happenstance.

Imagination

Einstein famously said, 'Imagination is more important than knowledge.' Recognizing its crucial role in shaping our futures, we've formulated five laws for harnessing imagination:

- **Ask broad, open questions:** 'What if?' and 'How might we?'
- **Break from the present:** Imagine longer time horizons.
- **Be bored:** Embrace moments of boredom and playfulness without an immediate goal. Cultivate environments that lack judgement or possibility of failure.
- **Allocate time to explore the edge:** Spend 20 per cent of your time outside your domain or daily routine.

- **Use science fiction:** Challenge assumptions, reframe perceptions and suspend disbelief with science fiction, the ultimate catalyst for imagination. Additionally, design fiction is a valuable process, combining science fiction with design thinking and foresight to create narrative prototypes.

Improvisation

Improvisation can unlock spontaneity and the courage to express our true selves, key to forging new insights.

One quickly learns the five laws of improvisation:

- **Permission to act on ideas:** Give your brain permission to play with bold ideas you might usually dismiss, then use that experience to reframe your approach to everyday life. Remember, stability is illusory; embrace uncensored ideas, ambiguity and change.
- **See mistakes as gifts:** Unusual additions bring new opportunities.
- **Accept issues and move on:** You can't stop the show because you flubbed a line.
- **It's better to give than receive:** Improving the experience of those around you, including scene partners, audience and peers, is more fulfilling than self-promotion.
- **Trust:** We're all performing together; we must have faith in our collective ability.

Invention

Innovation refines or expands upon something existing, while *invention* brings something entirely new into existence. They, along with failure and discovery, are intertwined in the vast potential futures.

Once we understand the extent to which the futures are open, we can invent.

- **Indeterminacy is a catalyst:** Unknown futures are a prerequisite for inventing.
- **Agency drives invention:** Make free choices and invent implicitly.
- **Your superpowers:** Individuals now have the same inventive powers as any large organization. How will you use them?
- **Failure and invention go hand in hand:** The more you fail, the more relevant you will become.

- **Ditch hard-held beliefs.** See beyond established assumptions and legacy models.

Impossible

Once we are inspired to drive change, we no longer see it as impossible. Our existing assumptions shift to invent what seemed unimaginable. New ideas often seem impossible until they become part of everyday life:

- **Be audacious:** Foster unwavering self-belief and translate ambitious goals into actionable short-term steps.

- **The mind enables the impossible:** Comfort with ambiguity helps form new mental models.

- **Exercise your 'impossibility muscles':** Practise thinking of the impossible things you could do. Then apply first-principles thinking to imagine how you might do them.

- **Grit:** Make the sacrifice to show up. Tenacity makes the difference; don't underestimate anyone – especially yourself.

- **Failovation:** Failure is often the path to innovation. We call this 'failovation'.

Zen Buddhism and the 6 i's

If you're aiming to improve your comfort with impermanence, transformation and change, Eastern philosophy and Zen Buddhism can help.

Greater practice of *shoshin* (beginner's mind) improves *intuition*, *imagination* and *invention* capacity, while comfort with *mujō* (impermanence) aids *improvisation* and enables us to achieve a more *inspiring ikigai* (flourishing or valuable life) than we ever thought *possible*.

Applying the 6 i's toolkit

Each 'i' serves as a tool that can be used as a pathway. Think in terms of short-term initiatives and long-term goals (Figure 12.6).

Figure 12.6 Applying the 6 i's toolkit

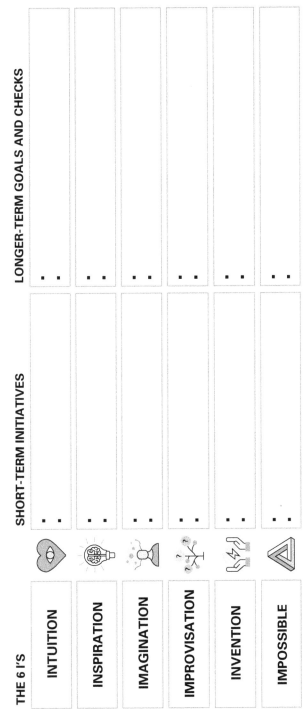

Applying the 6 i's Toolkit

Each "i" serves as a tool that can be used as a **pathway to affecting change.** Think in terms of short-term initiatives and long-term goals and checks in relation to each.

THE 6 I'S		SHORT-TERM INITIATIVES	LONGER-TERM GOALS AND CHECKS
INTUITION			
INSPIRATION			
IMAGINATION			
IMPROVISATION			
INVENTION			
IMPOSSIBLE			

Step 4: Dissent and alignment

OBJECTIVE

Constructive disagreement for alignment

The objective of the fourth step is to increase alignment to effect change, while challenging the status quo to respond better to disruptions.

In a world of disparate entities, alignment is more important than ever. To achieve real innovation, we must imagine novel ideas, question assumptions and offer diverse perspectives.

Aligning values while challenging conventional wisdom creates new solutions. Since resistance is fundamental to change, you will benefit by embracing this dissent, rather than fighting it.

To harness the virtues of disagreement, you need trust. Without trust, alignment is impossible.

Four archetypes of assumptions

Treating flawed assumptions as sacrosanct results in ineffective systems, institutions and governance. This approach makes the world more vulnerable than it ought to be.

To appreciate how prevalent these fragile assumptions are, we categorize them into four archetypes.

Normalcy

The presumption of a predictable world, where the future is a linear continuation of the past. Formulaic playbooks are perceived to be magic potions.

Risks and errors

The beliefs that if risks are invisible they are suppressed, that low probabilities can be reliably determined and that unlikely impacts can be ignored. A worldview where errors and failures must always be suppressed.

Time and space

The assumption that the universe is a predictable clockwork and the only timeframe to consider is the immediate horizon.

Alignment

The systems implicitly relying on decision-makers acting in good faith, with aligned incentives ensuring effective governance.

These implicit beliefs are neither accurate nor helpful. They do not acknowledge the increasing cost of relying on assumptions. *In non-linear environments, assumptions amplify.*

Steps to challenging assumptions

Building the capability to evaluate assumptions and biases is critical to achieving alignment. There are steps for challenging tacit beliefs which may be presented as fact:

1 **Identify the underlying assumptions:** Isolate and identify the assumptions. These could be specific beliefs, statements or generalizations.

2 **Critically assess assumptions:** Challenge the validity of assumptions. Offer diverse perspectives and opposing views.

3 **Adopt the beginner's mind by asking questions:** Antifragility requires one to ask questions, instead of succumbing to answers. Ask: *Why? Why not? How? What if?*

4 **Learn, unlearn, relearn:** Prototype and test beliefs to compare them with reality. Use any failures to spark new ideas and to update assumptions as an evolutionary process. The purpose of testing assumptions is not only to differentiate between belief and fact, but also to imagine alternative ways of doing things.

5 **Be imaginative and generate new approaches:** Innovation and creativity rely on opening new doors with novel ideas which cannot always be tested. This exploration, including into the seemingly impossible, is virtuous, especially when you can delineate what is validated versus what is assumed.

6 **Understand cognitive bias:** With confirmation bias, we're more likely to believe things that reinforce already-held opinions. Herd behaviour leads us to follow others under the assumption that they are correct. Understanding the nature of cognitive biases can help critically assess the underlying assumptions we rely on.

Figure 12.7 Challenge and test assumptions toolkit

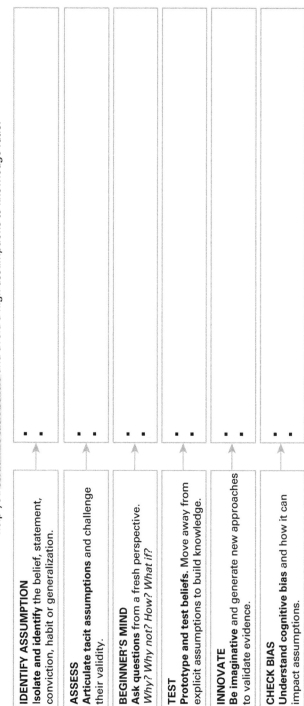

Challenge and Test Assumptions Toolkit

Challenging and testing assumptions is essential to becoming AAA⁺. This toolkit is designed to help you **scrutinize tacit beliefs** and avoid a high *assumptions to knowledge* ratio.

IDENTIFY ASSUMPTION
Isolate and identify the belief, statement, conviction, habit or generalization.

ASSESS
Articulate tacit assumptions and challenge their validity.

BEGINNER'S MIND
Ask questions from a fresh perspective.
Why? Why not? How? What if?

TEST
Prototype and test beliefs. Move away from explicit assumptions to build knowledge.

INNOVATE
Be imaginative and generate new approaches to validate evidence.

CHECK BIAS
Understand cognitive bias and how it can impact assumptions.

Challenge and test assumptions toolkit

Challenging and testing assumptions is essential to becoming AAA+. This toolkit is designed to help you scrutinize tacit beliefs and avoid a high assumptions-to-knowledge ratio (Figure 12.7).

Aligning disagreements through beneficial arguments

Alignment does not mean agreeing on everything. Healthy disagreements are important for generating new ideas.

Aligning societal values should not be confused with simply achieving consensus. There is an art to robust debate, thoughtful questioning and the creative outcomes which arise from candid exchanges. Alignment encourages broad sets of opinions that foster new solutions.

Innovation arises from cognitive diversity. In productive arguments, opinions are exchanged, ideas are debated and beliefs are challenged.

Socratic arguments enhance collaborative outcomes

Critical debate was seen by Socrates as the fundamental philosophy of life. Socratic inquiry stimulates critical thinking by generating ideas and investigating the underlying assumptions.

Beneficial arguments also make us wiser. Questioning our convictions through debate protects us from simply confirming our own beliefs.

Challenges for balanced perspectives

Warren Buffet considered that companies only receive objective advice if they hire a second advisor for their acquisitions, who would make a case *against* the transaction. By debating arguments for and against a deal, outcomes can be more nuanced. Relying on one heavily incentivized adviser invariably offers limited objectivity.

Misaligned incentives can foster herd mentality. Incentives do not often go to those who challenge core assumptions and question consensus. As the adage goes: *great minds think alike, but fools seldom differ.*

Stakeholder analysis

One key aspect to achieving alignment is stakeholder analysis. Integrate who can influence the outcomes of the disruptive project under consideration.

Aligning values while challenging conventional wisdom creates new solutions.

Step 5: Decision-making and driving change

OBJECTIVE
Decision-making in uncertainty and levers for change

In the fifth step, we aim to understand the nature of decision-making in deeply uncertain environments and how to effect change in a systemic context.

Building on our antifragile foundations and anticipatory thinking, this fifth step hinges upon cognitive, emergent and strategic agility:

- **Decision-making in deep uncertainty:** Understand the difference between reversible and irreversible decisions, as well as the degrees of uncertainty.

- **Driving effective change in complex systems:** Use leverage points effectively.

Reversible decisions

For decision-making, complete information is never available. Regardless of expert consultations and data analysis, perfect clarity persists as a mirage.

Considering whether a decision is reversible is powerful, as articulated by Jeff Bezos in one of his annual letters to Amazon shareholders. Two questions can help evaluate the nature of a decision: What are the consequences of this decision? Can this decision be reversed, and if so, for how long?

With limited consequences, we can make reversible decisions rapidly and gain a competitive advantage. *Reversible decisions are two-way doors, allowing for agility in the face of uncertainty.*

Conversely, when assessing consequential irreversible decisions, we must defer commitment in order to delve deeper because the stakes are higher. These decisions are one-way doors, with no turning back.

Bezos believes that you can make most reversible decisions with 70 per cent of the information you wish you had. For irreversible decisions, you should not require more than 90 per cent optimal knowledge. If you wait for more information than that, you may be too late.

CHECKLIST
Reversible versus irreversible decisions

Questions to filter reversible versus irreversible decisions:

- What is the greatest risk: deciding too late or too early?
- Is the decision fragile or antifragile?
- Is it easy or difficult to reverse the decision?
- How much is at stake?
- How important is the decision's speed? What is the opportunity cost of waiting?
- How high is the cost of making the wrong decision?

Decision-making in deep uncertainty

Given the features of our complex, uncertain and non-linear world, any decisions should be carefully evaluated. Some consultants, analysts and forecasters claim to have data-driven predictive capabilities. However, they simply extrapolate the past or, at best, the present. To avoid arbitrary decision-making, we outline the 'six degrees of (un)predictability' as an agile frame for decision-making.

1 **Know your knowns:** *Critically assess the drivers of any predictions to ascertain the ratio of assumptions to knowledge.* Isolate the underlying assumptions to separate fact from fiction. Our Complex Five, a matrix of animals, represent highly impactful events according to their degrees of uncertainty: Black Elephant (known unknowns), Black Jellyfish (unknown knowns), Black Swan (unknown unknowns), Gray Rhino (known knowns) and the Butterfly Effect. Being an effective decision-maker requires appreciating these levels of uncertainty.

2 **Qualify your unknowns to map uncertainties:** *Challenge the validity of assumptions, of what is not certain.* Investigate which assumptions may be flawed. Offer diverse perspectives and opposing views to critically examine these assumptions. Ask yourself what you have to believe for assumptions to be substantiated. Test assumptions not only to differentiate between belief and fact, but also to imagine alternative possibilities.

3 Impact cascades: *Consider systemic interconnections and next-order implications from initial change.* These should include scenarios that run counter to the deeply ingrained assumptions about how the world evolves. Leverage the wisdom of diverse contributors to map out impact cascades, which may further collide to amplify future changes, creating even more in the process.

4 Imagine the broad range of possibilities: *Seek a fresh perspective by asking questions instead of relying on answers. Why? Why not? How? How else? What else? What if?* Be imaginative and generate new approaches.

5 Assess stakeholders and interests: Stakeholders are individuals, organizations and entities that can influence prognostications. They are often incentivized to form a given point of view. *Ascertain stakeholder incentives, biases and track records.*

6 Inform decisions and take action: *Be agile in decision-making – there may be no right answers.* The environment is constantly updating, offering novel opportunities. Disconfirm what is no longer valid. Understand that certain decisions may be susceptible to cognitive biases and adjust where relevant.

Six degrees of (un)predictability toolkit

Use this critical approach to evaluate a decision for your project or business.

Explore the opportunities of the unknown futures ahead as they evolve in our UN-VICE environment (Figure 12.8).

Leverage points to drive effective change

Small shifts at the appropriate levels can produce greater changes through-out systems.[1] Using effective levers for change is a prerequisite for impact. But the higher the level, the greater the challenge to pull it:

- **Transform mental models:** Deeply held assumptions formed as children manifest during adulthood. A focus on both education and values (shared visions) can change the mindset with which current misaligned structures function.

- **Design underlying structures:** Change the structure that supports, creates and influences the system. Laws and policies can be rewritten to reward an environment conducive to effective change. Incentives determine outcomes.

Figure 12.8 Six degrees of (un)predictability toolkit

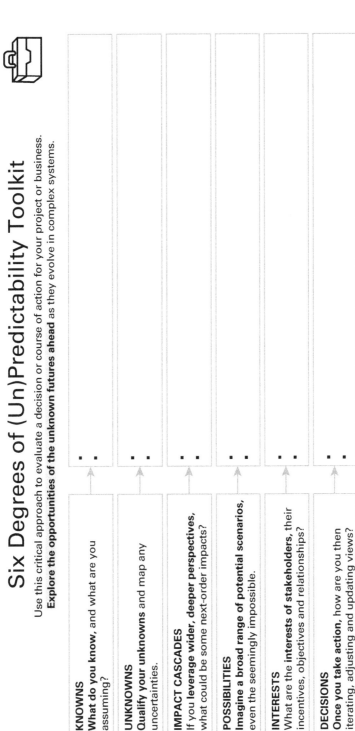

Six Degrees of (Un)Predictability Toolkit

Use this critical approach to evaluate a decision or course of action for your project or business. **Explore the opportunities of the unknown futures ahead** as they evolve in complex systems.

KNOWNS
What do you know, and what are you assuming?

UNKNOWNS
Qualify your unknowns and map any uncertainties.

IMPACT CASCADES
If you **leverage wider, deeper perspectives,** what could be some next-order impacts?

POSSIBILITIES
Imagine a broad range of potential scenarios, even the seemingly impossible.

INTERESTS
What are the **interests of stakeholders,** their incentives, objectives and relationships?

DECISIONS
Once you take action, how are you then iterating, adjusting and updating views?

- **Anticipate patterns and trends:** By monitoring patterns over time, we can better anticipate what might arise, providing further options to address short-termist and ineffective systems. Requiring effective and systematic disclosure (transparent communication on how an organization prioritizes agile decision-making and long-term success) can enhance the awareness of what is happening and what further changes might be required.

Changes must be applied to high leverage points and in the right direction, to be effective. *Incentives are strong leverage points because they represent the rules of the system and its boundaries.*

CHECKLIST
Decision-making and change

Key questions in relation to decision-making in uncertainty and driving change:

- What are the most effective levers to drive the contemplated transformations?
- How can we make informed decisions despite deep uncertainty?
- What are the consequences of this decision to drive change? Is the decision reversible?
- What are the degrees of uncertainties within which we will act?
- What could be the impacts of these uncertainties?
- How do we use leverage points for maximal effect?
- How to anticipate the next-order implications and monitor the impact of change?

Step 6: Iterating

OBJECTIVE
Iterating and feedback loops

Step 6 focuses on applying specific changes, assessing their impact, incorporating new information and actively utilizing feedback to continuously adapt in a dynamic environment.

Reconciling short-term goals with long-term aspirations demands change agents make effective decisions on both horizons simultaneously.

There isn't a singular path to cultivating the agility necessary to bridge disparate time horizons. Agility facilitates sense-making and decision-making, enabling us to emerge with relevance.

Abolishing the dualism between short-term and long-term goals necessitates iteration and the integration of feedback in our dynamic world.

OODA Loop: Decisions with speed, despite uncertainty

John Boyd's OODA Loop uses continuous feedback loops at every stage:

1 Observe: We observe the outside world and the result of previous actions. This helps us understand the big picture by separating signals from noise.

2 Orient: We orient, analysing and synthesizing what we learned in the observation phase. We must see the world as it is and find mismatches to re-orient.

3 Decide: Orientation guides the review of alternative actions and informs our ultimate decisions.

4 Act: The results of these actions interact with the environment to generate more information, beginning the next cycle.

Strong opinions weakly held

Paul Saffo's 'strong opinions weakly held' approach empowers informed decision-making, even when faced with incomplete information.[2]

Quickly form an initial view based on your perception of the environment as a tentative hypothesis. Intuition plays a key role in guiding you to this 'strong opinion', which may be influenced by personal bias. Then, gather evidence that supports or contradicts the hypothesis, allowing you to constantly update your views.

The discovery process should not be solitary. Effective engagement with stakeholders entails actively seeking evidence that challenges your perspectives. Proactively pursue contradictory insights to continuously enhance your decisions.

Cognitive, emergent and strategic agility

We shape our futures by connecting actions to our desired outcomes. While maintaining a long-term vision is crucial, daily experimentation is important in paving a path towards that vision. This continuous engagement creates a feedback loop of new information, requiring us to discern their relevance and adapt our plans. Embracing this dynamic nature of change prevents us from being trapped in reactions and instead allows us to actively explore.

Cognitive, emergent and strategic agility thrive on this principle. They demand a clear longer-term vision coupled with adaptability and judgement to make timely decisions based on emerging information. Anticipating market shifts, exploring new opportunities and evaluating fresh ideas are all facets of this approach.

Fast-changing environments drive new opportunities and gaps. Agility means finding those gaps and exploring them.

CHECKLIST
Bridging agility

The following questions help us navigate our dynamic journeys:

- What are feedback loops and how can we use them to account for constant changes?

- How do you operate in an emergent process which is constantly evolving?

- How do you use sense-making in an increasingly systemic environment, incessantly bombarded with information?

- How can you bridge the present with the longer-term future?

- What are the implications of the world being described as 'complicated' rather than 'complex'?

- What do you rely on to make decisions in UN-VICE environments?

Iterate and feedback loops to inform interventions

The Disruptive Thinking Canvas is a living process. Interpreting disruptions, scanning horizons and creating positive value doesn't stop after you do it once. The sixth step of the Disruptive Thinking Canvas serves as a catalyst for this continuous iterative framework.

Feedback loops offer emergent adaptation

Feedback loops are critically important to the Disruptive Thinking Canvas. Each step of the process is a developing phase that must be revisited as new information emerges.

Disruptive Thinking Canvas dashboard

We have developed a dashboard to help you evaluate the changes you make and integrate the information you come across during your implementations of the Canvas (Figure 12.9). This dashboard is useful at every stage, as challenges can, will and should arise at any of the six steps.

Approaching the dashboard by column:

- **Step:** The table's sections showcase the first five steps. Step 6, vital for gathering feedback across all sections, has its own dedicated column.
- **Meter:** Track your progress for each step with its dedicated meter. Completing a step raises its meter. Curate salient feedback within each step (see column 6) to capture developments.
- **Next few days:** What key actions can you take to start implementing each step?
- **Next few months:** Here, you can begin outlining your longer-term plans. As you initiate immediate actions and receive feedback, regularly update both your current priorities and your forward-looking vision. Consider: What new initiatives will I launch, building on my initial steps? What is the anticipated progression and impacts of initiatives? How might feedback from initial initiatives shape future plans?
- **Feedback loop:** This column represents the sixth step of the Disruptive Thinking Canvas. It is for capturing, iterating and learning. Through trial and error, you'll discover that some plans won't work, while others emerge unexpectedly. Capture this learning in the feedback loop to iterate and inform your next approaches.

As you progress, you'll move through different stages, enacting changes and generating feedback. Iterate to incorporate new ideas and learning as you go; remember that change is always messy.

Figure 12.9 Disruptive Thinking Canvas™ dashboard

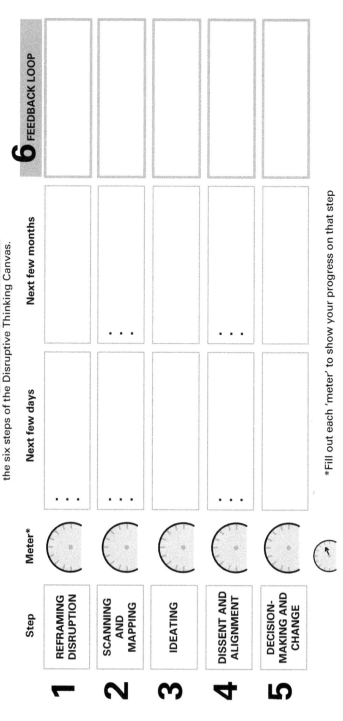

Disruptive Thinking Canvas™ Dashboard

Use this dashboard to track your **plans, progress and iterations** across each of the six steps of the Disruptive Thinking Canvas.

Step		Meter*	Next few days	Next few months	**6** FEEDBACK LOOP
1	REFRAMING DISRUPTION		...		
2	SCANNING AND MAPPING		...	...	
3	IDEATING				
4	DISSENT AND ALIGNMENT		...	...	
5	DECISION-MAKING AND CHANGE				

*Fill out each 'meter' to show your progress on that step

Shape your futures

With the Canvas, you become the architect of your futures. As you apply its steps, consider what each word in the Disruptive Thinking Canvas represents:

- **'Disruptive':** The Canvas's power lies not in its disruptiveness, but in its ability to unlock new possibilities. In our UN-VICE world, creating impactful change necessitates shake-ups to break from the shortcomings of the status quo.

- **'Thinking':** Tools can help plan for the expected future, but the Disruptive Thinking Canvas goes further. Fostering critical thinking in the face of constant change while exploring multiple possible futures requires challenging assumptions, imagining how to move beyond business-as-usual and developing effective mental models.

- **'Canvas':** As you engage with the Canvas, you exercise agency, recognizing our capacity to make choices thanks to uncertainty. The Canvas acts as your compass, guiding you in a world where, for the unprepared, every swerve feels like nothing that's ever happened before.

Notes

1 D Meadows. Leverage points: Places to intervene in a system, Academy for Systems Change, The Donella Meadows Project, 1999. www.donellameadows.org/archives/leverage-points-places-to-intervene-in-a-system (archived at https://perma.cc/LAJ5-FY32)

2 P Saffo. Strong opinions weakly held, Paul Saffo, 26 July 2008. https://web.archive.org/web/20240208002934/https://saffo.com/02008/07/26/strong-opinions-weakly-held/ (archived at https://perma.cc/UB7A-25EX)

INDEX

The index is filed in alphabetical, word-by-word order. Numbers are filed as spelt out, except for Horizon categories, which are filed chronologically. Acronyms and 'Mc' are filed as presented.

Looking for another book?

Explore our award-winning
books from global business
experts in Business Strategy

Scan the code to browse

www.koganpage.com/business-
strategy

Also from Kogan Page

ISBN: 9781789664706

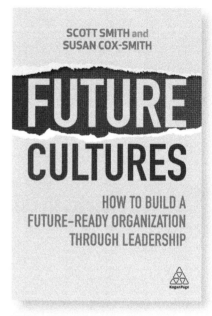

ISBN: 9781398612389

ISBN: 9781398614321

ISBN: 9781789666335

www.koganpage.com

Printed in the USA
CPSIA information can be obtained
at www.ICGtesting.com
JSHW042104030924
69236JS00024B/503